PEASANTS, POWER, AND APPLIED SOCIAL CHANGE

LOCAL COMUNAL

TODOS LOS SERES HUMANOS NACE
LIBRES E IGUALES EN DIGNIDAD Y DE
RECHOS Y, DOTADOS COMO ESTAN DE
RAZON Y CONCIENCIA, DEBEN COMPOR
TARSE FRATERNALMENTE LOS UNOS
CON LOS OTROS"

[Art. de la Derechos Humanos UNESCO]

Social Change—community farm enterprise director Celso León H. (right) and community official Pablo Cilio stand at the entrance to the Vicos community council meeting rooms on the ground floor of what was once the manor house. The Spanish text lettered on the wall to the right is a passage from the Declaration of Human Rights placed there by school teachers preparing for a local holiday celebration.

Peasants, Power, and Applied Social Change

VICOS AS A MODEL

Henry F. Dobyns
Paul L. Doughty
Harold D. Lasswell

Editors

 S A G E   PUBLICATIONS

Beverly Hills / London

For information address:

SAGE PUBLICATIONS, INC.
275 South Beverly Drive
Beverly Hills, California 90212

SAGE PUBLICATIONS, LTD
St George's House
44 Hatton Garden, London E C 1

Printed in the United States of America
International Standard Book Number 0-8039-0049-X
Library of Congress Catalog Card No. 76-162437
First Printing

To Allan R. Holmberg

Pioneer in blending knowledge with action

and crossing societal and disciplinary boundaries

CONTENTS

INTRODUCTION

As citizens of the United States of America face the decade of the 1970s many of them are intensely concerned over relationships between their country and numerous foreign nations. Many of them are not aware that, as we approach the twenty-first century, peasantry still exists in large areas of the world. This book is addressed to one key topic in that generalized concern, the nature of such peasants and the response of oppressed populations to opportunities for changing their relative social position.

One central fact in U.S. foreign relations during the 1970s is that the whole system of foreign affairs has altered in the three decades since the beginnings of the second World War. The conquests, reconquests, and failures to reconquer colonial dependencies during that global conflict produced a post-war era of rapidly increasing numbers of politically independent nations. Pre-war colonies and protectorates became self-governing everywhere. Thus, the United States must deal with considerably more independent nations than it did thirty or even twenty years ago.

A second cardinal fact about the post-war world is that the majority of the residents of the newly independent nations—as well as many older ones—are peasants. The editors of this volume, aware that Americans generally do not understand the nature of peasantries, feel overwhelmingly that such an understanding is vital to formulating reasonable national foreign policy.

This book analyzes the results of a project to improve the standard of living of a few thousand rural Peruvian highland Indians undertaken jointly by the national Indian Institute and anthropologists from Cornell University in the United States. The anthropologists provided their skills as data collectors to find out what the Indians themselves wanted, their knowledge of general principles of social and cultural change as defined by social scientists at the time, and furnished research funds granted by U.S. foundations. The Peruvian Indian Institute provided official governmental status for the project in Peru, and necessary coordination with other official organizations.

It is worthy of note that this project began under a Peruvian president who as an army general had deposed a constitutionally elected civilian government in 1948. The general then won an election held by his regime in 1950 and served the six-year term specified in the Peruvian constitution. The "Cornell Peru Project" was officially organized late in 1951 and began to operate in Vicos early in 1952. Within a short time, newspaper and magazine publicity made the project fairly well known to Peruvian intellectuals and the literate public.

By the end of the initial five years of the Cornell Peru Project's work, rapid and pacific change had occurred nationally and among the Vicos Indians. An elitist engineer, Manuel Prado Ugarteche, was elected to the presidential term beginning in 1956 and took office on July 28 of that year. During the Prado administration the Cornell Peru Project recommended, and the Peruvian Indian Institute sought, the expropriation of Vicos for its inhabitants. During the Prado administration agrarian reform became a burning political issue in Peru; under a fiscally responsible and conservative prime minister, a commission was established to study the problems of agrarian reform and housing. Conservative cabinet members blocked both the Vicos expropriation and a large-scale scheme to launch national agrarian reform by conveying range lands owned by the Cerro

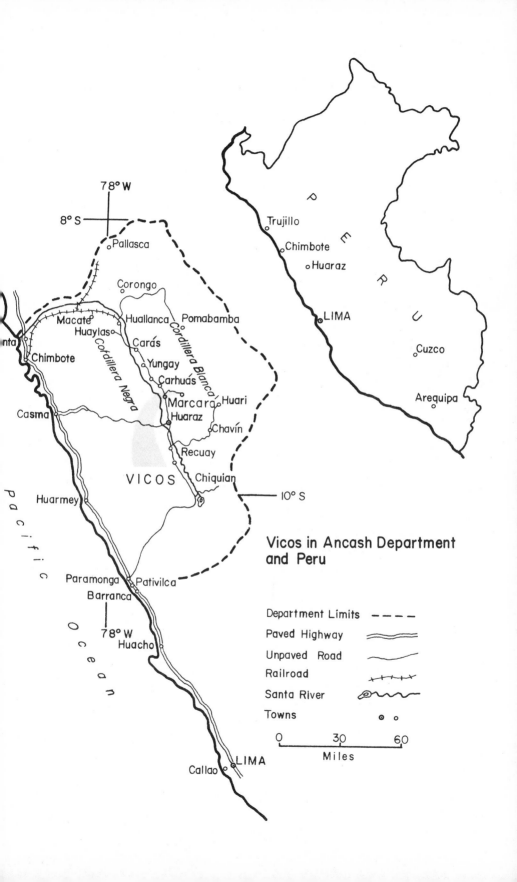

78° W

8° S

Pallasca

Corongo

Macate
Huaylas
Huallanca
Pomabamba
Carás
Yungay
Carhuás
Marcara
Huari
Huaraz
Chavín
Recuay
VICOS
Chiquian

Chimbote

Casma

Huarmey

Paramonga
Pativilca
Barranca

78° W
Huacho

nta

Cordillera Negra

Cordillera Blanca

Pacific

Ocean

10° S

Trujillo

Chimbote

Huaraz

LIMA

Cuzco

Arequipa

P E R U

Vicos in Ancash Department and Peru

Department Limits	– – – –
Paved Highway	
Unpaved Road	
Railroad	+–+–+
Santa River	
Towns	∘ ∘

0   30   60
Miles

Callao

LIMA

de Pasco Corporation (a Delaware corporation) to members of neighboring "Indigenous Communities."

Toward the end of the Prado administration, nonetheless, the good offices of the Hon. James I. Loeb (then United States Ambassador to Peru) and the Hon. Edward M. Kennedy obtained Peruvian presidential approval for a direct sale of Vicos to its Indian inhabitants with Peruvian governmental financial assistance. Meanwhile, the Vicos locally elected governing board provided aid in kind to nearby serfs who rented the estates on which they labored and lived to avoid landlord exploitation.

The military junta that deposed President Prado a few days before the end of his constitutional term of office displayed an official interest in changing the basic rural social structure of Peru by issuing decrees labeled the "bases" for agrarian reform legislation. That junta, having annulled the results of the 1962 presidential election, purged the lists of registered voters and supervised another election in 1963. An architect, Fernando Belaunde Terry, emerged victorious in the presidential contest but his party gained only a minority of seats in either house of parliament.

At the beginning of the Belaunde administration, the president and cabinet restrained the national police forces when members of indigenous communities began to "recuperate" their lands from neighboring landlords. The large landholders accused the communal organizations of "invading" privately owned lands, but the typical movement occupied land whose ownership had long been disputed in the courts. For a few months the constitutionally recognized Indigenous Communities energetically shifted the balance of power in some areas of rural Peru.

During this period of land recuperation, numerous community leaders followed to a greater or lesser degree the Vicos pattern of community farming enterprise instituted to raise community funds. Knowledge of the Vicos experiment was one of many factors fostering change, since descriptions of the program had been disseminated to every officially registered Indigenous Community. Leaders from numerous communities of this kind visited Vicos at one time or another.

After the Belaunde administration began to dispatch contingents of the national paramilitary police force to halt these peasant movements going on all over the country, increasing political pressures on the government demanded additional legal reforms in the tenancy systems. Following a great deal of partisan maneuvering, the Peruvian parliament managed to pass agrarian reform legislation. Officials in a series of Belaunde cabinets then implemented that legislation to some degree, but only in certain areas of the country. As few Belaunde cabinets held office very long, rapid turnover in policy-making offices of the executive branch probably delayed effective tenancy reform materially.

The Belaunde regime focused its efforts on several other major programs, including an Interministerial Committee for Popular Cooperation, an organization to promote and logistically support rural community self-help projects, and an Amazon basin penetration highway, plus settlement of a long-simmering dispute over ownership of oil fields exploited by the International Petroleum Company.

Public discontent over the agreement negotiated with the oil company precipitated a national scandal, and another military coup d'etat followed when Belaunde was ousted from the country on October 3, 1968, and General Juan Velasco Alvarado was sworn in as president. He appointed an entirely military cabinet which has remained relatively stable.

Within days, the military regime, following the lead of Mexico in nationalizing oil resources, expropriated International Petroleum Company properties. Within months, the regime issued decrees instituting reforms in the Peruvian system of higher education—long wracked by student strikes, demonstrations, and intense partisan activity and divisions within student bodies and faculties. By the "Day of the Indian," June 24, 1969, the military regime was ready to announce its most radical measure. Changing the title of the occasion to "Peasant Day," the military junta decreed a thoroughgoing agrarian reform. To prove how seriously it meant its radical executive-order reforms, the junta immediately seized most of the large sugar-growing plantations on the Peruvian coast. A majority of these strong earners of foreign exchange credits turned out to be owned by foreign interests, although some of the largest were Peruvian feifdoms.

By the end of August, 1969, the military junta had recruited the author of one chapter in this volume to serve as director of its new Bureau of Peasant Communities. Thus, the changing agrarian and Indian policy of Peruvian national administrations came full circle. An intellectual, scientific, anthropologist— forced into virtual exile under one general-president, accused by some of being a Communist and by others of being an "imperialist lackey" because of his efforts on behalf of Indians under the elitist engineer-president, and merely one among numerous more or less alienated intellectuals under an architect -president—joined the new administration. With extensive powers he was able to implement, on a national scale, many of the kinds of measures tested and proved during the Vicos experiment toward developing a prototype for improving peasant life by increasing the peasant share of power.

In a word, the research and development program at Vicos, officially or not, has played a significant part in the changing national policy of Peru's traditional land tenancy systems. At times Vicos stood at the forefront of reform, a lonely and isolated show-piece for conservative governments to cite as evidence of a "sincere interest" in discovering whether integration of backward and exploited Indian populations could be achieved. As national sentiment solidified in favor of more and more effective agrarian reform, Vicos was itself affected by shifting national policies. It became only one project among many agrarian reform programs exploring several alternative approaches to such fundamental social and economic problems as how to free serfs from onerous labor and social obligations to landlords, how to convert small-scale serf and peasant poor, from under-employed gardeners producing less than subsistence from their plots and eking out their income with unskilled wage labor, into commercial farmers; or how to create truly national loyalties among hitherto physically and socially isolated rural populations so as to avoid more serious guerrilla-style peasant armed movements such as the one that occurred in 1965 with Communist leadership.

This volume describes, then, one of the fundamental influences toward agrarian reform in Peru and its consequences for wider participation in the political process, for wider sharing of economic benefits from the capitalistic market system operating in the country, and for wider appreciation of human dignity and respect flowing from these.

In organizing this volume the editors have followed a format designed to demonstrate to the reader the multiple ramifications of key or strategic acts of intervention on the part of the Cornell Peru Project or other agents acting on its behalf. The authors present their data as they bear upon eight important areas of human value preference, areas in which not only the quantity aspects but also the quality of life-ways might be reflected. We were concerned with showing how the Vicosinos came to achieve a "wider sharing" of positive values than they had had under the manorial regime.

We begin, consequently, with the value-institutional area which seemed to be the key to obtaining positive change effects in other areas. This variable was power, so we examine all the other value changes in terms of this one. The theoretical framework here follows the innovative lead of Lasswell and Kaplan(1) and the later work of Lasswell and Holmberg,(2) who set forth the value-institution groups of power, wealth, skill, enlightenment, affection, respect, rectitude, and well-being. By doing this, we attempt to demonstrate the complex interplay of institutions in terms of the attributes of human relationships as they develop and change in the context of power. The reader will recognize at once that it would have been possible to visualize everything in light of any one of the other value institutions, but this would, we felt, not be the most direct way of handling the case. The undeniable and irresistible importance of power in this context dictated otherwise—a fact that others have recognized in similar social situations elsewhere in the world.

The role of power in opening the door to change was appreciated by the Cornell Peru Project leadership right from the beginning when it assumed the position of patron of the Vicos manor with all the absolute privileges that the role contained. Through the planned devolution of that power to the people of Vicos, Project leadership was able to modify other areas of life which had been very rigidly controlled. Thus, power is the key factor whether one speaks of peaceful or of violent change. Writing in a comparative context of peasant revolutions of this century, Eric Wolf says:

"The poor peasant or the landless laborer who depends on a landlord for the largest part of his livelihood, or the totality of it, has no tactical power: he is completely within the power domain of his employer, without sufficient resources of his own to serve him as resources in the power struggle. Poor peasants and landless laborers, therefore, are unlikely to pursue the course of rebellion *unless* they are able to rely on some external power to challenge the power which constrains them."(3)

The Cornell Peru Project provided that important external source of power, constituting a social umbrella under which the people of Vicos were able to alter their lives to their greater satisfaction, and without the imminent threat of tragedy and retribution to discourage them as it had before.

For these reasons we have taken the power-value category as the proper springboard from which to launch our analysis of the events at Vicos during a fifteen-year period. To be sure, the method of presentation will perforce involve some repetition of fact and event as we study some of the same happenings in the light of different value institutions and the resultant and varying consequences they produced. We have tried to avoid redundancy in doing so, hoping that the many sides of particular situations will become clearer and thus more understandable. This approach is consistent with the holistic and functional analytical methods of anthropology vital to the integral comprehension of human society in a rapidly changing terrestrial system.

Finally, this collection of value-institutional analysis does not attempt to present a full and definitive description of Vicos culture. To do so would require several substantial volumes, and indeed, much of this detail has already been presented elsewhere. Instead, we have striven to provide the reader with a concise factual analysis which draws from the large accumulated body of data to highlight what Vicos represented in 1951, what the Cornell Peru Project did, and the result after fifteen years. Again, in doing this, the power variable is primary to our presentation, since Vicosinos as a special variety of peasant grouping (serfs) represented, in absolute terms, the bottom of the national social, political, and economic hierarchy. In other words, since the Vicosinos were exploited by everyone else, to treat them as an isolate or simply as marginal to Peruvian society would avoid dealing with the most salient feature of their life—powerlessness—necessary to the understanding of their internal attributes at the time the Project began to work in Vicos. The Vicosinos were not only part of the national society in 1951, they were in their condition essential to it—a necessary subordinated complement to the dominant oligarchy.

Henry F. Dobyns
Paul L. Doughty
Harold D. Lasswell

REFERENCES

1. H. D. Lasswell and A. Kaplan, *Power and Society: A Framework for Political Inquiry.* New Haven: Yale University Press, 1950.

2. H. D. Lasswell and A. R. Holmberg, "Toward a General Theory of Directed Value Accumulation and Institutional Development," in H. W. Peter (Ed.), *Comparative Theories of Social Change.* Ann Arbor: Foundation for Research on Human Behavior, 1966. Available with slight changes in Ralph Braibanti (Ed.), *Political and Administrative Development.* Durham, N.C.: Duke University Press, 1969, chapter 8.

3. E. R. Wolf, *Peasant Wars of the Twentieth Century.* New York: Harper and Row, 1969, p. 290.

A NOTE TO ANTHROPOLOGISTS

Because this book attempts to convey a message, relevant to fundamental issues of our times, that derives from a large-scale anthropological research program, it carries special importance for anthropologists. It directs the attention of social scientists to the basic importance of studies of peasantries and the processes of change affecting peasants and serfs all over the world.

This volume describes what one group of social scientists accomplished when it acted from a strong personal feeling of responsibility for carrying the findings of social science into the world of practical affairs. As the number of anthropologists virtually skyrockets, and as the discipline becomes dominated by young degree-holders—a high proportion of whom entertain grave doubts about the "relevance" of their professional activities and cry out for social, economic, and political reforms in their own and other countries—it strikes us as vitally necessary to place before the concerned younger generation this record of research and development conducted by a team of highly motivated anthropologists.

This experience suggests to us that the truly "revolutionary" anthropologist is not he who most frequently publishes papers pleading for economic and social reforms, or seeks to find occasions for physical confrontation with officialdom to shout

provocative slogans. Rather, the really revolutionary anthropologist seems to us to be the one who employs his best
disciplinary skills as both data collector and theorist, working
directly both with decision-makers and the people in seeking to
broaden in fundamental ways the distribution of power within a
national society. The late Manuel Gamio conducted key
research on peasant villagers during a critical phase of the
Mexican social revolution and significantly influenced the
leaders who formulated revolution philosophy—and then executed and interpreted it. We regard him as a prototype
revolutionary anthropologist.

Very clearly Jomo Kenyatta also stands at the pinnacle of
success as a revolutionary anthropologist. Trained by Bronislaw
Malinowski at the very center of the British Empire, Kenyatta
applied his anthropologist's skills to the task of winning
political freedom for his fellow Africans, and then making them
socially dominant within their own country.

Compared to Kenyatta, the first holder of a doctorate in
anthropology to head his nation, any other anthropologist's
achievements in this respect seem minor indeed. Nonetheless,
we similarly regard the late Allan R. Holmberg as a truly
revolutionary anthropologist. Whereas Kenyatta worked with
native activists to confront colonial authorities and wrest power
from them by force, Holmberg chose to prove a prototype for
peaceful social reformation. This book offers a description and
partial analysis of that prototypical program led by Holmberg
with the decisive support of the late Carlos Monge Medrano,
M.D., as Co-Director of the Cornell Peru Project representing
the Peruvian Indian Institute.

It goes almost without saying, therefore, that we regard
Mario C. Vázquez V. as another truly revolutionary anthropologist. A student of Holmberg's and his (and our) colleague,
Vázquez has stood at the forefront of the Vicos program
throughout its tumultuous fifteen-year history of direct action.
He has, therefore, remained the principal symbol of the Vicos
program during the post-Cornell Peru Project period even
though he was working in other central Andean social and
cultural contexts. Since mid-1969 he has occupied a position in
the Peruvian revolutionary government rather like that of
Gamio in Mexico half a century earlier, devising administrative

measures to improve the relative position of peasant communities in Peru while continuing research into their characteristics.

We take great personal pride in our own minor roles in this revolutionary anthropological program at Vicos as associates of Holmberg and Vázquez. We feel strongly that pioneering works such as those of Gamio and Kenyatta and this one at Vicos merit attentive study by the young anthropologist unsure about the function his discipline plays in society. We have no apologies for placing social science in the service of men who seek the wider and equitable sharing of political, economic, and social power among citizens of any nation.

Henry F. Dobyns
Paul L. Doughty

Chapter I

EXPERIMENTAL INTERVENTION

IN THE FIELD

Allan R. Holmberg

I

Traditionally, anthropologists have approached the study of culture change from the perspective of the outside observer of a naturally on-going process. By contrast, few attempts have been made to approach the study of change from the perspective of the intervening participant; in other words, as both the designer and activator of a socio-cultural process. It is the purpose of this chapter to explore some of the potentialities of this latter method—called here the method of participant intervention—as a possibly fruitful approach to further investigation of the dynamics of culture change. Specifically, there are three points on which the chapter will focus:

1. The characteristics by which the method of participant intervention may be distinguished from other approaches to the study of change.

2. The role of the investigator in the application of this method in the field

3. Some of the possible contributions of this approach to theory and method in the field of cultural change.

Editors' Note: This chapter originally appeared as "Participant Intervention in the Field" in Human Organization, vol. 13 (1955), pp. 23-26. Reproduced by permission of the Society for Applied Anthropology.

II

In 1952, as part of a research program in Culture and Applied Science, Cornell University, in collaboration with the Indigenous Institute of Peru, arranged to rent Vicos, a publicly owned hacienda on which previous observational studies had been made, for an initial period of five years. Broadly speaking, the purpose of embarking on this experience was twofold: on the theoretical side, it was hoped to conduct some form of experimental research on the processes of modernization now on the march in so many parts of the world; on the practical side, it was hoped to assist the community to shift for itself from a position of relative dependence and submission in a highly restricted and provincial world to a position of relative independence and freedom within the larger framework of Peruvian national life.

The assumptions and expectations on which the study was based were essentially as follows:

In the first place, we assumed that Peru would never be able to reach the much-desired goals of national unity and modernization unless more attention were paid to the masses of Indians who now constitute over 50 percent of the total population and who fall largely outside of the framework of national culture;

Secondly, we assumed that the hacienda Indian, if offered an opportunity to broaden his relations in the outside world, would, within a reasonable period of time, adjust to modern conditions and take a productive and respected place in Peruvian national life;

Thirdly, we expected that the Indians themselves, through the development of new organizations, would take over the operation of the community after our period of research and experimentation had ended;

Finally, we were intrigued by the possibility of conducting investigations in a hacienda system such as Vicos, where as both agents and students of change we might be able to exert somewhat more control over the subjects and the variables than is usually the case and, thus, gain new insights into the socio-cultural process. This last point should be stressed, because it is here that our approach in Peru departs from the traditional methods already referred to, for by taking control of

Skill—A young Vicos matron uses a community sewing machine to embroider a new cape, employing a skill she learned from the seamstress instructress on the staff of the Peruvian National Plan for Integrating the Aboriginal Population.

the hacienda we placed ourselves in the position to apply the method of participant intervention which has been little employed in anthropology, either because of a strong value notion that the people one studies should not be tampered with, or because the opportunities for controlled intervention have been neither easy to find nor simple to study.

III

The *Hacienda Vicos,* where the work was ultimately carried out, lies in the Inter-Andean valley of Callajon de Huaylas in north-central Peru, about 250 miles from the capital city of Lima. Surrounded by snow-capped peaks of the Andes, some of them over 20,000 feet in height, it contains a land area of from 30,000 to 40,000 acres, about 2,500 of which are now under cultivation and another 4,000 of which are utilized for grazing purposes. It is very rocky and hilly, rising in elevation from about 9,000 to 14,000 feet. The lower parts of the hacienda are used largely for agricultural purposes, the upper parts, almost exclusively for grazing.

Like many properties of the Andes, Vicos belongs to the state. Formerly it was leased for exploitation to the highest bidder at public auction every 10 years. Attached to the land but owning none of it are about 380 families of Quechua-speaking Indians—2,250 people—most of whom live on the lower part of the hacienda on scattered farmsteads ranging from one to 15 acres in size, occupying roughly 90 percent of the arable land. The remaining 10 percent of the land was previously farmed for commercial purposes by the lessee of the hacienda, with Indian labor supplied without charge—by custom, of long standing, one adult member of every household was obligated to pay a labor tax of three days a week for the right to occupy a small plot of land for subsistence purposes. In addition to the labor tax, the Indians were obliged to supply domestic animals for agricultural work on the hacienda, and the peons and their families were obligated by turn to supply certain free services to the hacienda and its employees, such as shepherds, grooms, watchmen, cooks, and servants.

The Indian community itself is divided into some 50 kinship groups named *castas* or *sibs.* It is presided over by an indigenous mayor who assumes office for a period of one year, by a process we might loosely call election, and who appoints a number of assistants. The indigenous officials, however, perform largely a religious function. In economic and political matters they are dependent on and subordinate to, respectively, the Patron and government officials in the outside world. Moreover, the Indian community as a whole is by no means a united group; individualism runs high and allegiances are largely to immediate kin groups. In brief, this was the state of affairs at Vicos when Cornell assumed control.

As a result of this system, which has been in operation for several hundred years, the lot of the Indians at Vicos has not been a particularly favored one. Power had been concentrated in the hands of the Patron or the Mestizos in the outside world, and it has been to their advantage to keep the Vicosinos in a depressed socio-economic state. This, together with other undesirable conditions, has produced in the Indians attitudes of distrust, suspicion, fear, and even hate of the outside world. Such in fact were the prevailing attitudes at Vicos at the time our work began.

IV

A full statement of all steps of the Vicos operation is presented in the chapters that follow, and in Appendix C. Essentially, however, we were concerned with the development and study of two major processes: (1) changing the initial (and expected) image of ourselves from that of hostile Patrons to friendly consultants and observers; and (2) developing independent problem-solving and decision-making organizations among the indigenous population which could gradually assume the control and direction of community affairs in a rational and humane manner. To start these processes in action, a great many specific steps were designed, all of which emerged from a thorough base-line study of the community and the surrounding area. The following are a few measures that we took at Vicos:

1. Indian leaders were given responsibility (for example, supervision of the labor force) formerly held by outside employees against whom there was felt great hostility.

2. Free services to the hacienda (cooks, shepherds, and so on) were abolished and paid employees were hired for strategic jobs.

3. Returns from Indian labor on the hacienda were invested in the interests of community development (improved agricultural practices, education, and so on).

4. A body of Indian leaders, known as *mayorales,* was organized for the purpose of sharing responsibility for planning and executing an integrated program of change drawn up by the Cornell group in consultation with the Indian leaders.

5. Weekly meetings of the labor force as a whole were initiated for the discussion of hacienda and community affairs.

At the beginning our mode of operation can perhaps best be summarized in the following terms: As problems arose they were brought up for discussion with the committee of Indian leaders with whom we met in a seminar for a couple of hours each week. As agreements or compromises were reached, they were discussed with the labor force as a whole so that modifications could be made if necessary. In establishing meetings with the labor force, we took advantage of an ancient custom of the hacienda, that of *mando,* a weekly meeting at which the hacendado assigned work tasks to the labor force for the ensuing week. We also utilized this meeting as a sounding board for new ideas and responses to any introductions or changes made, and as a means of feeding back to the people the results of our studies and the progress of the program. How new responses and organizational innovations have been initiated and established by these techniques can perhaps best be illustrated by an example.

When we first began to work at Vicos, we soon discovered that one of the principal causes of in-group strife among the Indians was disagreements and fights over the ownership of cattle. Many of the 380 families own a few animals at least, the majority of which graze together in a sheltered area in the upper part of the hacienda. Since the ownership of cattle is a highly desired form of wealth and economic security, cattle rustling was apparently one of the best ways to increase the size of the herds. Consequently, a great deal of time and money went into the settlement of disputes over the ownership of animals—time and money that the community expressed a desire to spend in other ways. In view of this, it occurred to us—as it had not apparently occurred to the Indians—that one of the best ways to solve this problem would be to initiate a program of branding. This was suggested to the Indian leaders who heartily agreed, as did the people themselves with whom we discussed the matter in a general assembly. Consequently, a series of branding irons were made and offers were made to brand the cattle. At first no takers arrived. Again, the matter was brought up for discussion in a meeting of the Indian leaders, at which time one *mayoral* suggested to the others present that perhaps the reason most of the people had not responded was because some of the Indian leaders themselves had not brought their cattle down for branding, and that possibly the reason they had not done so was that some of them who possessed the largest herds had acquired them largely by rustling. This was heatedly challenged by another Indian leader, the largest and most powerful cattle owner on the hacienda, and to prove his innocence he began to brand his own cattle. Within a short time, most of the others followed suit. Suffice it to say that in the year following not a single dispute over the ownership of cattle arose and that the practice of branding animals has since become firmly established at Vicos.

What did we accomplish and what did we learn by this intervention? Here we believe we see the emergence of an institutional practice for the solution of a problem on a community-wide basis where previously there had existed only a wide variety of individual techniques, none of which had apparently been very effective in controlling the theft of cattle. Moreover, by studying the action we initiated we were able to test a number of hypotheses derived from earlier observation and interviewing, such as the following: (1) That the greatest resistance to branding would occur among the most powerful people of the community—the wealthiest, and the owners of the most cattle; or (2) that the least resistance would occur among the people who were most acculturated to the ways of the outside world. At the same time, the results of this intervention provided us with basic information about what steps to take next in the organizational growth of Vicos. For example, we subsequently gave serious thought to the introduction of the annual round-up as an additional way of stimulating community-wide action for the solution of a wide variety of other problems.

V

Enough has now been said about our mode of operation at Vicos to hazard a few general statements about the method of participant intervention as compared with other approaches to the study of change. The first of these has to do with the degree of involvement of the investigator himself. In purely observational studies of the natural process of change, it is generally assumed that the investigator stands outside of the socio-cultural process he is studying, that he himself is not a part of it. In such approaches the investigator is little concerned with the means or ends of a socio-cultural process; he tries hard not to affect the situation; he minimizes his influence as much as possible. In fact, he aims for complete objectivity.

The same cannot be said, however, for the method of participant intervention, where, for the most part, just the opposite holds true. The investigator becomes a vital part of the process he is studying; he defines and manipulates both means and ends; he tries strategically and economically to influence the situation. In fact, we might almost say that he aims for completely "objective" subjectivity.

Of course, the fact that the investigator is deeply involved in the process raises a second and very important point, namely, the values of the investigator himself. The outside observer of change can usually avoid this problem by rationalizing that his values have little effect on the situation under study, although I doubt that this is so. On the other hand, the participant interventionist must face up to the value problem—he must take responsibility for the action he initiates.

While it is impossible here to consider all facets of the value problem, I would like simply to state this with respect to our work at Vicos: we took a value stand, one that has since been defined in great detail: we were concerned with helping the Vicosinos to transform the hacienda on which they lived in a dependent and submissive state into a "just, peaceable, morally and intellectually progressive community of . . . responsible men and women." While, of course, no such value position can be justified scientifically, we—and many Vicosinos—believe these to be good and desirable ends. Actually, beyond a clear statement of one's value position, little further need be said about the value problem.

A third point to which I would like to call attention has to do with the matter of control. In many respects the Vicos situation was like a laboratory, and by this I mean more than a natural laboratory. We were trying to manipulate and control large and complex blocks of reality (environment, society, and culture) in their natural setting. At the same time, we were trying to conduct our experiments and our interventions by dealing with substance that has real meaning to the Vicosinos (like potatoes, cattle, land, or health). And we were trying to deal with this substance within the total context of culture. This, of course, is not experimentation in the laboratory sense of the measurement of the precise effect of a single variable, but rather the development of a strategy for the manipulation and control of systems or sets of variables in the direction of meaningful and purposeful ends. Let me cite an example of what I mean.

When we first arrived at Vicos we found that the Indians' potato crop had failed. The potato is one of the principal sources of food at Vicos, and is, therefore, a strong variable. Thus, a desirable and meaningful end-point or goal for the Vicosinos as subjects, and ourselves as experimenters, became the production of more and better potatoes within the shortest possible period of time and with the least amount of money. On the basis of excellent technical advice, the Vicosinos were informed that a good crop would be assured if they planted certain kinds of potatoes under certain conditions, with certain kinds of techniques. The fact that this was so, to be sure, rested on the evidence of many precisely controlled technical experiments of which we and they simply had to have the knowledge and skills to apply. But I wish to emphasize that the production of many large and healthy potatoes involved the interaction of a complex set of variables—including people, land, fertilizer, insecticide, techniques of plowing, planting, hoeing, irrigating, etc.—all of which were necessary to reach the goal. It would have been possible to carry out a set of perfectly controlled experiments in which the precise effect of any one of the above-mentioned variables on the production of potatoes could have been determined (and where knowledge is lacking, experiments of this kind are necessary). But it would have been meaningless to conduct them in the context of the goal that we and the Vicosinos wanted to reach.

I should like to make a few other remarks about this matter of control, for it is here, I believe, that the participant interventionist in the field has a significant contribution to make. Depending upon the approaches used by the investigators, and the situations and problems studied by them, studies of the dynamics of culture and behavior vary a great deal with respect to two major characteristics—degrees of control, and richness of context. If we were to set up a continuum or scale for dealing with each of the characteristics, say from little to much control, and from little to much context, I think we would find that most studies in the behavioral sciences cluster toward the extreme ends of the continua. This can best be illustrated by taking two quite different approaches to the study of the dynamics of culture and behavior—that of the experimentalist and that of the observer.

Typically, the experimentalist, as exemplified by the experimental psychologist, has very much control and very little context, while the typical observer, as exemplified by the field anthropologist, has very little control and very much context. One of the major problems of the behavioral sciences is how to combine these two approaches into one so as to deal with much control and much context. (I do not mean to suggest that much good work along this line is not being done or has not already been done by sociologists, particularly industrial sociologists, and social psychologists.) But it is precisely here, I think, that the participant interventionist in the field has something further to contribute, for in a situation like Vicos he can manipulate and control larger blocks of context than can ever be done in the laboratory. This does not mean that all approaches are not necessary for a thorough understanding of the socio-cultural process. It simply means that the participant interventionist in the field, building on the work of the experimentalist and observer, attempts to control somewhat more complex sets of variables in the natural setting of the total culture. Moreover, his approach differs from that of the administrator in at least two significant ways. In the first place, his focus is on the study and analysis of the process he initiates, and in the second place, he is concerned with the total context in which it occurs.

VI

Let us now turn to a brief consideration of the role of the investigator in the application of the method of participant intervention in the field. I can think of no more summary or illuminating way to do this than to resort to analogy to indicate something of what I have in mind. The analogy concerns the psychoanalyst in the therapeutic situation. What does the analyst do? He starts with a patient who desires but is unable to function to his fullest capacity in the world in which he interacts. The fact that he cannot do so may be the fault of the society in which he lives, but if the patient is to make a satisfactory and desirable adjustment to life, he must change his behavior in various ways. The analyst cannot change this behavior for him; the patient must do it for himself. Ideally, what happens is this: through a process of self-enlightenment, with occasional strategic intervention by the analyst, the patient cures himself so that he can face up to his anxieties and shoulder his responsibilities to the best of his native abilities. When he reaches this point, the analyst is out of a job.

It seems to me that the role of the participant interventionist in the process of community development is much the same. His job is to assist the community to develop itself, and to study this process while it is taking place. He cannot "cure" the community as a surgeon cures a patient; the community must perform the operation on itself. At first, to be sure, as our experience in Vicos indicates, the investigator may have to intervene frequently and boldly, but as problem-solving and decision-making skills are developed, the investigator intervenes less and less until he works himself out of the role of intervener and into the role of consultant and observer.

VII

While it is probably much too soon to assess the over-all scientific results of our application of the method of participant intervention in the field at Vicos, our experiences thus far would seem to indicate that the method has a number of advantages as an approach to the theoretical and practical problems involved in programs of modern socio-economic development. In the first place, we have been able to carry out a great many scientific studies of the broad experimental type that would have been impossible to conduct under other conditions.

Of a great variety of such studies, I need mention only that from the very beginning we have been able, first, to conduct experiments on the acceptance and rejection of innovations which we have been able to follow up by observation and interviewing.

In the second place, we were in a position to test hypotheses that have been derived from other cultural systems and by other methods of study.

In the third place, we were in a position to speed up the processes of change and collapse within a relatively short period of time, changes that might have taken years to effect by natural processes.

In the fourth place, we have been able to test our predictions and improve our methods as the program advanced.

Finally, by being in a position of control—both political and scientific—and by having a continuing program of intervention and study (partially self-financed—no small item these days) we felt that we were able to isolate, integrate, and study at first hand the factors relevant to the transformation of a socio-cultural system like that of Vicos, which is an anachronism in the modern world, to a level of maturation in keeping with the high potential of its people and basic dignity of mankind the world over.

Chapter II

THE ROLE OF POWER IN CHANGING VALUES

AND INSTITUTIONS OF VICOS

Allan R. Holmberg

More than 50 percent of the world's population is peasantry, the large majority of which lives in the so-called underdeveloped countries or newly emerging nations, under natural conditions and social structures that have denied peasants effective participation in the modernization process. In the context of a modern state, this peasantry plays little or no role in the decision-making process; its members enjoy little access to wealth; they live under conditions of social disrespect; a large majority of them are illiterate, unenlightened, and lacking in modern skills; many are victims of ill health and disease. Characteristic of this sector of the world's population is a deep devotion to magico-religious practice as a means of mitigating the castigations of a harsh and cruel world over which it has little or no control. Such, in fact, were the conditions of life on the *Hacienda Vicos.*(1)

Operating on the assumption that these conditions of human indignity are not only anachronistic in the modern world but are also a great threat to public and civic order everywhere, Cornell University, in 1952—in collaboration with the Peruvian Indian Institute—embarked on an experimental program of induced technical and social change which was focused on the problem of transforming one of Peru's most unproductive, highly dependent manor systems into a productive, independent, self-governing community adapted to the reality of the modern Peruvian state.

Up until January, 1952, Vicos was a manor or large estate, situated in a relatively small intermontane valley of Peru, about 250 miles north of the capital city of Lima. Ranging in altitude from about nine thousand to twenty thousand feet, Vicos embraced an area of about 40,000 acres(2) and contained an enumerated population of 1,703 monolingual Quechua-speaking Indians(3) who had been bound to the land as serfs or peons since early colonial times. Vicos was located in the civil administrative district of Marcará, one of several such manors in Carhuaz Province which with thirteen others make up Ancash Department, one of twenty-three such units in the country. A Roman Catholic parish priest resided beside the parish church in Marcará, visiting Vicos and other outlying settlements a few times during the year.

Vicos was a public manor,(4) a type not uncommon in Peru. The title of Vicos was held by the Public Benefit (Charity) Society of Huaraz which rented the manor out to the highest bidder at public auction for periods ranging from 5 to 10 years. Vicos was one of 56 such properties owned by the Public Benefit Society of Huaraz which used its income from rent to maintain the largest, though woefully inadequate, hospital in the Andean area of the department of Ancash. The rent paid for Vicos amounted to approximately $500 a year. The Benefit Society board, appointed by the Minister of Health and Social Service and in theory responsible to the ministry, was in fact autonomous to a large degree. Members of the Benefit Society board were of the regional upper class residing in the departmental capital of Huaraz and were often themselves *patrones* of similar estates.

Each manor such as Vicos has particular lands, usually the most fertile bottom lands, reserved for commercial exploitation by the successful renter who utilizes, virtually free of charge for several days of each week, the serf-bound labor force—usually one adult member of every family, to cultivate his crops. Under the contractual arrangements between the renter and the Public Benefit Society the former was legally but not always functionally bound to supply, in return for the labor tax paid by his serfs, plots of land (usually upland) of sufficient size to support the family of each inscribed peon.

Power—Luis Moreyra y Paz Soldan, Prime Minister of Peru in 1963, and Luis Alvarado Garrido, then Foreign Minister and Acting Minister of Labor and Indian Affairs, examine documents connected with the purchase of Vicos land title by its Indian occupants. Cornell University Professors Allan R. Holmberg (fourth from right) and William F. Whyte, with Mrs. Whyte, look on with Vicos leaders Francisco Valerio, and Celso León H.

Vicos as a typical manor of the region was organized along similar lines. At the head of the hierarchy stood the renter or *Patrón* (Patron), usually absentee, who was always an outsider and non-Indian (that is, a "white" or Mestizo). He was the maximum authority within the system and all power to indulge or deprive was concentrated in his hands. Under his direction was an administrator, or overseer, also an outsider or Mestizo, responsible to the renter for conducting and managing the day-to-day agricultural or grazing operations of the property. Depending on the operations of the manor, the administrator employed from one to several Mestizo foremen (*Capataces*) who were responsible for the supervision of the labor force. They reported directly to the administrator on such matters as the number of absentee members of the labor force, and the condition of the crops regarding such factors as irrigation, fertilization, and harvest.

Below and apart from this small non-Indian "power elite" stood the Indian society of peons, bound to a soil they did not own and on which they had little security of tenure. The direct link between the labor force and the administration was through a number of Indian straw bosses, appointed by the Patron and responsible for the direct supervision of the labor force in the fields. These men in turn supervised the Vicos Indian "straw bosses" (called *mayorales* or *mandones*), each of whom had specific duties on the manor. Most of these men were field bosses (*pampa mayoral*) but one was in charge of maintaining the manor house and household (*ruri-mayoral*). Each *Mayoral* had under his direction a certain number of peons from a particular geographic area of the manor. In 1952 there were eight straw bosses at Vicos, with a total labor force of about 380 men obliged to work three days a week for the manor, being paid a "ration" of coca(6) and/or twenty centavos, about one penny for a day's labor. Although most of the time this work was at Vicos, sometimes the Vicos labor force would be "loaned" or hired out to other persons in the region. In such cases either the Patron or the administrator pocketed the salary earned by the Vicosinos as day laborers. In addition to the "labor tax" paid by the Indian community, its members were obligated to supply other free services to the manor, such as those of cooks, grooms, swineherds, watchmen, and servants who were supervised by the *ruri-mayoral.*

The whole system was maintained by the application of sanctions ranging from brute force to the impounding of peon property. Whipping serfs by labor bosses reportedly ended about 1928 when an Indian protest over this practice brought a central government order to end it. The hacienda still maintained its own jail into which recalcitrant or erring peons were placed, without recourse to the national laws or judicial system. Thus, the renter of Vicos and his administrator decided who was to be committed and for how long. Such actions were supported by the local officials in the district capital of Marcará or the nearby provincial and departmental capitals as well. When Vicosinos ventured to the local Sunday market to sell or buy the few things they could, they were likely to be put to work against their will by private persons in Marcará, often without pay. Vicosinos who refused to work would customarily be fined in some manner or incarcerated by the police. In such instances, the Patron or his surrogate might intervene, obtaining the peons' release and, of course, in so doing, increase the "social debt" of the peon to the Patron.

In matters not associated directly with manor operations, the Indian community of Vicos was organized along separate and traditional lines. The principal indigenous decision-making body consisted of a politico-religious hierarchy of some seventeen officials known as *Varas* or *Varayoc,* so named from the custom of carrying a wooden staff as a badge of office. The organization had been created as a system of "indirect" rule by the Spaniards in the sixteenth century, and similar ones were established throughout the colonial empire from the pueblos of the American southwest to Chile.(7) Over the many years the *varayoc* system in Vicos had become very elaborate since it was, in conjunction with the celebration of religious festivals which the *varas* managed, the only organization in which Vicosinos could participate. Through service in the *varayoc* institution, men (and only men) could achieve greater social prestige and status in the community ultimately, perhaps, with the opportunity of becoming a *mayoral* of the hacienda. Persons whose service as a *varayoc* had been long and distinguished were (and still are) called *yayas* (father of fathers) and constituted an

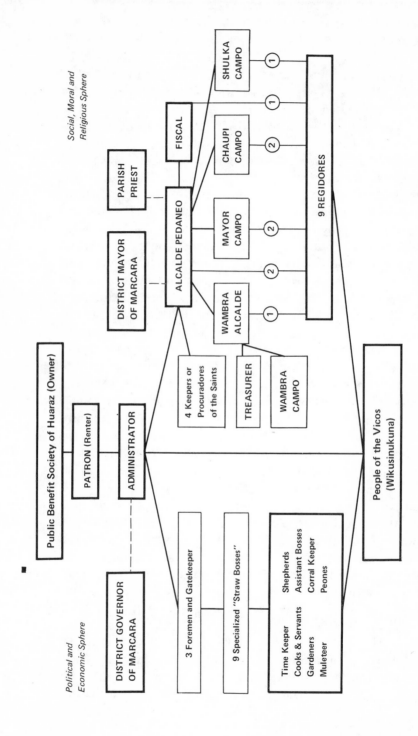

Political and Economic Sphere

Social, Moral and Religious Sphere

Public Benefit Society of Huaraz (Owner)

PATRON (Renter)

ADMINISTRATOR

DISTRICT GOVERNOR OF MARCARA

DISTRICT MAYOR OF MARCARA

PARISH PRIEST

ALCALDE PEDANEO

FISCAL

4 Keepers or Procuradores of the Saints

WAMBRA ALCALDE

TREASURER

WAMBRA CAMPO

SHULKA CAMPO

CHAUPI CAMPO

MAYOR CAMPO

9 REGIDORES

① ① ② ② ② ①

3 Foremen and Gatekeeper

9 Specialized "Straw Bosses"

Time Keeper   Shepherds
Cooks & Servants   Assistant Bosses
Gardeners   Corral Keeper
Muleteer   Peones

People of the Vicos (Wikusinukuna)

Figure I. ORGANIZATIONAL STRUCTURE OF VICOS MANOR IN 1951.

informal but well-defined council of elders much consulted and respected by all Vicosinos. From the Vicos side of things, the authority and power wielded by the *varayos* was legitimatized through the approbation of the *yayas,* although all power and authority of the *varayoc* really depended upon the Patron, who could veto any decision they might make. Consequently, service in the *varayoc* system provided the principal vehicle for achieving social distinction, respect, and power, although the *varayoc* activities were approved and ultimately controlled by the Patron.

The major functions of this body included the settling of disputes over land and animals in the Indian community, the supervision of public works such as the repair of bridges and the community church in Vicos(8), and the celebration of religious festivals. Prior to 1952 the *varayoc* also executed the penalties imposed by the Patron on the people either for failure to fulfill their obligations to the manor or for disputes among the serfs which the Patron or administrator mediated and judged. The *varayoc* might thus administer public whippings to adulterers, commit disobedient peons to the manor jail, or give public denunciation of breaches of respect to authority or parents.

Because the *varayoc* fulfilled various administrative, religious, and judicial functions and, in so doing, exercised more power than any other Vicosinos could through an organization, let us examine some details of the complex hierarchy diagrammed in Figure I. The nine statuses in the system and the roles of the persons attached thereto are arranged in a hierarchy which we can summarize in order of seniority:

> *Fiscal* (controller): serves as the organizer of many religious activities and in the recruitment (prior to 1952) of servants for the Patron. This personage is usually the one of greatest seniority and a former *alcaldi.*
>
> *Alcaldi* (mayor, also called, *chontayoc, alcaldi pedaneo, alcaldi penario,* or *warangayoc*): responsible for the activities of the other *varayoc* and supervises their acts, maintaining discipline and respect for the authority they symbolize. This is the most prestigious position even though second in seniority rank.
>
> *Mayor campo* (major "campo"): alternates and substitutes for the *alcaldi,* sharing his responsibilities.

> *Chaupi campo* (middle "campo"): shares responsibilities and alter-
> nates with the *mayor campo.*
>
> *Shulka campo* (minor "campo"): assists the *chaupi campo.*
>
> *Wambra alcaldi* (children's mayor): assigned various religious duties
> and helps to manage the Vicos cemetery.
>
> *Wambra campo* (children's "campo"): assists the *wambra alcaldi.*
>
> *Tesorero* (treasurer): named by the *wambra alcaldi* and assists in
> maintaining the cemetery.
>
> *Regidor* (councilman, also known as *brazo* = "arm", and familia =
> family): lowest ranking of the *varayoc* whose task is to assist
> those to whom he is assigned. There are nine *regidores;* during
> fiestas and rituals they act as waiters (*kamachicos*) serving the
> other, higher-ranking *varayoc.*

Finally, there are the *procuradores,* numbering four to six, who are named by the *alcaldi* from among his friends and sympa-thizers. These persons are charged with registering volunteer sponsors of religious fiestas and seeing that these persons fulfill their promises the following year. *Procuradores* are not con-sidered as *varayoc* and do not carry staffs of office.

As can be appreciated by the above list, the *varayoc* are organized in a hierarchical fashion with the lower ranks serving the upper ones. In all their acts the *varayoc* must exemplify the guiding values of Vicos life, including respect for authority and age, reverence of holy things, loyalty, obedience, manliness, and morality. In going from place to place, for example, the *varayoc,* carrying their staves, walk in single file by order of rank; they bow and tip their hats to one another and kiss the hands of higher-ranking personages in the system, and are originally selected (in theory at least) on the basis of their correct marriage, proper family life, and actions.

Ideally, one is promoted through the ranks of the organiza-tion over a period of as many as thirty years, rising from the rank of *regidor* to that of *fiscal* in order of seniority as noted above. A man may serve as *regidor,* then ten or so years later, become *shulka campo,* and later, *chaupi campo,* and so on. Actually, the order of promotion is only closely observed in the case of the three final offices. Some idea of the complicated activities and ritual involved in being a *varayoc* is conveyed by the following account:(9)

"All the *varayoc* change in January of each year. The new *Alcaldi* is elected previously, his designation constituting a ritual which begins in the last week of October with 'voting.' Adult males are consulted as to whether the office of *Alcaldi* shall be occupied by the senior *campo mayor* or by him whose turn it is, or another. This consultation is effected during the repair of the largest bridge of the locality for which task the *varayoc* invite the former *varayoc* and all the men, who after exchanging opinions, ratify the senior *campo-mayor* or another person who possesses the necessary attributes to function as *Alcaldi*. That is, he must be married, an adult, hold a comfortable economic position and enjoy prestige. After the event the newly elected is plied with liquor by the *varayoc,* who officially pay him the same attention again on All Saints' Day. During the month of November, the outgoing *Alcaldi* obtains from the Mayor of the Municipality of Marcará a 'commission' or written certification of the designation of the new *Alcaldi*. This petition used to be made with prior consent of the *Patrón* of the hacienda. The 'commission' is conveyed to its recipient on the main day of the festival of St. Andrew (November 30th). Later, on the night of December 31st, the *varayoc* effect the 'capture' of the *alcaldi*-elect, who is plied with liquor and a meal in the house of the outgoing *varayoc* until sunset on January 1st. On that day the ceremony of transmission of office is carried out in the door of the Vicos chapel. Until 1956 the conveyance consisted of the *Patrón* swearing in the new *Alcaldi* and handing over to him his *vara,* and his swearing in his *campo-mayor* and giving him his *vara.*

"In effect the conveyance ceremony initiated the subordination of the *varayoc* to the *Patrón*. When the hacienda system was abolished in 1956, the intervention of the *Patrón* disappeared, and since then the conveyance has been effected without swearing in and the staves are handed over directly by the outgoing to the incoming *Alcaldi* and *campo-mayor*.

"During the days following the conveyance the *Alcaldi* and *campo-mayor* are preoccupied with the formation of their respective squads of *varayoc,* endeavoring to make them up of persons who live in the different zones, since oral transmissions of orders and supervision of their fulfillment is in this way facilitated. Later the *varayoc* repair to Marcará for the ceremony of *requinákuy* or mutual getting acquainted by the *varayoc* of the neighboring towns in the District. On this occasion, they agree on the date of the benediction imparted to all the *varayoc* of the district of Marcará by the priest at the parish church."

The *varayoc* were organized in a kind of "pecking order" in which, through ritual, their often servile and inconsequential activity was dignified and elevated to a condition approaching sanctity. Under the hacienda regime, the *varayoc,* although wielding considerable power as the highest native authorities in Vicos, reflected not only the hierarchical structure of the larger society that ultimately controlled them, but in ritualized procedure, formally acknowledged their subordination to the Patron, the constitutional mayor of the district of Marcará (at that time appointed by the Prefect) and the parish priest. This ceremonial acknowledgment was reinforced by the kind of activities directed and performed by the *varayoc* during their period of office: repair of paths, roads, and bridges for the district as a whole, executing orders and applying penalties given by the Patron, and supporting, servicing, and managing religious events for the priest. What power they exercised, then, was, in last analysis, dependent entirely upon the Mestizo, non-Indian authorities.

The principal process for gaining respect in traditional Vicos society was to grow old and to participate in the politico-religious hierarchy, the top positions of which could be occupied only after many years of faithful service to the community. Wealth was also a source of gaining prestige and recognition, but it could not be amassed in any quantity, by native standards, until one's elders had died or until an individual himself had worked very hard and lived frugally for many years. In other words, the principal role to which high rank was attached was that of hard-working, virtual subsistence farmer who placed little or no value on other occupations or skills. Consequently there was just no place for a rebellious or symbolically creative individual in traditional Vicos society. The manor system was, of course, in large part responsible for this. It needed few skills beyond brawn; enlightenment could not be tolerated because the more informed the population, the more it might become a threat to the traditional manor system. Records show that all protest movements of Vicos had been squelched by a coalition of the landlords, the clergy, and the police.(10) As a result, over a period of several hundred years the community remained in static equilibrium—and completely out of step with anything occurring in the modern world. The rule at Vicos was conformity to the status quo. It pervaded all institutions and dominated the social process. The peon was subservient to the overlord, the child to the parents; both were cowed into submission. Even the supernatural forces were punishing, and the burdens one bore were suffered as if naturally ordained by powers beyond one's control.

In 1952 all Vicosinos were virtual subsistence farmers, occupying plots of land ranging in size from less than one-half to about five acres. The principal crops raised were maize, potatoes, and other Andean root crops, wheat, barley, rye, broad beans, and quinoa (pigweed, used as a cereal). In addition, most families grazed some livestock (cattle, sheep, goats, and swine) and all families raised small animals like guinea pigs and chickens as a way of supplementing their diets and their incomes. After thousands of years of use and inadequate care, however, the land had lost its fertility, seeds had degenerated, and the principal crops and animals were stunted and diseased. Per capita output was thus at a very low level, although the exact figure is not known.

In addition, many Vicosinos suffered from malnutrition; most were victims of a host of endemic diseases. Studies in parasitology(11) demonstrated that 80 percent of the population was infected with harmful parasites, and epidemics of such diseases as measles and whooping cough had been frequent over the years. There were, to be sure, native curers employing magico-religious techniques and herbal remedies to cope with these problems of well-being, but it can be said that the community had little or no access to modern medicine. The goal of the traditional Vicosino was simply to survive as long as he possibly could, knowing full well that he might be a victim of fate at any moment.

INTERVENTION
FROM WITHOUT

In 1952 the Cornell Peru Project intervened in this context in the role of Patron. Through a partly fortuitous circumstance— the industrial firm which was renting Vicos on a ten-year lease with still five years to run went bankrupt—the property and its serfs were available for sublease for a five-year period. For a couple of years prior to this time, however, the Peruvian anthropologist, Dr. Mario C. Vázquez, had conducted a very detailed study of this manor as a social system, part of a larger comparative study of modernization of peasant societies that the Cornell University Department of Anthropology was conducting in several areas of the world. Thus, when opportunity to rent the hacienda arose, the university seized upon it to conduct experiments in modernization. In its negotiations prior to renting the hacienda, Cornell received full support of the Peruvian Government through its Institute of Indigenous Affairs, a semi-autonomous agency of the Ministry of Labor and Indigenous Affairs. In December, 1951, a formal Memorandum of Agreement was drawn up between Cornell and the Institute of Indigenous Affairs, and the Cornell Peru Project became a reality at Vicos on January 1, 1952.

Several months prior to assuming the responsibilities of the power role at Vicos, a plan of operations was drawn up,(12) focusing on the promotion of human dignity rather than indignity and the formation of institutions at Vicos which would allow for a wide, rather than a narrow, shaping and sharing of values for all participants in the social process. The principal goals of this plan thus became the devolution of power to the community, the production and broad sharing of greater wealth, the introduction and diffusion of new and modern skills, the promotion of health and well-being, the enlargement of the status and role structure, and the formation of a modern system of enlightenment through schools and other media. It was hoped that, by relying on institutions specialized to these values as independent variables, this focus would also have some modernizing effect on the more dependent variables, namely, the institutions specialized to respect, affection (family and kinship), and rectitude (religion and ethics), sensitive areas of culture in which it is generally more hazardous to intervene directly.

In designing our program and a method of strategic intervention, we were very much aware of two, among many, guiding principles stemming from anthropological research: first, innovations are most likely to be accepted in those aspects of culture in which people themselves feel the greatest deprivations; and second, an integrated or contextual approach to value-institutional development is usually more lasting and less conflict-producing than a piecemeal one. Consequently, we established our operational priorities on the basis of the first principle but tried to optimize change in all areas at the same time, realizing, of course, that with scarce resources all values could not be maximized concurrently. Perhaps a few examples will best illustrate our use of the method of strategic intervention.

Our first entry into more than a research role at Vicos coincided with a failure of the potato harvest of both the Patron and the serf community due to a blight which had attacked the crop. The poor of the community were literally starving, and even the rich were feeling the pinch. Complaints about the theft of animals and food were rife. At the same time, previous study of the manor had forewarned us about the major grievances of the serfs against the traditional system. These turned out not to be such things as the major commitment of each head of household to contribute one peon to the labor force for three days each week, but the obligation of the Indian households to supply the extra, free services (such as swineherds and cooks) to the manor. Since we were in a position of power, it was relatively easy to abolish these services. A decision was made to do so, and volunteers were hired to perform these jobs for pay as needed. Thus an immediate positive reinforcement was supplied to the community in our power relationship with it.

An added incentive to collaborate with the new administration resulted when, as Patrons, we reimbursed the serfs for labor they had performed under the previous administration but for which they had not been paid for approximately three years. Under the traditional system, each peon was entitled to about three cents per week for work performed under the labor tax. In some Peruvian manors this is paid in the form of coca leaves, which most adult males chew, but at Vicos it was supposed to have been paid in cash. By deducting the back pay from the cost of transfer of the manor to our control, we fulfilled earlier commitments with the money of the previous administration and received the credit for it. Through such small but immediately reinforcing interventions, a solid base for positive relations with members of the community was first established. In this regard, of course, Dr. Vázquez, who had previously spent almost two years in the community living with an Indian family, and who personally knew and was trusted by almost every one of its members as well as many others, played a key role.

INCREASING AGRICULTURAL PRODUCTIVITY

One of the most immediate and urgent tasks at Vicos was to do something about its failing economy which, even without blight, in reality meant increasing its agricultural productivity. Manors like Vicos are never productive because the renter during his period of tenure puts as little as possible into the operation and exploits the property for as much as he possibly can. The serfs, on the other hand, make no improvements or other capital investments on their lands, because they, too, have no security of tenure. As a consequence, most such manors are in a very bad state of repair.

Since the Cornell Peru Project possessed funds only for research and not for capital development, the wealth base had to be enlarged by other means. It was decided, in consultation with Indian leaders, who were early informed about the goals of the Project, that no major changes would be initiated immediately in the day-to-day operations of the manor. We even retained the former Mestizo administrator, a close friend of the Project Director and Field Director, who agreed to reorient his goals to those of the Project.

The principal resources available to the Project were the labor of the Indian community and the lands which had been formerly farmed by the overlord. By employing this labor to farm these lands by modern methods (the introduction of fertilizer, good seed, pesticides, proper row spacing, etc.), and by growing marketable food crops, capital was accumulated for enlarging the wealth base. Returns from these lands, instead of being removed from the community, as was the case under the traditional system, were plowed back into the experiment to foment further progress toward our goals. Profits from the

Project's share of the land were not only employed further to improve agricultural productivity but also to construct health and educational facilities, to develop a wider range of skills among the Indian population, and to reconstruct what had been a completely abandoned administrative center of operations. At the same time, new techniques of potato production and other food crops, first demonstrated on Project lands, were introduced to the Indian households which, within a couple of years, gave a sharp boost to the Indian economy. In short, by 1957 when Cornell's lease on the land expired, a fairly solid economic underpinning for the whole operation had been established, and the goal of considerably enlarging the wealth base had been accomplished.

DEVOLUTION
OF POWER

From the very first day of operations, the process of power devolution was initiated. We decided it would be impossible to work with the traditional *varas* as a leadership group, because they were so occupied during their terms of office with religious matters they would have no time to spend on secular affairs. On the other hand, the former straw bosses, also elderly and respected men with a great deal of direct experience in conducting manor affairs for the Patron, were available. We decided not to bypass this group even though we knew its members had enjoyed the greatest indulgences under the traditional system and, being old, were less likely to be innovative than younger men. Under prevailing conditions, however, this seemed to be the best alternative to pursue. As it turned out, it proved an effective transitional expedient. Gradually, as success was achieved in the economic field, it became possible to replace (by appointment) the retiring members of this body with younger men more committed to the goals of modernization. For instance, men finishing their military service—an obligation we encouraged them to fulfill— returned home with at least an exposure to other values and institutions in Peruvian society. In pre-Cornell days the few such returning veterans were forced back into the traditional mold within a few days' time, with no opportunity to give expression to any newly found values they may have acquired. Insofar as possible, we tried to incorporate people of this kind into decision-making bodies and tried to provide them opportunities to practice whatever new skills they had acquired (the Peruvian army, when dealing with highland Indian recruits and draftees, provides literacy and often technical training in agriculture, mechanics, and so on).

Moreover, the Cornell project directors took the opportunity to develop needed leadership qualities among the *mayorales* by conducting meetings with them and encouraging their participation. This marked a startling innovation for them since in matters of hacienda management or life, the Patron in past years not only ignored Vicosino wants or opinions but actively discouraged any true leadership initiatives that might be shown by individuals. By the same token, the traditional *mando* or gathering of serfs to receive their weekly orders also served as a kind of forum at which time Vicosinos were advised of project activities and the people encouraged to offer their views. In the first five years of the Project, not only did age composition of the governing body completely change, but decision-making and other skills had developed to a point where responsibility for running the affairs of the community was largely in indigenous hands.

Between 1957 and 1962 the Cornell Peru Project supported the Vicosinos in their effort to buy the estate of Vicos and to become its proprietors, culminating in its complete purchase on July 13, 1962. At the same time it sponsored the change in land tenure, the Cornell Peru Project assisted in a reorganization of the process of public decision-making to allow for the democratic participation by the former serf population. Methodical preparations to this end followed.

Between May and September, 1956, Cornell Peru Project staff members consulted Vicosinos either individually, in small groups, and by family or in zonal and general assemblies about what they wished for the future of Vicos upon the conclusion of the university's rental contract. The opinion of the majority was to purchase the manor, and, to this end, they suggested collective work on the manor lands with the proceeds of this labor going to pay the cost of the purchase. Since this operation would require organization, which had the prior approval of the Vicosinos, it was decided to divide the manor-community into ten geographic zones in accord with the ten most important areas of population concentration. Each zone would have its respective representative or delegate elected democratically. The ten delegates would then form the "Communal Directive Board" *(Junta de Delegados).*

In October of 1956 the first zonal elections were held. The ten elected councilmen chose their own officers, namely president, secretary, and treasurer. These officers then made contact (with the aid of the Cornell Peru Project) with the Peruvian Indian Institute and through the action of the Institute an official resolution for the expropriation of the Vicos manor on behalf of the Vicos serfs was obtained. The expropriation resolution did not become effective. Quite the contrary, a long and sterile struggle began between the Vicosinos and the Public Benefit Society of Huaraz, owner of the manor. From 1956 to July, 1962, when the purchase finally was officially approved, the Vicosinos were aided and protected by a "power umbrella" consisting of the Cornell Peru Project and the Peruvian Indian Institute (later Plan for Integrating the Aboriginal Population) to implement their attempts to achieve either purchase or expropriation of the manor in their favor. In this period of uncertainty and struggle, the people of Vicos became more united and cohesive behind their elected representatives. The first elected delegates were replaced in 1959 by others elected in the same way. Since that year, the delegates have been democratically elected annually in the month of June.

Based on his observations of the first elections, Vázquez in 1960 persuaded the Vicosinos to introduce some changes into the electoral process. In 1956 and in 1959 the delegates had been elected by acclamation of the candidate proposed by an individual with the most prestige and local power. Naturally, under this system, those elected did not always represent the majority opinion, but rather those individuals with the most power and wealth. In 1960 the advisory staff asked that the election be made between two candidates, previously nominated, and that each person verbally express his vote for his preference. This innovation did not aid in solving the problem, because it almost always resulted in the election of the candidate of greatest power and prestige, since godchildren vote for their godfathers, younger brothers for older brothers, debtors for their creditors, and so forth.

In 1961, therefore, two other changes were made. A secret ballot was introduced using colors to identify the candidates. The Vicos public participated in the direct election of the president and other officers of the Communal Directive Board. At first the Vicosinos had difficulty picking up the thin colored-paper ballots which they selected from boxes in which they were stocked, later depositing them in the ballot-box slot. Their rough farmers' hands and fingers were unaccustomed to such delicate operations and this occasioned the final use of thick cardboard ballots about two inches square which could easily be grasped by calloused hands. To some extent the people were disoriented by the "secret chamber" for voting despite the many explanations that were offered them. These difficulties have been overcome, and in succeeding years have not caused such problems.

The reason for changing the manner of electing the council officers stemmed from complaints that certain zones would be favored in communal work as the result of election "agreements" among delegates. Moreover, the president's authority was limited to the delegates and to his own zone constituents, so that the great majority of people in the other zones were even unaware of the existence of such an office. Under these circumstances emerged the decision that such officials should be elected by everyone, and not just the delegates. Another fact to be noted is that the council candidate from a particular zone who ran second in the election would act as alternate to the delegate in the case that the latter became sick or absent.

This of course resulted in the inclusion of even more persons in the formal processes of the community. The annually elected council is now accepted by some 94 percent of the people as the best instrument of government.(13) As Montoya reports, this acceptance was due directly to the widespread discontent the Vicosinos felt with regard to the conditions under which they were forced to live on the hacienda. When asked if they like to vote for delegates, and why, the response was likely to be: "Yes, voting is better, because now we can not be slaves. In this way we ourselves choose our leaders."(14)

As a result of the evolution of a council of delegates in the place of the former *mayorales* and *capataces* (roles which have disappeared altogether) a number of important changes have taken place and continue to transform the former structure of the manor. Today the scope of council activities has grown to include some of those formerly dealt with by the *varayoc*—some public works, settlement of internal community disputes over land, and other matters. In addition, and very importantly, membership on the council of delegates gives not only prestige, but also power in a more real sense than ever exercised by the *varayoc*, or indeed even the *mayorales*. The elected council, further discussed in the following chapters, is the maximum authority in the community today, no longer superseded by outsiders in the manner of the Patron and administrator of former years.

A vivid demonstration of the role of the delegates, and their prestige in the community, took place in 1961 when the *varayoc* had an argument among themselves over cattle belonging to the church. Unable to mediate or settle the dispute themselves, they called upon the elected manager and secretary of the community to do this. Today, therefore, *varayoc* activities have narrowed to where they are concerned largely with religious festivals and conduct of the marriage system. Despite this change, however, the *yayas* and other older persons in general continue to exercise much influence in Vicos life although the delegates increasingly represent the younger elements in the population—particularly those who have achieved primary or secondary schooling.

The power structure of Vicos has changed in other ways as well. In 1951, as we see in Appendix B, the people of Vicos occupied few positions of power *(varayoc, mayorales* and one man as *teniente gobernador)*. All of these personages were entirely subordinate to either Mestizo members of the hacienda staff *(capataces,* administrator, and Patron), or to complete outsiders such as the *gobernador* (official in charge of rural law enforcement) who named a "reliable" Vicosino as his lieutenant *(teniente gobernador),* the district municipal mayor, the police, the judge, the priest, and finally, any other private member of the Mestizo community of Marcará. Since the school in Vicos was scarcely operational (see Chapter VI) neither the teacher nor the educational system played any role worthy of mention.

During the course of the project in the mid-1950s the Cornell Peru Project, by virtue of its official status under the then Ministry of Labor and Indian Affairs, not only completely assumed the role of hacienda Patron and his assistants, but also, because of the prestige and nationally based sources of power, was able to influence official affairs in the district of Marcará with reference to Vicos. In this manner the people of Vicos came under an umbrella which shielded them somewhat from the complete arbitrary and often illegal control formerly exercised over their lives by Mestizos in the district capital.

It was no longer possible, for example, for someone from Marcará to force a Vicosino to work against his will and without pay or to incarcerate people without due cause. In the same manner, dealings with higher authorities were also filtered through Project staff. In the course of establishing the Project programs in agriculture, education, and health, other Peruvian governmental agencies were brought to Vicos, a place their representatives had never before visited. A new dimension was added to the picture. Here were other agencies also seeking to assist rather than exploit the people. There was, of course, the danger—which still continues—that these new outside agencies would simply replace the old ones in a well-meaning, but paternalistic way. New faces in Vicos included, after 1957, nine school teachers and a Ministry of Labor and Indian Affairs-Ministry of Education program director for the new "nuclear school" and the "Ancash Program" (one man directed both programs) and his staff of five or six persons.(15) This program of the combined ministries was designed to take over the operations of the Cornell-Peru Project insofar as its development role was concerned. Cornell personnel remained at Vicos, after 1957, as advisor to the Ministerial programs and as a research operation, represented by a field director and, upon occasion, numerous students. In actuality, the Cornell field director played a somewhat wider role than existed "on paper," since Cornell still maintained not only its power base in Lima at the ministries, but also as the former Patron of Vicos. This power image was further enhanced since Dr. Vázquez, with the longest and most profound contact with Vicos, was the field director until 1962. By this time however, he had already begun to withdraw both physically and operationally from Vicos (he, and all Cornell representatives, save occasional students, left Vicos completely by the end of 1963, except for sporadic short visits).

Although the Ministerial representatives, and the Ancash program in particular, officially held responsibility for the entire operation at Vicos after 1957, their role was at times somewhat diminished by continued Cornell presence, as well as by the increasingly aggressive Vicosino participation in the management of their own affairs. Thus, the people of Vicos, through their elected delegates, made their wishes manifest for a new school principal to replace the incumbent whom they greatly disliked. When the director of the Ancash Program (who at that time was also director of the nuclear school) as well as the Cornell field representative were unable to obtain this change at the Ministry of Education, the Council of Delegates padlocked the school and sent a commission to Lima, where they convinced the national office to make the change desired.

By 1966 the ministerial programs had waned greatly. The Vicos school and the small rural schools in the vicinity continued to function fully, but the new Ancash program director and his personnel were often absent from Vicos engaged in the operations of the expanded regional program.(16) Moreover, the "director" of the nuclear school program had been transferred to Lima in 1965 even though he continued to draw a salary and "occupy" the position at Vicos (a bureaucratic situation referred to by Peruvians as *"destacado"*). This condition continued through 1967, and the nuclear school program was left in the hands of an underpaid acting director who had been a member of the program for some years. The programs of both ministries therefore suffered, perhaps, but in fact the betterment of the community was effected, since the Vicosinos, by 1966, were virtually running their affairs without any outside supervision.

Thus, with the disappearance—planned and unplanned—of outside agencies, the power continuum with relation to the people of Vicos presented a radically altered picture. Vicosinos now occupy several new positions of power which had not been open to them in 1952 (Council of Delegates with their own officers; a municipal agent representing the district mayor, an elected position of the Marcará district council) in addition to that of *teniente gobernador* which had formerly existed. Gone were the positions of Patron, administrator, *capataz*, and *mayoral* of the old hacienda. With the sale of Vicos in 1962 the Public Benefit Society also ceased to have a controlling influence in Vicos life. The school system on the other hand became more closely involved with the community, especially when the first Vicosino assumed teaching responsibilities at Vicos in 1966. Finally, the arbitrary and extra-legal power exercised by the townsmen of Marcará over the Vicosinos in former days was vastly diminished.

In sum, the picture of the power structure with reference to Vicos in 1966 showed the elimination of extra-legal external controls, an increase in the official stature of the Vicos community and leaders, an integration of Vicos into the formal political and administrative organization of the nation, a shortening of the distance between the people and the sources of national power, and access to those sources. In the years of the Vicos Project the people had increased their share of power from what could be considered a zero point with reference to the "outside" world in 1952, to one which, given the rural, undeveloped context of the region as a whole, placed them in a position to defend their interests successfully and to develop those other aspects of their lives they deemed important. The formal evidence of this new power first emerged in 1963 when a Vicosino became a candidate (though not elected) for the office of municipal councilman in Marcará. In 1966 the first Vicosino in history to occupy public elective office was elected to a councilman's position in Marcará District, despite continuing local prejudice against Vicosinos and Indians in general.(17)

In the area of well-being it was much more difficult to devise a strategy of intervention that would show immediate and dramatic payoff. This is a value area, to be sure, in which great deprivation was felt at Vicos, but it is also one in which the cooperation of all participants in the community was necessary in order to make any appreciable impact on it. The major standard of living problems at Vicos, even today, stem from public health conditions. All individuals are deeply concerned about their personal well-being but many are unwilling to forego other value indulgences to make better conditions a reality for the community as a whole. In addition, even had the community demanded improvement, the resources available to the Project and the Peruvian government at the time the Project began were grossly inadequate—even as they are today.

A variety of attempts were made to tackle the most urgent health problems, however, In collaboration with the Peruvian Ministry of Health and Social Welfare, a mobile clinic was organized to make at least one visit to the community each week. Support for this effort came from the community itself through the construction of a small sanitary post at which the sick could be treated. It was hoped to staff this clinic through the public health services of Peru and nuclear school personnel but all attempts to do so were frustrated by lack of budget and responsibly trained personnel. In Peru, such services seldom extend into rural areas because the preferred values of the medical profession are, as almost everywhere, associated with city life. Consequently, no major public health effort was launched and the medical and sanitary state of the community has shown little net gain. What advancement has been made stems principally from improved nutrition and higher levels of living. As enlightenment about the germ theory of disease diffuses, and the results of modern medicine are not only clearly demonstrated but made readily available through the application of public health measures that take native beliefs into account, we expect a sharp rise in the well-being status of the community to follow.

OPTIMIZING
GOALS

Strategies for optimizing Cornell Project goals for the respect, affection, and rectitude values first rested heavily on the examples set by Project personnel. From the very beginning, for example, an equality of salutation was introduced in all dealings with the Vicosinos; they were invited to sit down at the tables with us; no segregation was allowed at public affairs; Project personnel lived in Indian houses. At the same time, we attempted to protect the constitutional rights of Vicosinos which previously had been flagrantly violated by Mestizo society. Abuses by Mestizo authorities and army recruiters were no longer tolerated. The draft status of all Vicosinos was regularized; young men were encouraged to fulfill their legal obligations to the nation. While not directly intervening in the family or tampering with religious practice, the indirect effect of optimizing other values on the respect position of the community soon became evident. As Vicosinos mastered modern techniques of potato production, for example, they were approached by their Mestizo compatriots in the surrounding area, seeking advice as to how to improve their own crops.

Even the rectitude patterns at Vicos began to change. When we first took control of the manor, rates of theft were extremely high. Every peon farmer, as his crops approached maturity, had to keep watchmen in his fields at night. As the Indian economy rose and starvation was eliminated, this practice virtually disappeared. Even the parish priest became an enthusiastic supporter of the Project, for his services were more in demand—to say nothing of their being much better paid.

A strategy of promoting enlightenment at Vicos was initiated through the adaptation of a traditional manor institution to goals and values of the Project. In most Andean manors run along the line of Vicos, the peons, after completing their three days' labor, must report to the manor house to receive their work orders for the following week. This session of all peons, straw bosses, and the Patron was known as the *mando*. We devised a strategy of meeting, the day before the *mando*, the *mayorales* or decision-making body and utilizing the *mando* to communicate and discuss the decisions taken. Since heads of all households were present, the *mando* provided an excellent forum for the communication of news, the discussion of plans, and progress toward goals.

A long-run strategy of enlightenment rested on the founding of an educational institution at Vicos that could provide continuity for Project goals, training of leadership dedicated to the process of modernization, and the formation of a wide range of skills. Through collaboration with the Peruvian Ministry of Education and the Vicos community itself, this became a possibility. Within the period of Cornell's tenure, levels of advancement and skill rose sharply and their effects have been substantial throughout the society.

TRANSFER OF
TITLE

In 1957, at the time Cornell's lease in Vicos expired, the Project made a recommendation to the Peruvian Government through its Institute of Indigenous Affairs, to expropriate the property from the holders of the title, the Public Benefit Society of Huaraz, in favor of its indigenous inhabitants. By this time we felt that a fairly solid value institutional base, with the goals of modernization we had recently formulated, had been established in the community. The Peruvian government acted upon the recommendation and issued a decree of expropriation.

It was at this point that the experiment became especially significant, both in the local area and throughout the nation, for national development. Prior to this time, although considerable favorable national publicity had been given to the Project, little attention had been paid to it by the local power elite, except in terms of thinking that the benefits of its developments would eventually revert to the title holders. It was inconceivable in the local area that such a property might be sold back to the indigenous inhabitants. Consequently, local power groups immediately threw every possible legal block against the title reverting to the Indian community. They set a price on the property that would have been impossible for the Indian community ever to pay (seven million soles); members of the Project were charged with being agents of the communist world; the Vicosinos were accused of being pawns of American capitalism; Peruvian workers in the field were regarded as spies of the American government. Even such a "progressive" organization as the Rotary Club of Huaraz roundly denounced the Project, accusing its field director of being an agent of communism.

Fortunately, the Project had strong support in the intellectual community of the capital and among many of Peru's agencies of government. The co-director of the Project and President of the Indigenous Institute of Peru (also an internationally recognized scholar in high-altitude biology), Dr. Carlos Monge M., was tireless in his effort to see justice done to the Vicosinos. Even his efforts did not bear fruit until almost five years had passed, and the Institute's integration program had been absorbed by the Peruvian National Plan for Integrating the Aboriginal Population, established in 1959. The reason for this delay was that not only was legal resistance formidable, but the central government of Peru at this time was an elitist government, which, while giving great lip service to the cause of the Vicosinos, was reluctant to take action in their favor. It is a matter of record that many high officials of government were themselves *hacendados*, hesitant to alter the status quo. In fact, efforts to negotiate the sale of Vicos to the people had led the Cornell staff to explore "philanthropic" offers for loans to Vicos (at 20 percent interest!) and to seek means of applying political pressures. All such efforts came to total frustration when, in the spring of 1961, the Prime Minister of Peru (Pedro Beltrán E.) informed the United States' Charge d'affaires that he would never approve the Vicos sale for fear of the precedent it would set in land reform matters throughout the country.(18)

Meanwhile the Vicosinos, now renting the manor directly by using their own earnings, were reluctant to develop Vicos because of the danger of their not being able to enjoy the fruits of such labor. While agricultural production rose through the stimulation of annual crop loans from the Agricultural Bank of Peru, other capital investments were not made for fear that the price of the property would rise with every investment made. The first estimates of the value of Vicos made by the Public Benefit Society included, with the price of the land, such things as the estimated value of the Cornell Peru Project staff housing, teachers' living quarters (built by the Vicosinos), each serf's house and animals, trees planted by the people, and communally built bridges. Thus, one estimate of the value submitted by the Public Benefit Society was S/7,000,000 (in contrast to a ministerial estimate which set the value at S/700,000!). Consequently, for several years, doubt over the outcome impeded infrastructural investments and slowed the pace of development.

Then, in the summer of 1961, a series of events took place which led to the final sale of Vicos on July 13, 1962. The people of Vicos had by this time grown tense over the delays, and adding to their frustration was the fact that the Public Benefit Society was preparing to auction the Vicos estate (and peons) to a new renter as it had in days prior to the Project. In addition to this situation the nation as a whole had been experiencing considerable peasant unrest during much of the year. In Vicos, these tensions were heightened when the national police killed three serfs and wounded others on the adjacent manor of Huapra in August, 1960. This incident stirred the Vicosinos to the point where they bitterly talked of purchasing arms in the event that the Public Benefit Society should actually proceed with its reported plan to restore the hated hacienda system.

At this point, in the summer of 1961 two U.S. political leaders who were to play roles in creating an opportunity for Vicosinos to insure their continued social autonomy, visited Vicos. First came James I. Loeb, U.S. President John F. Kennedy's first Ambassador to Peru, who expressed his concern over Vicos to Peruvian government officials. Next, Edward Kennedy, then only a private citizen (but, importantly for the kinship-conscious Peruvians, the brother of much-admired President Kennedy) paid a vist to Peru, including Vicos and other places in the Callejon de Huaylas. Here he became absorbed with the dilemma of the Vicosinos and upon return to Lima, in an interview with Peruvian President Manuel Prado, demanded that action be taken to proceed with the sale of Vicos.(19) This initiative had its effect, and shortly serious negotiations for the sale of Vicos began. Through the constant pressure exerted by the President of the Institute of Indigenous Affairs of Peru, U.S. government officials in Peru, and the Cornell Peru Project, an agreement was reached between the Public Benefit Society and the Vicos community for the direct sale of the property to the Vicosinos. The price was two million soles ($74,626) to be paid in the following manner: S/500,000 payable immediately from Vicos community savings and another similar amount to be paid in three years. The final one million soles was loaned by the national government to be repaid over a twenty-year period at no interest.

In addition, the national government of Peru agreed to procure financing for a new regional hospital in the departmental capital of Huaraz to compensate the Public Benefit Society for the "loss" of the rent-producing property of Vicos and to meet a genuine need for the medical facility. By 1968, the Vicosinos had paid the initial heavy installments entirely from their community earnings. They quite literally purchased their freedom: their homes and other belongings, their lands, animals, and themselves.

Thus, after a five-year wait following the devolution of power, the community actually became independent in July, 1962. Since that time the Cornell Peru Project played a diminishing research, advisory, and consultant role.

RESULTS

The initial reaction to the sale of Vicos was one of euphoria. To provide palpable and irrefutable evidence of their new status, the Vicosinos purchased a large, deluxe Ford model 600 truck on which they painted the phrases, "Vicos Communal Property" and "Cry of Reform," designed to impress skeptics in Marcará and the region. With the controversial assistance of Peace Corps volunteers stationed in Vicos from 1962 through 1965, they also succeeded in obtaining the purchase of lands of the adjacent estate of Chancos (which had formerly been part of Vicos and on which 65 Vicosinos still lived in serfdom) which they incorporated into their community.[20] Other opportunities have continued to develop, which, over time, will add to the changes already introduced. In 1967, for example, with the assistance of the regional Indigenous Development Program, the community began work on a new vehicular road which would connect Vicos with the remote but heavily populated region on the far side of the Cordillera Blanca, the great chain of snow-capped peaks at the foot of which Vicos rests. Diversification of Vicos economic life continued apace and numerous Vicosinos were attaining the educational requisites for effective participation in regional and national life.

What can be said in a general way about results of the Vicos experience so far? In the first place, if one criterion of a modern democratic society is a parity of power and other values among individuals, then vast gains have been made at Vicos during the past decade. Starting from the base of a highly restrictive social system in which almost all power and other value positions were ascribed and very narrowly shared, the Vicosinos have gradually changed that social system for a much more open one in which all value positions can be more widely shared and in which they can be attained through achievement. This in itself is no mean accomplishment, particularly since it was done by peaceful and persuasive means.

In the second place, the position of the Vicos community itself, vis-à-vis its immediately surrounding area and the nation as a whole, has undergone a profound change. Starting at the bottom of the heap, and employing a strategy of wealth production for the marketplace and enlightenment for its people, the community of Vicos has climbed to a position of power and respect that can no longer be ignored by the Mestizo world. This is clearly indexed by the large number of equality relationships which now exist at Vicos (and in intercommunity relationships between Vicos and the world outside) where none existed before.

Finally, of what significance is Vicos in the context of national development? Peru is a country with a high degree of unevenness in its progress. The highly productive agricultural coast, with its off-shore fishing grounds among the richest in the world, is moving ahead at a modern and rapid pace. In contrast, the overpopulated sierra, containing major concentrations of indigenous populations, many of whom live under a medieval type of agricultural organization such as existed at Vicos, is lagging far behind. The major lesson of Vicos, for Peru as a whole, is that its serf and suppressed peasant populations, once freed and given encouragement, technical assistance, and learning, can pull themselves up by their own bootstraps and become productive citizens of the nation. The Vicos experience also proved that this development did not require, in essence, vast investments of capital from outside sources. Rather it showed that with the appropriate opening of opportunity and strategic intervention from the outside (particularly technical assistance), such an impoverished and exploited community as the serfs of Vicos could actually finance, to a large degree, the changes necessary to provide for a greater sharing of human values. The element of power proved to be the key that permitted the

Cornell Peru Project to open the door to change; the devolution of power to the people of Vicos proved to be the mechanism which made the new system viable. In the following chapters my coauthors will consider the role of power in the changes which took place by design or consequence of the act of making the Vicosinos wielders of power.

NOTES

1. M. C. Vázquez, "La Antropologia y Nuestro Problema del Indio," Peru Indígena, vol. II (1952) Nos. 5 and 6, pp. 7-157; A. R. Holmberg, "Changing Community Attitudes and Values in Peru," in *Social Change in Latin America Today* New York: Harper and Bros., 1960, pp. 63-107.

2. Earlier publications on Vicos estimated acreage as much smaller. This figure is correct, based on accurate measurements made by Gary Vescelius. Of the total acreage however, approximately 6,700 acres are high-altitude pastures and the inhabited and arable portion is comprised of 3,850 acres. The rest is uninhabited wasteland at the foot of the snow peaks. In 1963 Vicos added an additional 110 acres of arable land which it purchased from the neighboring estate of Chancos.

3. J. Oscar Alers, "Population and Development in a Peruvian Community," Journal of Inter-American Studies, Vol. VII (1965), no. 4.

4. Throughout this and other chapters we shall use the terms manor or estate as equivalents of the Spanish word *hacienda*. In highland Peru, a hacienda refers to a large landholding containing a resident population of serfs and employees or share croppers who serve the needs of the land owners or renters (Patrons). Although not formally defined, a smaller landholding with similar arrangements is referred to in Peru as a *fundo*.

5. The political structure of Peru is as follows: the country is divided into departments which are then subdivided into provinces and these into districts. Each of these has its respective capital. Vicos is a rural community under the jurisdiction of the district of Marcará (capital, Marcará), Province of Carhuaz (capital, Carhuaz), Department of Ancash (capital, Huaraz).

6. The leaf of the plant Erythrozylon coca, which is chewed by the Indians. The use of coca is further discussed in Chapters III and IV.

7. M. C. Vázquez, "The Varayoc System in Vicos," Ithaca: Cornell University Comparative Studies of Cultural Change, 1964, mimeo. The position of *varayoc* in other places had different names such as "captains," "corporals," "inspectors," "principals," and so on. This institution has survived to the present with modifications throughout the Indian areas of the Andean regions as well as in Mexico and Central America, particularly among the Mayas. For example see Frank Cancian, *Economics and Prestige in a Mayan Community,* Stanford: Stanford University Press, 1965. In Vicos the terms *varas, varayoc, envarados, varayos, alcaldes,* are used interchangeably to refer to the persons holding positions in this organization.

8. For a full description of the Vicos marriage system and kinship organization see Richard Price, "Trial Marriage in the Andes," Ethnology, Vol. IV (1965), no. 3, pp. 310-322, and M. C. Vázquez and A. R. Holmberg, "The Castas: Unilinear Kin Groups in Vicos, Peru," Ethnology, Vol. V (1966), pp. 294 ff. Also see Chapter III.

9. M. C. Vázquez, "Local Authority on a Peruvian Andean Hacienda." Paper delivered at the annual meeting of the American Anthropological Association, Philadelphia, 1961, pp. 21-23.

10. C. Barnett, *"Indian Protest Movements in Callejon de Huaylas."* Ph.D. thesis, Cornell University, 1960.

11. Ch. C. Collazos, H. S. White, R. L. Huenemann, E. Reh, P. L. White, A. Castellanos, R. Benites, Y. Bravo, A. Loo, I. Moscoso, C. Caceres, and A. Dieseldorff, "Dietary Surveys in Peru, Chacan and Vicos: Rural Communities in the Peruvian Andes," Journal of American Dietetic Association, 1954, vol. 30, pp. 1222 ff. E. H. Payne, L. Gonzalez M., and E. M. Schleicher, "An Intestinal Parasite Survey in the High Cordilleras of Peru," American Journal of Tropical Medicine and Hygiene, 1956, vol. 5, No. 4, pp. 696-698.

12. A. R. Holmberg, "Proyecto Peru-Cornell en las Ciencias Sociales Aplicadas," Perú Indígena, vol. II (1952) Nos. 5 and 6, pp. 158-166.

13. R. Rodrigo Montoya, "Elección de Dirigentes: Aceptación y Resistencia," Cuadernos del Centro de Estudiantes de Anthropologia (Universidad Nacional Mayor de San Marcos, Lima), vol. II, no. 1 (1963), pp. 80 ff.

14. Ibid., p. 72.

15. The nuclear school staff consisted (in theory) of a medical doctor, an adult education expert, a public health teacher and sanitarian, an agricultural engineer, plus a director. At no time, however, was this staff complement ever complete. The "Ancash Program" staff of the Ministry of Labor and Indian Affairs consisted of a warehouseman-handyman, an administrative assistant, and a social worker-home economist.

16. Since all schools are controlled by the regional representatives of the Ministry of Education, the (3) schools of Vicos will always be under this centralized administration.

17. M. C. Vázquez, "Un caso de discriminación en las elecciones municipales de 1966," Wamani (Ayacucho, Perú) vol. I, no. 2, pp. 30-44.

18. Private communication from the Hon. Douglas Henderson.

19. Personal observations and private communication from Dr. John Plank and the Hon. Douglas Henderson.

20. While the Peace Corps volunteers played a key role in this operation, they also provoked or exacerbated much internal conflict between elements in the community, the Peruvian government staff, and other outsiders connected with the community at that time. The Chancos episode is too involved to discuss here in detail but readers may refer to the following accounts for a history of these events: Richard W. Patch, "Vicos and the Peace Corps," American Universities Field Staff; Paul L. Doughty, "Pitfalls and Progress in the Peruvian Sierra," in Robert Textor (Ed.) *The Cultural Frontiers of the Peace Corps,* Cambridge: MIT Press, 1965; and Henry F. Dobyns, Paul L. Doughty, and Allan R. Holmberg, *The Measurement of Peace Corps Impact in the Peruvian Sierra,* Ithaca: Cornell University Department of Anthropology, 1965.

Chapter III

THE INTERPLAY BETWEEN

POWER AND WEALTH

Mario C. Vázquez

WEALTH AND POWER BEFORE THE INTERVENTION OF THE CORNELL PERU PROJECT

In the course of our studies, carried out from 1949 to 1951,(1) it was found that Vicos was characterized by a predominantly subsistence economy. Savings and profits were the prerogative of the few who owned great numbers of livestock, especially cattle. Large amounts of cash could be obtained quickly only by selling livestock to dealers outside the manor. The relatively few families who did possess cattle to sell were regarded by their fellow serfs as "rich" although no serfs could be considered very well-to-do in terms of the national economy.

Those who had no cattle to sell obtained cash in the form of daily wage work from Thursdays through Saturdays in neighboring towns where salaries were low because of the superabundance of Vicosinos seeking work during the same three days of the week. Others migrated seasonally to plantations on

Author's Note: This chapter is an expansion of an American Behavioral Scientist article, an earlier version of which was prepared for the Comparative Studies of Cultural Change Project, Department of Anthropology, Cornell University, under Contract AID/csd-296 with the Office of Technical Cooperation and Research of the U.S. Agency for International Development. The data analyzed were collected under the direction of the late Professor Allan R. Holmberg with grants from the Carnegie Corporation of New York and an anonymous donor. The conclusions are those of the author and do not necessarily reflect opinions or policies of any supporting agency or organization.

the coast as contract laborers. Others served as harvest nomads in the upper Casma River valley, exchanging their labor for a share of the grain harvest, paid in kind. Finally, on Sundays the women obtained a few soles in cash by selling eggs, cheese, and other produce, and by hiring out as domestic servants to the Mestizos. A few men sold baskets, charcoal, and glacial ice.

Thus the principal source of serf wealth, and its primary symbol among the serfs, was the number of head of cattle that each family possessed. Cattle constituted the only marketable property available to the Vicosinos for sale at a given moment. Since Vicos was a manor operated under a peonage system, houses, trees, other improvements, and lands which constitute a source of wealth and a form of savings in free societies had value in name only. They could be transferred only by the operator of the manor and not by the serfs even though the latter had actually constructed the dwellings they occupied. The serfs were mere usufructuaries during the time they carried out their manorial obligations of working three days per week for the overlord of the manor.

According to the census taken of the Vicos population by the Cornell Peru Project at the beginning of 1952, and utilizing the local criterion of wealth—the number of animals owned—twenty-eight families or 7.7 percent of the total number of families at that time were found to be wealthy. That is, they owned more than eleven head of cattle or their equivalent in other animals, reckoned in terms of sales prices(2) rather than grazing units.

The wealthy Vicosinos were considered specially privileged individuals because they were lucky; they enjoyed divine protection which caused their herds to increase and made them successful in other activities. This was the case in the realm of agriculture, where the crops of the rich were superior as a rule to those of other farmers, because their animals were utilized more opportunely to fertilize their fields (which have probably been under continuous cultivation for at least 3,000 years and therefore require fertilization to yield well), and in the operations of plowing and planting. In the latter tasks, the animal owners naturally had first call on the power of their beasts. Also, the wealthy farmers could obtain the supplemental human labor necessary to cultivate their fields at the proper

Wealth—Agricultural produce such as the maize these women are breaking from the cobs and livestock constituted the traditional sources of wealth in Vicos.

time in exchange for lending their oxen or beasts of burden to those without animal resources. In addition to all these advantages, the wealthy farmers had more free time to tend personally to their crops and animals, while those who lacked animals had to wait upon the grace of the wealthy before they could initiate their own plowing and planting, while at the same time they had to obtain cash by hiring out by the day in order to provide for the primary subsistence needs of their families.

Besides being considered as people blessed by fortune, the wealthy were viewed by their fellow serfs as constituting the highest status social group within the manor. They were regarded as "the powerful ones," and "the monied ones," or "the cattle barons." Of course, their status was higher if they were elders and had occupied positions of local authority. They were then the *yayas,* men with the highest prestige, the most power and authority, whose opinions were in many matters decisive during discussions of the internal affairs of the serf population.

Class distinctions obliged the wealthy to possess certain objects symbolic of their status, to behave differently, and to accept the responsibilities of fictive kinship and local authority. If they did not, the became subject to the social controls of satire and hostility. So the wealthy had to dress better than their inferiors—to own at least two sets of clothes, to possess homes with several rooms made of sun-dried bricks and roofed with clay tiles, and closed by wooden doors made by professional carpenters. The wealthy had to disdain serving as daily wage workers in neighboring towns or coastal plantations, to participate as functionaries in the local religious festivals and those of the nearby towns, to accept positions of local authority in the administration of the manor and its serf population, and to accept the responsibilities of sponsoring weddings.

The factor that imbued the wealthy with the greatest social visibility and power was not their possession of a large number of animals per se, nor the bearing of the rich man, but rather their ability to have cash on hand ready to be used at a moment's notice. That is to say, they commanded the ability to carry out any kind of transaction and so to dominate, by means of their money, those situations that might affect them or their families, and to "assist" the needy by granting them loans.

The Vicosinos knew that with cash in hand they could obtain better prices in commercial transactions, whether buying or selling. Thus, in selling cattle the wealthy owner held out for the best offer, while the poor owner was apt to sell at lower prices, being pressed for cash. In the same fashion, the wealthy person obtained the best discounts while making purchases, especially in the case of peripatetic peddlers, who preferred to sell on a cash basis and not on credit, which was the traditional practice.

The wealthy stood out, and they demonstrated their superiority over other individuals by acting as local bankers. They were able to grant loans to those who needed money. The loans were granted under diverse terms—with or without interest, over a fixed or an indefinite time period—with arrangements subject to the type of relationships that existed between lender and borrower.

A loan granted by a rich Vicosino did not constitute a simple monetary transaction with its corresponding paperwork, but was rather the beginning of a state of dependency of the borrower on the lender, and it lasted for the entire period during which the debt remained to be paid. By virtue of having loaned a sum of money varying between fifty and five hundred soles (between $2 and $20 at the then current exchange rate), the rich man felt he had the right to use the person of his debtor, who became his permanent *minka* or unpaid laborer for various enterprises. Should the debtor fail to do the bidding of the lender, he was obligated to return the amount of the loan plus any accrued interest. Usually this was done through local Indian authority, the *varayoc,* whose intervention was in itself embarrassing and a bad precedent for the debtor, since upon public notice that he was a bad risk he could no longer obtain loans from other serfs.

The power of the wealthy Vicosinos was not limited only to other serfs, but extended to the manor overlords and overseers and to the Mestizos living in neighboring towns. In several instances the wealthy Vicosinos obtained land from the manor above and beyond what the other serfs received, in exchange for animals or money turned over to the overseers or employees of the manor. These transactions were frequent when the rich man held a job with the manor administration such as *mayoral* (straw boss) or *repuntero*.(3) In the case of Mestizo authorities under whose jurisdiction the Vicosinos found themselves, it was common knowledge that the wealthy Indians were never punished. On the contrary, the Mestizo authorities usually favored them, and thus the sons of the wealthy were not pressed into military service although it was legally compulsory for all able Peruvian citizens.

The giving of gifts or bribes to the Mestizo authorities or the patron was institutionalized to the point of acquiring a Quechua term, and was known as the *senyi*. The Vicosinos who could best satisfy such Mestizo demands were, of course, the wealthier ones. This advantage was further enhanced by some who established symbolic kinship ties through *compadrazgo* with a number of key authorities such as the justice of the peace, district council secretary, and district governor.

It should be pointed out that despite these "advantages" enjoyed by the few wealthier men of Vicos, this group was still impoverished by regional standards. Their ascendency in Vicos can be understood in terms of their roles as "brokers" between the dominant Mestizo class and the bulk of the Indian serfs. The wealthier men of Vicos were in one sense an artifact of the exploitative system. The condition and status of the rest of the population—92 percent—thus stands in its real dimension. Whatever wealth they controlled was limited by the Patron and the native "rich" since it was held in terms relative to their own positions.

Despite the fact that it would appear logical to treat the rest of the Vicosinos as a monolithic socio-economic unit, it would be incorrect to do so, for, as our studies revealed, there were still other distinctions made by the people themselves. In actual physical manifestation, these differences appear to have been largely a matter of degree rather than of kind, revolving especially around the ownership of animals, and to some extent participation in the civil-religious hierarchy described in the preceding chapter.

Thus, the "rich" group consisted of twenty-eight families (7.7 percent) whose wealth was determined by their ownership of at least eleven cows and bulls, or their equivalent in small animals calculated on sale value. The wealthiest families of this group owned herds of more than sixteen cattle, several horses, and as many as twenty-five sheep. The "middle" sector of 146 families(40 percent) was characterized by ownership of six to ten large animals and considerably fewer numbers of sheep or pigs. The 189 families (52.3 percent) constituting the really "poor" of Vicos were those with no large animals such as cows, no changes of clothing, and a constantly ragged appearance relative to others, and, importantly, were frequently those who incurred debts either in cash or labor to the others. Moreover, the poor were characteristically stereotyped as being worthless, lazy, irresponsible, and drunken by the rest.(4)

Work Psychology. Living in a social and economic system whose rewards were so limited, many Vicosinos developed fatalistic self-images of themselves as men unable to possess material objects or who adopted extremely utilitarian pragmatism in this matter. In the latter category, two men in a sample of ten reared under manorial conditions who were in 1960(5) intensively studied, regarded wealth as more important than people, or regarded objects as simply aids to survival. Two others did not feel that they could own anything, while a third felt that one obtains nothing that is not given to him by someone in a position of authority. Two more individuals regarded possessions as dangerous because they arouse envy in others, and a third (who evidently did own something) lied to avoid such envy. Yet he regarded money as magical. This man also felt that he could own no more than had his father—a significant attitude for development efforts. Another fellow in the sample joined in this type of fatalism, believing that God placed him in life-long poverty. Just as serious from a developmental point of view, the repressive manorial society actually engendered feelings of shame over ownership in at least some individuals. One man in the intensively analyzed sample reported that he would be ashamed to own anything, and professed to believe that if he did it would rot!

Although this sample is small and its representativeness unknown, it is suggestive that six of the ten men were either ashamed to own things, felt their possessions were limited by external authorities, or that they could own nothing.

On the other hand, these psychological attitudes were counterbalanced by a strong motivation to work stimulated by the same hacienda conditions. The men in the intensively analyzed sample agreed almost completely upon the necessity for working. Eight of them felt they had to work—three in order to survive, three to avoid punishment, one to please the woman who fed him, and one who looked forward only to eating, to support his family. On this score, one other man saw himself characterized by inability to master the physical world, and the tenth in the sample felt himself to measure up to his father's standard. Thus, there was one significant motivation upon which to build economic improvement and cultural change.

THE CORNELL PERU PROJECT AND THE INTRODUCTION OF TECHNOLOGICAL CHANGE

Between 1952 and 1956 the Cornell Peru Project introduced modern agricultural production techniques into Vicos. These innovations included new varieties of seed for the locally important crops such as potatoes and maize. At the same time, the "medieval" system of servitude and peonage was gradually abolished.(6) Then, when the Indians took over direction of their own affairs, the obligation to work three days each week for the management disappeared. In its economic aspects at the present time, the Vicos community is a type of production enterprise, organized along cooperative lines, in which its members receive the profits of their labor. In the course of achieving this it was necessary for Vicos to become more directly related to the national and regional economic networks and markets. Therefore, where feasible and appropriate the Cornell Peru Project actively fostered greater contact between Vicosinos and the outside world.

Supervised Community Farm Credit. In 1957, when the Vicos manor passed into the power of the Vicosinos who wished to acquire title to it, they faced the problem of obtaining community funds with which to pay for the estate. They had lands and labor to dedicate toward winning their liberation from the manorial system, but they needed capital and technical assistance if they were to carry on a large-scale agricultural enterprise. Under those circumstances, the Technical Committee of the Peruvian Indian Institute established contact with the Inter-American Cooperative Food Production Service (SCIPA) whose technicians became interested in establishing a Supervised Agricultural Credit program at the community level in Vicos.(7)

The SCIPA technicians carried out preliminary studies, and organized the CAS-VICOS (for Credito Agricola Supervisado Vicos),(8) which began to operate in June of 1957 after obtaining a crop loan from the Peruvian Agricultural Development Bank.

For these purposes, the community was represented by its ten elected councilmen, who chose one of their members as their "agricultural representative" to manage the funds together with the technician assigned by the Inter-American Cooperative Food Production Service. The initial crop loan was for S/223,500, but only S/123,892.75 was actually withdrawn from the bank to grow potatoes on thirty hectares formerly cultivated by the Patron of the manor. In 1958, the area planted to potatoes was increased to forty-five hectares, and the crop loan authorization raised to S/250,000, not all of which had to be withdrawn.

In 1963 the community farm enterprise ceased to count upon the technical assistance of the former SCIPA organization,

Table I. VICOS COMMUNITY FARM ENTERPRISE POTATO PRODUCTION

Season	Hectares	Gross Sales	Profit	Reference	
1956-57	10	———	———	11	(9)
1957-58	30	263,639	137,073	12	(10)
1958-59	50	312,371	91,161	13	(11)
1959-60	45	603,453	162,739	13	(11)
1960-61	45	———	206,000	14	(12)
1961-62	45	334,732	146,855	15	(13)
1962-63	45	472,615	———	16	(14)
1963-64	53	258,560	222,290	16	(14)
1964-65	53	184,989	−32,989	17	(15)

which had been nationalized and reorganized. Instead, Vicos began to operate more on its own with assistance from personnel connected with the Ancash program of the Ministry of Labor and Indian Affairs. The Vicos leaders by then understood the general nature of the banking and commercial transactions involved and the technical management of the crops. They could count, moreover, upon the confidence of the Agricultural Development Bank, whose officials had never encountered problems with the Vicosinos, despite the relatively large sums loaned to them.

The profits obtained during the several community farming seasons were employed for purchasing the manor.

SUPERVISED FAMILY
FARM CREDIT

From the beginning of the Project its leaders intended to introduce a modern system of credit along with the new technology required to raise the levels of living. Unfortunately, the Vicosinos were unfamiliar with any but the most exploitative types of credit arrangements extant on the hacienda at the time, and in the early 1950s they still did not fully trust Project personnel sufficiently to be able to accept suggestions without question.

It was necessary, therefore, to utilize the credit-in-kind-for-new-seed system common to the Vicos area which the people themselves understood as a device by which some new farming skills and economic relationships might be introduced without too great disruption. In other words, the Project planned to syncretize new methods with a familiar process until reaching the point where a new organization and economic system could be instituted.

Because the potato is a preferred food in Vicos, and since there is almost always a good regional and national demand for quality potatoes, it seemed that potato cultivation would prove to be an appropriate vehicle through which to introduce the desired changes.

The Vicosinos were familiar with a type of local credit-in-kind arrangement to which they resorted in desperation in order to obtain seed to plant, after a total crop failure or famine during which they consumed potatoes or grain reserved for seed. Mestizo merchants who advanced Vicosinos seed under such circumstances dictated agreements that they recover an amount of the harvest equal to the quantity of seed advanced before dividing the remainder of the harvest equally with the Vicos debtor gardener.

The Cornell Peru Project proceeded, therefore, in the traditional role of merchant supplying a new seed supply, which was in this case both selected and disinfected. Moreover, the Project introduced the use of fertilizers, insecticides, and the proper spacing of rows and of seed within the rows. These operations were supervised by the author, utilizing technical information obtained from the SCIPA. In contrast to traditional credit-in-kind arrangements, then, cultivation was guided in new ways which were to alter the Vicos image of the possible and the real.

A companion step to the guided diffusion of technical knowledge to family gardeners during the 1952-53 potato season was the utilization of the commercially farmed fields of Vicos as demonstration areas for the innovations. Since all the serfs still had to perform three days of work weekly for the manor, this obligation provided an opportunity for them to observe, under conditions of no risk to their own crops, and to see the results that their hands produced.

Despite energetic attempts by Project personnel to make known the offer of new seed, fertilizer, and insecticides to Vicosinos, only seventeen of 363 families chose to experiment with the innovations on the subsistence plots allowed them traditionally by the hacienda.

The first harvest was carried out amidst great interest on the part of the Vicosinos. With one exception, the participating farmers obtained important economic advantages. The one who obtained the best harvest, after paying the cost of production of S/361.00, achieved a net profit of S/627.00. This was the equivalent of 122 days' wages—about S/5.00 per day at that time. The Cornell Peru Project received a net profit of S/475.00, since its investment was S/512.00, or greater than that of the Vicosino.

As a natural consequence of that success, the number of participants increased in the two following seasons to eighty-seven families in 1953-54, and 158 families of a total of 180 intended cooperators inscribed in 1954-55. (All could not be accommodated because of a lack of seed potatoes and fertilizers.) That is, in a period of two years almost 40 percent of the families adopted the new techniques, seeds, and fertilizers for potato production, furthermore meeting their primary needs for subsistence and began to sell their surplus harvest commercially.

Seeing the success reached in the first three seasons of Cornell Peru Project-supervised crop loans in kind, and at the request of several participants who considered the division of the harvest into equal portions unjust, the Cornell Peru Project abolished the transitional system and established a more conventional agricultural credit arrangement. The Project continued to extend credit-in-kind in the form of seed potatoes, fertilizers, and insecticides to be repaid after the harvest. Seventy-two families participated in the 1955-56 agricultural season, and only thirty-five in the 1956-57 season. The number diminished in that year because the participants in the previous season (1955-56) did not receive adequate orientation for the sale of their crops, and this resulted in many not obtaining money, despite their having raised good crops, to pay their debts. Although this awakened a fear on the part of some in continuing to participate in the credit system, Vicosino demand for crop loans greatly expanded again after 1959, and became the norm thereafter as the new community organization assumed management of the program.

Crop Loan Consequences. When the Cornell Peru Project ended its term as sub-leasor of Vicos in 1956, crop loans to family gardeners were briefly suspended. By extending crop production credit to Vicos "paleotechnic" farmers who learned and adopted "neotechnic" cultivation, the Project provided the serfs with experience they did not forget in profiting from a kind of credit arrangement they had not known in manorial times. After the Indians shed the status of serfdom and took over management of their own affairs, they showed how well they had learned from the Cornell Peru Project credit model. The first demonstration occurred during the 1957-58 potato production season when the elected Council of Delegates began to extend credit-in-kind from community farm enterprise funds. Eighteen Vicos families received crop loans in kind, and one neighboring community, Llipta, obtained similar credit when it sought technical assistance from the Vicosinos. The Inter-American Cooperative Food Production Service extension agent reported visiting the eighteen Vicos farmers to assist their production efforts.(16)

The availability of community credit for commercial farming on the part of individuals formed an important stimulus to increasing family potato production and sales from former less-than-subsistence plots. The credit-in-kind extended in 1958 utilized community funds to purchase seed potatoes, fertilizers, and insecticides which were taken by farmers on credit to b. repaid after the harvest together with an annual 9 percent interest charge. This was identical to the rate the community farm enterprise paid the Peruvian Agricultural Development Bank for its crop loan.

The number of families farming in this style nearly tripled the following year. In the 1958-59 potato season, fifty families took part in the credit program. This number then increased progressively. Eighty-five Indians received community credit for the 1962-1963 season, a good one for profits. Forty-five families shipping 43,704 kilograms of potatoes to market grossed S/99,026.60 or an average of S/2,200 per family.(17) Such success brought a record 248 families into the community credit program during the 1963-64 season (53 percent of all Vicos families at the time), who obtained credit-in-kind worth S/54,491. This considerable increase was due to the participants receiving adequate guidance in the sale of their crops, which were dispatched to Lima for sale on the wholesale market together with the community farm enterprise's harvests. The Vicosinos themselves supervised the transportation and sale of their produce.

One example of Vicos commercial farming success drawn from the 1959-60 potato season illustrates how community crop loans fostered individual profits. One Vicos entrepreneur obtained on credit seven sacks of seed potatoes worth S/910, and then fertilized with seven sacks of guano worth S/467. He received a sack of Aldrin valued at S/105 and half a kilogram of

Dhitane worth S/28, for a total loan value of S/1,510. He paid 4.5 percent interest, or S/67, on this crop loan. This farmer's family consumed the third-grade potatoes he grew, and he kept ten sacks of commercial grade tubers. Still, he marketed enough potatoes to repay his crop loan plus interest and turn a cash profit of S/3,500,(18) a return of 230 percent on the investment!

Many Vicosinos already farmed entirely with their own capital by the 1963-64 season, eschewing community crop loans, and by March of 1964 no fewer than 111 self-financed potato growers who dispatched their commercial crop to the metropolitan market under community supervision had realized an average profit of more than S/1,000 each.(19)

The family crop loan program was again suspended in 1964, in fact, since a majority of the Vicosinos by then held sufficient seed potatoes and sufficient capital of their own to acquire fertilizers and insecticides.

One idea of the importance of Vicos potato production to Peru, after its former serfs learned scientific farming practices, may be gained from a comparison of tuber sales in Vicos and the nation. According to the Lima newspaper El Comercio for May 17, 1959, the country produced 63,532 metric tons of commercialized potatoes during the 1957-58 season. Vicos sold 182.9 metric tons of potatoes on the Lima market, from its season's production with only thirty hectares. That tonnage amounted to 0.283 percent of the reported commercial total. In other words, only 346 other production units of Vicos scale would have been required to grow the potato supply that was marketed. Thus the traditional myth about commercial crop production inevitably falling as a consequence of agrarian reform can be laid to rest in light of this experience. Not only did production dramatically increase, but when integrated even superficially into the national market Vicos peasants showed they could and would play an active and important role. Given the technical tools with which to increase production, they did so, while still awaiting legal reform of their tenancy status.

Installation of Community Sewing Shops. Initiated by the Cornell Peru Project in 1960 and carried on under the direction of the Peruvian National Plan for Integrating the Aboriginal Population of the Ministry of Labor and Indian Affairs, the women's workshop provided sewing instruction and made sewing machines available for use. In addition to apprentice training the women received, participants, for example, made 844 garments during 1964, mostly for their families' use but some for sale as well.

The Chancos Venture. A property adjacent to Vicos known as Chancos had been originally part of the manor. Because it contained a popular thermal bath and small hotel, the Public Benefit Society of Huaraz (the owner) separated it from Vicos and rented the properties independently. Chancos also contained some hectares of land under cultivation and had 114 serfs attached to it who, by kinship, were Vicosinos. Consequently, the Vicos community was long interested in freeing its relatives from serfdom and in acquiring the good bottom land that formed part of Chancos. Under the tutelage of several Peace Corps volunteers in 1963-64, the Vicosinos were able to accomplish this goal, thus expanding the community base in terms of its land and human resources.(20) The people of Chancos voted to join the community, and participated in elections for council delegates for the first time in 1964. The former manor lands of Chancos were added to those of the community and put into production accordingly, with the people of Chancos retaining usufruct over their family plots and gaining the advantages of Vicos collective resources.

In 1963 the hotel at Chancos, located at the lower boundary of the Vicos community, was re-opened under the direction of a Peace Corps volunteer. One of its aims was to provide work opportunities for the youth of Vicos, and eight young men participated in operating the Chancos installation under volunteer management.

When Peace Corps volunteers were no longer available to supervise the hotel, restaurant, and thermal spring-water baths, the Public Benefit Society of Huaraz found itself unable to auction off the right to operate the Chancos resort facilities (which had not been acquired by Vicos). It turned, therefore, to a Vicosino to operate the hotel and baths, choosing a man who had efficiently managed the Vicos community farm enterprise for several years and had lived six months on a farm in the United States under a U.S. Agency for International Development training program. The Public Benefit Society also permitted another Vicosino with extensive experience outside the manor to operate the Chancos restaurant, significantly called the "Thirteenth of July" after the date of Vicos independence when final central government approval of the sale of the estate was granted in 1962.

Forestation Program. Begun by the Cornell Peru Project in 1952 on an experimental basis, a massive forestation program was launched in April, 1964, under the direction of the Forestation Administration of the Ministry of Agriculture with financial backing from Alliance for Progress funds from the United States. This was designed to improve the tree-poor quality of the local environment and to provide for future economic advantages.

The work was directed by trained technicians from the Peruvian Bureau of Forestry. The program consisted of forming a stand of several million eucalyptus trees, under an agreement for the proceeds of the expected harvest of these plantings to be divided between the Ministry of Agriculture and the Vicos community.

As a result of this experience several Vicosinos have gained further employment with the Forestry Bureau in other areas of the region where forestation projects were in progress.

WEALTH AND
POWER SHARING

As already mentioned, the Cornell Peru Project was initiated with the explicit practical objective of improving the standard of living of the Vicos population.(21) That original goal has been achieved. Vicos is no longer a society with essentially a subsistence economy. It is far exceeding its former little-more-than-subsistence agricultural structure, because both the community as a farm enterprise and the majority of its members work the land not only for the sake of subsistence, but also for commercial purposes. At the same time, the Vicosinos devote themselves to other economic activities that are new sources of monetary income. Economically, the Vicosino no longer depends solely on the agricultural production of his farm plots or on the sale of his livestock, or, in the absence of these, on the daily wages earned in neighboring towns and coastal plantations.

By 1964 the Vicosinos were in effect shareholding members of a production enterprise called, officially, the Andean Community of Vicos. That organization operated with its own capital of approximately S/1,200,000 (or U.S. $45,000) created during the previous seven years through the commercial exploitation of community-held farm lands in Vicos. Seventy percent of that capital was utilized to pay for the purchase of the Vicos estate. Its total price of S/2,000,000 (or U.S. $75,000) was paid to the former owner in 1967, with the aid of a loan for half the amount made to Vicos by the government of Peru for this purpose in 1962.

Besides accumulating capital toward the purchase of the Vicos estate itself, the Vicosinos each year participate in the distribution of a certain percentage of the community farm enterprise's harvests. Thus, in 1964, 93 percent of the families were beneficiaries of 25 percent of the gross production of potatoes on the communal lands—87,768 kilograms for their own consumption. This made it possible for 65 percent of the families to sell potatoes raised on their own farm plots through the community farm enterprise marketing program in the national capital. These families earned an average income of S/1,000 (or U.S. $37.50) from the sale of their agricultural products. These and other families sold additional potatoes directly to Mestizo buyers who sought them out in Vicos, to buyers in the capital city of the department where they hauled them, and to local storekeepers who had established fictive kinship relations (see Chapter IV) with them.

In addition, 75 percent of the families purchased the total grain production of the community farm enterprise in maize, wheat, and barley, at prices lower by 20 to 50 percent than those current in the regional market. The community farm enterprise policy in growing cereals for sale to Vicosinos at subsidy prices removes some pressure on individual families to produce all subsistence needs. This frees some plots for commercial production, a factor visible in Table 2.

Twenty percent of the Vicos families also had an income of from eight to thirty soles (U.S. $0.30 to $1.12) per day during 1964 by virtue of wages received by some of their members

Table 2. CHANGES IN THE NUMBER OF HOUSEHOLDS CULTI-
VATING FOUR MAJOR CROPS(22)

Crop	1951 (a)	1963 (b)	Index Number (b/a) 100
Potatoes	324	440	136
Maize	359	450	125
Wheat	357	428	120
Barley	356	338	95
Number of crops	1,396	1,656	119
Number of households	363	461	127

who worked on the forestation program or in the Chancos hotel. In 1965 this figure rose to about 87 percent when a massive transplanting of 500,000 eucalyptus seedlings was carried out. Only 15 percent of the Vicos labor force will be required during the ten-year period up to the first tree harvest, however, and then possibly a greater number of workers will be needed.

Twelve percent of the Vicosino families participated in the local credit union. Members deposited their savings monthly and most of them had already obtained loans during the initial two years for purchasing sewing machines, tools, musical instruments, business inventories, and so on. Finally, there are several Vicosino residents who annually earn more money (S/25,000) than the richest Vicosino of the traditional type who sells a yearly average of five head of cattle for an approximate cash income of S/15,000.

Despite the increase of the daily wage rate from twelve to fifteen soles for men and from five to eight soles for women in neighboring towns in the past few years, few Vicosinos accept these jobs since they prefer to work on their own farm plots cultivating potatoes and the major cereal crops listed in Table 2. Because of the commercial value of potatoes, farmers have focused their energies on this crop at the expense of others which can now be obtained at low prices from the community farm enterprise.

On the other hand, it should also be mentioned that in 1964 several Vicosinos returned from the coast to live in Vicos, continuing a current of return migration that began some years earlier with the improvement of the Vicos economy.(23) They became steady workers in the forestation program, in the Chancos hotel, and in other specialized capacities in this region.

CONCLUSIONS

The Vicosinos have been freed through the effort of the Cornell Peru Project not only from the manor system and peonage, but also from the conservative plutocracy upon which most of them depended by virtue of having solicited or having needed to solicit monetary loans. These had all but converted them into servants of the wealthy for as long as the loan was outstanding. As a consequence of the previously outlined changes, there may now be observed:

(a) An increase in commercial activity in Vicos and the region. In 1953 thirty-two persons devoted themselves to the resale of merchandise obtained in Carhuaz and Marcará. In 1963 seventy-eight persons sold a greater variety of articles acquired for the most part in Huaraz at lower prices, or purchased from Huaraz wholesalers who deliver merchandise to Vicos.

(b) The use of personal capital for the cultivation of potatoes, using new seed potatoes and guano fertilizer.

(c) The purchase of chickens and cattle for breeding purposes, and donkeys and horses of high quality, which are used not only to move the internal agricultural produce of Vicos, but are also hired out to pack ore from nearby mines to trucking terminals. This appears clearly in Table 3. Changes in animal ownership patterns are especially significant in view of traditional socio-economic values and class structure. With the introduction of commercial farming and the ability to achieve economic improvement through this medium, ownership of cows is relatively less important than previously. The large increase in donkeys and horses reflects their increased use in farming and for transporting produce.

(d) The increased purchase of cotton clothing and manufactured cloth for making clothing for women and children.

(e) The acquisition of modern appliances, tools, and furnishings, such as sewing machines, bicycles, radios, record players, musical instruments, tables, chairs, cots, trunks.

Table 3. CHANGES IN NUMBER OF VICOS HOUSEHOLDS POSSESSING MAJOR DOMESTIC ANIMALS(24)

Domestic Animal	1951 (a)	1963 (b)	Index Number (1951 = 100) (b/a) 100
Chickens	352	406	115
Cows	328	388	118
Sheep	320	338	106
Pigs	293	353	120
Goats	122	163	134
Donkeys	38	113	297
Horses	40	62	155
Guinea pigs	308	360	117
Number of animals	1,801	2,183	121
Number of households	363	461	127

(f) The utilization of Mestizo style materials in house construction, as in plaster to whiten walls, and ceramic roof tiles purchased in the valley outside Vicos.

(g) The formation of new institutions such as the St. Andrew's Band of Vicos, the Community Cooperative, and the Vicos young men's soccer club.

(h) The participation of youths and poor individuals in local government with the single prerequisite of obtaining a majority of the votes of their fellows.

Finally, it may be said in summary that before the Cornell Peru Project intervened in Vicos, 52 percent of the families were poor(25) with extremely limited sources of income. Wealth in the form of livestock and the money accumulated by their sale was in the hands of only 7.7 percent of the families. Now, however, wealth in the form of monetary income is within the reach of essentially all Vicosinos.

Although the majority of the Vicosinos still lack the animals to fertilize and cultivate their fields, they now have the cash with which to hire or buy draft animals and to purchase natural and chemical fertilizers and seeds. Approximately 70 percent of the families no longer need to beg the wealthier few to lend them money because, in addition to their traditional sources of income, they receive income from the cash sale of their commercial agricultural products and in the form of wages for work obtained in programs sponsored by their own community and (now) by the national government. In situations such as the credit union and the community sewing workshops there also exist means of saving which permit Vicosinos to invest in purchasing more food, clothing, and modern commodities of diverse uses, including capital goods such as a truck and sewing machines.

It should also be mentioned that, in the sector not participating actively in this technological progress, there are still poor men and widows who continue to depend on the traditional rich to whom they are subordinated not only for economic reasons, but also by kinship ties.

In conclusion, wealth, which gave a small group of Vicosinos the power to exercise several types of economic oppression and to dominate most individuals in the serf population through reprisals and moral sanctions, is now represented in the form of money coming from new sources of income and is shared by the majority of the Vicosinos. They are gradually freeing themselves from their oppressors and at the same time participating in the economic life of the region and of the country. A new type of formal power has been created, represented by the elected council of the community, which established its improved position of wealth by purchasing the former estate lands and is responsible for the various programs for the development of Vicos.

This experience with the relationship between changing production of wealth and sharing social power in Vicos shows that investment and political techniques already tested there can solve many of the most acute social and political problems of the Andean region.(26) Cornell Peru Project participant intervention in Vicos production, and social organization of information diffusion and produce marketing, provides a prototype that can be modified to fit many local situations where lower-than-subsistence productivity weakens socially subordinate peoples elsewhere in the world.

NOTES

1. M. C. Vázquez, "La Antropología Cultural y Nuestro Problema del Indio," Perú Indígena, vol. II, nos. 5 and 6 (1952), pp. 7-151.

Peasants, Power, and Applied Social Change

2. M. C. Vázquez, "Cambios en Estratificadión Social en una Hacienda Andina," Perú Indígena, vol. VI, nos. 14 and 15 (1957), p. 77.

3. *Repuntero:* a person assigned by the manor administration to care for the herds in the pasture lands and/or collect grazing fees from drovers for outside livestock pastured on manor lands.

4. Vázquez, 1957, op. cit., pp. 69-80.

5. Ralph Klein, "The Self Image of Adult Males in an Andean Culture." New York University Ph.D. Dissertation, 1963, pp. 61, 72, 88, 66, 54, 94, 107, 78, 101, 55, 102, 95, 67, 62, 89, 108, 73, 83.

6. A. R. Holmberg, "From Paternalism to Democracy: The Cornell Peru Project," Human Organization, vol. 15, no. 3 (1956), pp. 15-18.

7. It is appropriate to acknowledge here the important role played by Ing. Abelardo Baraco, Inter-American Cooperative Food Production Service extension agent and one of the members of the Technical Committee, and Ing. Carlos Chueca Sotomayor, Chief of Supervised Credit for the Inter-American Cooperative Food Production Service at that time.

8. C. A. Farromeque D., "Informe sobre el credito agricola supervisado, campaña 1957-58," Perú Indígena, vol. 8, nos. 18 and 19 (1959).

9. M. C. Vázquez, "Proyecto Peru-Cornell," Perú Indígena, vol. 6, nos. 14 and 15 (1957), pp. 223-224.

10. Farromeque, op. cit., pp. 243, 248-249.

11. Carlos Chueca S., "La Comunidad de Vicos (Ancash) Su Integracion a la Vida Nacional," typescript, October 6, 1961, p. 8. Also Carlos Chueca S., "Participacion del SCIPA en la Comunidad de Vicos, typescript no date, p. 1.

12. H. F. Dobyns, "Monetary Credit and Transculturation," Cornell Peru Project Papers Read before the American Anthropological Association 1961 Annual Meeting. Lima: Cornell Peru Project, 1962, p. 16.

13. P. Roman U., "Informe de actividades del Plan Nacional de Integracion de la Poblacion Aborigen en el Periodo del 1° de Enero de 1962 al 30 de Junio de 1963," Perú Indígena, vol. 10 nos. 24 and 25 (1963), p. 110, and H. F. Dobyns, "Eleventh Report of the Cornell Peru Project," Ithaca: Cornell University Department of Anthropology, 1962, p. 4.

14. P. Roman U., *Plan Nacional de Integracion de la Poblacion Aborigen: Informe Actividades Enero 1963-Junio 1964,* Lima: Ministerio de Trabajo y Asuntos Indigenas, 1964, pp. 101-102.

15. P. Roman U., *Plan Nacional de Integracion de la Poblacion Aborigen: Informe Actividades Julio 1964-Junio 1965.* Lima: Ministerio de Trabajo y Asuntos Indigenas, 1965, p. 41.

16. Farromeque, op. cit., p. 246.

17. Roman U., 1963, op. cit., p. 103.

18. Chueca, 1961, op. cit., p. 3.

19. Roman, 1964, op. cit., p. 103.

20. For further details about this event, see P. Doughty, "Pitfalls and Progress in the Peruvian Sierra," in R. B. Textor (Ed.), *Cultural Frontiers of the Peace Corps,* Cambridge: MIT Press, 1965, and R. W. Patch, "Vicos and the Peace Corps: A Failure in Intercultural Communication," American Universities Field Staff Reports, vol. 11, no. 2.

21. A. R. Holmberg, "La realizacion del Proyecto de Antropologia Aplicada en la Zona de Vicos, Marcara, Ancash," Perú Indígena, vol. 2, no. 4 (1952), pp. 88ff.

22. J. O. Alers, "Population, Attitudes, and Development: The Case of Vicos." Cornell University Ph.D. Thesis, 1966.

23. M. C. Vázquez, "Proceso de Migracion en la Comunidad de Vicos, Ancash," in H. F. Dobyns and M. C. Vázquez (Eds.), *Migracion e Integracion en el Peru,* Lima: Editorial Estudios Andinos, 1963, pp. 93-102.

24. Alers, op. cit.

25. Vázquez, 1957, op. cit., p. 77.

26. A. R. Holmberg and H. F. Dobyns, "The Cornell Program in Vicos, Peru," in C. R. Wharton, Jr., (Ed.), *Subsistence Agriculture and Economic Development,* Chicago: Aldine Publishing Co., 1969, p. 410.

Chapter IV

HUMAN RELATIONS:

AFFECTION, RECTITUDE, AND RESPECT

Paul L. Doughty

The theme of deprivation, found in many subordinate societies, was particularly strong at Vicos in 1952 as a pervasive characteristic of manorial life. It can be stated with certainty that it would be impossible to approximate, in the slightest way, the patterns of life as they were in Vicos, or as they are now without examining this factor as it affects interpersonal behavior.

The social condition of the Peruvian Indian was succinctly portrayed by the Mexican educator, Moises Saenz. In 1931 he was commissioned to survey the Andean Indian population and, especially, the "Indian Problem," as it has been so often called. During the course of his Peruvian travels he chanced to ask some Indians walking by the roadside where they were from, and to Saenz' distress they replied, "We belong to don Guillermo Pacheco."(1) This situation has persisted in wide areas of the Peruvian Andes and only within the last decade has it appeared to be changing significantly.

Author's Note: This chapter was prepared originally for the Comparative Studies of Culture Change Project, Department of Anthropology, Cornell University. The material was collected under the auspices of the Cornell Peru Project and its director, Allan R. Holmberg, and financed by a grant from the Carnegie Corporation of New York (1960-62), contract Number PC-(W)-155 with the United States Peace Corps (1962-64), and the Cornell-Columbia-Harvard Inter-University Summer Program in Latin American Culture (1960, 1961). While drawing on the work of many associates in addition to personal observations, the analysis and opinions expressed on these pages are the sole responsibility of the author.

The manorial society to which the Vicosinos "belonged" and in which they participated in 1952 was governed by a code which was feudal in origin and hierarchical in nature. Its philosophy and outlook dominated the economic and social life of the province of Carhuaz and particularly the district of Marcará in which Vicos is located. This was a dichotomized society, comprised of two all-encompassing social castes, the Indians and the Mestizos.

THE DIMENSIONS OF PEONAGE:
VICOS, 1952

As the district capital, the town of Marcará represented in microcosm the centralized character of Lima in national life.(2) The parish church, principal stores, government offices, schools, and modern means of transportation and communication were centered there in the houses and buildings set along the cobblestoned streets. The Mestizos living here were the literate, Spanish-speaking (but bilingual) representatives of the wider Peruvian society. They occupied all public offices in the district and determined and executed public policy, in so far as this was permitted by the national government at the time. Although most Mestizos were engaged in some agricultural activity, the manual aspects of such work were by preference delegated to Indian peons whenever possible.

As Indians, the people of Vicos showed their distinctiveness in many visible ways.(3) The traditional Vicos dress was of homespun, hand-woven woolen cloth, hand-sewn into a costume unique to Vicos although similar to that worn by other Indians in the immediate area. The men wore closely tailored, heavy, black or navy blue pants and jackets, broad sashes around their waists, and sandals made of discarded automobile tires on their scarred and cracked feet. Their generally ungroomed, shaggy hair was infrequently cut, but rather, was covered by a large stiff felt hat. The women wore elaborately decorated blouses and mantles, several—often ten or more—heavy woolen skirts, and sashes about the waist. Five or six brass rings were adornment for their fingers, and their hair was braided in a dozen narrow strands, sometimes intertwined with

Affection—A Vicos mother and her daughter.

bits of red cloth. Most women went barefoot in contrast to the men, although they wore the same type of hat, decorated, however, with bands of bright satin and other baubles. These quaint outfits, derived from 17th-century Spanish lackey uniforms, were soiled and tainted by the odors acquired through the unrelieved use which also left them in ragged condition. The style of dress assured Vicosino distinctiveness; the shabby appearance encouraged Mestizo disrespect.

The Vicosino homesteads were widely dispersed over the arable lands of the manor. For the most part, they were small and poorly constructed, being either conical or rectangular in shape. The stone and adobe walls, usually built through the cooperative efforts of one's neighbors and relatives in a work bee *(minga),* were often noticeably out of plumb. The thatch or crude tile roofs sheltered the well-used family belongings on wall pegs or suspended from the roof. Although built by his hands, on his own time and with his own resources, the homestead did not belong to the Vicosino. It was, instead, the property of the manor.

Only 23 Vicosinos were able to speak Spanish (the rest speaking only Quechua) and all were illiterate.(4) Vicosinos did not participate in public affairs, held no official public offices, and none would have been entitled to vote. As serfs and servants the Vicosinos formed the principal resource of the manor and were regarded as property rather than as citizens.

For the people of Marcará, social status and the contingent roles were a question of ascription rather than achievement. Classification as an Indian at birth(5) thus placed one permanently in the social shadow of the Mestizo. Social mobility in Marcará District was nil for the Indian, and Vicosinos were discouraged from migrating since this was not in the best interests of the manor.

The assumptions underlying this socio-economic arrangement took for granted the generic inferiority of the Indian as a being.(6) In its extreme form, the Mestizo declared that the Indian was "the animal closest to man" and that the Vicosinos were "savages" and "brutes." Less radical were opinions that the Vicosinos were merely ignorant, slow, drunken, humble or simple. Mestizo "respect" was earned through the faithful adherence to prescribed behavior; and indeed the Vicosino usually proved himself to be a tractable laborer and beast of burden. Failure to conform was fraught with difficulties of a psychological and physical nature since recalcitrant Indians received punishments ranging from tongue-lashings to imprisonment and flogging. Conformity to the ascribed role of the Indian, of course, tended to reaffirm the specious assumptions about the Indian and his place in society.

The prevalent Mestizo belief that the Indian was "childlike" was evident in the use of the familiar form of address—such terms as "boy" or "son"—with Vicosinos no matter what their age. Such usages in Mestizo society are normally employed with children only. For the few Vicosinos able to speak some words of Spanish, this situation was especially frustrating. Not only were they addressed as non-adults, but in Quechua. The Indians were thus reminded of their place in society and denied even the possibility of improving their command of the national language.(7)

One of the chief differences between Vicos and the Mestizo town of Marcará, where so many Vicosinos contracted "protective" relationships through fictive kin, was the fact that in Vicos there were only four events which allowed for the establishment of these ties. These were birth, baptism, first hair cutting, and marriage. In contrast, the people of Marcará, who often served as godparents to Vicosinos, themselves had developed fourteen types of occasions at which fictive kin could be gained.(8) This represented, in significant terms, a measure of the greater social movement and complexity of the district capital as opposed to the restricted life in the hacienda. Whereas the people of Marcará utilized the fictive kin system for many and diverse social aims, the Vicosinos' use of the system was for much narrower and defensive purposes. We may also note here that while a Vicosino might choose a godparent for his child in Marcará, the reverse would never happen. The patron-client relationship between Marcará and Vicos was well served through such enduring "spiritual" ties and obligations. Under manorial conditions, wealthier Vicosinos often preferred to seek Mestizo godsibs and godparents for their children outside Vicos in order to assure themselves of having some intercessors to protect them from abuses by the civil authorities and other Mestizos. This preference contrasted with the usual reinforcement of internal relationships between Vicosinos that ritual kinship accomplished for most of the serf population.(9) Reportedly about two-thirds of the godparents of marriage of Vicosinos are other Indians, and about one-third are Mestizos from Marcará. Besides providing protection for Vicosinos, Mestizo godparents perform other cultural brokerage functions. They confer somewhat more prestige on their godchildren than do Vicosino godparents. Commanding greater economic resources than Vicosinos, the Mestizos often make possible a costlier marriage ceremony than an Indian could afford, even providing a brass band on occasion. The marriage godparent or sponsor shares the cost of the wedding about equally with the groom's father.

Ritual kinship ties are strong among Vicosinos and involve significant reciprocal obligations. Godchildren haul wood and perform other services for their marriage sponsors for years after the ceremony. The godsibs of the marriage sponsor give him sheep, chickens, prepared food, and alcoholic beverages in quantity. On the other hand, the godparents provide counsel to and admonish their godchildren when the latter encounter marital difficulties. The ritual parents rather than the real parents intercede to seek solutions to marital problems.(10)

Very frequently, on the other hand, the intercessors on the side of conventional morality and local custom are the husband's grandparents or other close relatives. Fictive kinship relations typically strengthen the ties between members of the patrilineal *castas* (see below) to which Vicosinos belong. Such reinforcement comes about rather naturally. When couples live near the husband's parents in the customary patrilocal pattern, wives are usually attended during childbirth by their mothers-in-law. Thus, the latter become the midwife-godmothers of their own grandchildren, and when children are later formally christened in church, paternal in-laws are usually chosen for godparents.

When a young man marries, tradition calls for his grandparents to act as his sponsors, if considerations of establishing protectionist ties with Mestizos do not intervene. If a youth's grandparents are already deceased, his older brother and sister are preferred as matrimonial sponsors by local custom. Thus, family heads become godparents of their own grandchildren and godsibs to their own sons and daughters-in-law. In cases of matrilocal residence, which occur, a wife's mother becomes midwife-godmother and baptismal godmother of her off-spring.(11)

The selection of ceremonial sponsors for a marriage is a serious matter for Vicosinos, albeit significantly influenced by customary preference for certain relatives. They are formally solicited by the groom's parents with gifts of alcoholic beverages and ceremonial foods. If the young man and woman living in *watanaki* ("trial marriage") are rounded up by the traditional lay religious authorities of Vicos (the *varayoc*) while living or sleeping together during Lent, they are held with similar couples until their marriage sponsor arrives to vouch that they will marry in a church ceremony. This leads at times to godfathers being selected precipitously.

However quickly such a decision may be made, the ritual kinship relationship established is lasting and very important in structuring Vicos social networks. The fictive kinship relation-ship is serious enough for local subculture to define marriage between gobsibs as a crime against the community. Vicosinos believe that cohabitation by godsibs causes crop blights or torrential rains that damage crops. In the past, transgressions of this type were punished by public whipping, although punish-ment has shifted in recent years to fines and public disgrace. Vicosino repugnance toward sexual relations between godsibs is reflected in vivid folktales about women, living in the *ashma-naki* relationship, as it is termed locally, being transformed into frightening heads flying through the night air emitting hair–raising sounds while their decapitated bodies gurgle through a gaping esophagus only partially stoppered by a maize cob.(12)

Covertly, the Vicosino response to every-threatening and humiliating interaction with Mestizos (and all outsiders) was one of fear and great mistrust.(13) Mestizos were often thought to be *pishtakos,* human ogres who murdered Indians in order to make use of their bodily fat and organs as grease. As bogy-men in childhood tales and as domineering and abusive figures in real life, Mestizos were feared more than hated, and therefore shunned. If contact were unavoidable, however, a kind of passive non-cooperation would be adopted in the interaction situation. If the Mestizo wanted him to work, the Vicosino would have to be instructed repeatedly as to his chores.

"Dimwittedness" was the sanctioned mental state; lack of initiative and brightness its manifestation in behavior.

Despite their fears, the Vicosinos were not entirely passive under the manorial system. Obliged to work three days a week without effective remuneration, they took what they could whenever possible. The agricultural custom of gleaning and the patterns of work rhythms aptly illustrate this opportunism. Anyone was allowed to glean the manor fields after harvest. This being the case, Vicosino peons engaged in the harvest generally left uncounted numbers of potatoes behind for the gleaners who followed. The manor thus lost a very large percent of its harvest.(14) Indeed, anything belonging to the Patron or his representative was open to theft, or as a Vicosino might say, "grow legs and walk away."

The habit of Vicos men of chewing coca is a common and definitive Indian trait in the Andean regions. In the Mestizo view coca chewing is invariably considered to be a debasing and stupefying vice to which the Indian succumbs to alleviate his hunger and sorrow and to give him endurance to perform the heavy, menial work demanded of him. From the Vicosino point of view, however, coca fulfills an important social role as well as these assumed nutritional and psychological ones.(15) While working for the manor Vicosinos were normally permitted seven or eight opportunities to masticate coca during the work day.(16) These "coca-breaks" sometimes lasted as long as twenty minutes, reluctantly accepted by the operator as necessary for the Indians to be able to work. For the Vicosino, on the other hand, this was a social period, characterized by conversation and joking. Vicosinos rarely took even two such breaks during the day when working on their own fields, and persons who did might be accused of laziness. It cannot be said, therefore, that the Indians gave their all to the work of the manor.

Behind these defenses lay hidden the true culture of Vicos, both rejected and distinct from that of the Mestizo world. The Vicosinos recognized their uniqueness—in their clothing, speech, habits, and values.(17) They had a lively, bawdy sense of humor which they usually did not share with outsiders. One's worth in the society—for both sexes—was judged by his ability to work hard on his own and his family's behalf. Prestige and respect were "acquired" through the passive process of growing old, although the possession of wealth, sponsorship of religious festivals, ability to speak some Spanish or exercise some special skill were also means by which one might acquire prestige in the community. Acquisition of the latter attributes was thought to be a matter of luck as much as anything.

Family organization also differed from that of the Mestizos who reckoned their kin bilaterally. The Vicosinos were divided into 52 *castas* (in 1952; there are now 69) or unilinear descent groups which were rigorously patrilineal in character.(18) Within the family unit the man gave the "orders" and was considered to be "worth more" than his spouse, whose ideal role was conceptualized as essentially passive in nature, "like the soil in which man plants his seed to be nourished." At mealtime the women and girls serve the men their food and remain apart. Similarly, the woman inevitably walks behind her husband to show her respect for him in public. In speaking, women often employ a high-pitched, whining tone of voice, at times covering their mouths. Such "shyness" and vocal tension is particularly evidenced when talking to Mestizos, but is also common among the Vicosinos themselves.(19)

Marriage in Vicos was a relatively closely managed affair with the couple, their parents, godparents, and the *varayoc* all involved in the arrangements. In 1952 there was reportedly no importance attached to virginity, and adolescents normally had sexual experience prior to arranging marriage, beginning with a period of "trial" *(watanakuy)*. This usually lasted for about one year, and always culminated in a church wedding during the Lenten period. During this time the couple could separate if the relationship did not prove congenial. Children born under such circumstances were in no way considered "illegitimate" and received care equal to that received by others.(20)

Childhood, however, was not a particularly benign period of life in Vicos, but rather harsh and uncertain.(21) Attendance at the manor school was not even considered possible and certainly not encouraged (only thirty-nine students had been enrolled at the school since it was established in 1940). The parents feared that the children would become lazy or be ill-treated by teachers who considered them "savages."(22) Instead, children performed chores from the age of three or four years and were usually attired in the cast-off rags and clothing of others until ten or more years of age. The social horizons of the child were severely limited and the circle of playmates was small, being comprised principally of relatives. Many children (particularly girls) spent a substantial portion of their young lives herding the family animals in solitude or in the company of one or two siblings.

The admiration of one's parents was gained through work and obedience even into adult life. The main sources of affection and friendship lay in the nuclear family and the *casta,* although in certain circumstances the maternal relatives might prove important. An adjunct to the *casta* was the set of fictive kin acquired during the course of a lifetime. The godparents, godsibs, and godchildren extended the circle of confidence and friendship upon which one could rely for assistance or protection and so would be chosen with this in mind.

Conduct of family affairs was overseen by the older men and women, although not without the sometimes active participation of the older children (sometimes called *yayas*). Questions of incest and infidelity were handled within the *casta* if possible, and if this failed it would befall the community authorities, the *varayoc,* to mete out appropriate punishment to violators of the moral code.

Death in Vicos was, and is, a dramatic, emotional event. Funerals and wakes of adults usually last five days and are accompanied by an elaborate purification of the corpse(23) for the ascent to heaven, where many believed, the Vicosinos would occupy the roles played on earth by the Mestizos. The wake and procession continue to be serious—but not sober—events. The heavy drinking and dancing which accompany the ritual to the music of flutes and drums stimulate expressions of grief and frustration. Men rich enough to afford a simple, black wooden coffin were indeed well off, for many went to their unlettered graves in crude sacks—a final indignity. For children, particularly infants, death was often considered as a stroke of good fortune since the child would not have to suffer the hardships of life.(24) An Indian cantor, imitating the intonations of a priest in "Latin," accompanies the procession to the cemetery. Prior to the onset of the Cornell Project, few Vicosino deaths were recorded in the district registry of vital statistics nor did

the Mestizo authorities consider them worthy of any preoccupation.

The only community-wide internal organization permitted
among the Vicosinos was that of the *varayoc* or "petty
mayors."(25) This group of seventeen men, ideally the most
righteous and moral men of the community, were lead by the
alcaldi (mayor) who carried a silver-adorned stave as a symbol
of his office. They constituted a hierarchy of authority among
the serfs of the manor. In addition to this group, the *alcaldi* also
named at least four persons *(procuradores)* who were responsible for overseeing the conduct and organization of the principal
festivals. The selection of the mayor was a voluntary, annual
event at which only the Vicos men took part. Theoretically, one
must "rise through the ranks" in order to become mayor. Thus,
a minimum of seven years would be required to achieve this
position.

It was the responsibility of the *varayoc* to enforce the moral
code, regulate the trial marriage system, see that the religious
festivals were properly celebrated, care for church property on
the manor, execute public works, and judge and penalize crimes
ranging from breach of promise to homicide. It was important
for the mayor and his co-officials "to know how to give orders"
or "to know how to lead." Their authoritarian style of
leadership was clearly patterned after that of the Patron.

The mayor was accorded great respect. He walked ahead of
the other *varayoc* and occupied the preferred places in the
presence of the others. All of the *varayoc* roles, were, in fact,
greatly concerned with the conduct of various rituals accompanied by the practice of special etiquette with each other. The
former *varayoc,* especially those of great age (always of concern
in selecting the mayor) constituted a group of elders (called
vayas) who were the most respected persons in Vicos. The
elders were considered the repository of community knowledge
and were often called upon as "resource" personnel to help
settle disputes of various types.

The operator of the manor, however, could and did intervene
in *varayoc* affairs at any time and the latter were further
controlled by the legal mayor of Marcará who theoretically
appointed them and actually ordered them to see that certain
public works be carried out by Vicosinos. The *varayoc* survived

as a viable organization by carrying out these orders and being obedient to the manor operator in particular. Among their manorial duties, the *varayoc* were responsible for punishing recalcitrant serfs by seizing their tools or animals and providing adolescent girls to work as domestics at the manor house or at the house of the Patron (who often lived elsewhere). The mayor and vice mayor only assumed office upon approval of the Patron. *Varayoc* were in effect, therefore, the errand boys of Mestizo society and as such constituted a quaint but tragic mockery of the Vicosino and his cultural integrity.

The religious and festival activities of Vicos were not especially numerous, particularly when compared to those of the Mestizo towns of the region.(26) Indeed, if the intensity of religious celebrations as practiced in colonial times was as great as has been claimed, then contemporary Vicos religious practices represent a marked decline in this sphere of activity. Kubler has noted that during the colonial period(27)

> "Nearly one-fourth of each year, it is true, was consumed in its [the religious calendar] celebration . . . but it will be noted that the feasts invoke all the major events of the geneology and life of Christ, and that among them each and every one of the apostles is commemorated . . . [and] arduous preparations were undertaken for the appropriate celebration of the particular day. Individual prestige was accumulated by the discharge of the major-domo's responsibilities. . . ."

The principal feast days and Saints of Vicos are those of the conquerors: St. Andrew (Sacred Patron of Vicos), Our Lady of Ransom (Virgin de las Mercedes), Holy Week, and Carnival. The celebration of these events and the organization of activities was largely in the hands of the *varayoc,* their appointees, and the *mayordomos* (sponsors) who usually volunteered to underwrite the costs of the celebrations.(28) Serving as *mayordomo* at one of the festivals, which entailed the conspicuous expenditure of one's own or borrowed wealth, brought the respect of one's *casta* and neighbors.

The hierarchy of *mayordomos* and their helpers was populated by such personages as the "corporal," "wax corporal," "potato corporal," and "meat corporal." Each of these, as the titles imply, was responsible for supplying or managing the use of a particular item required for the celebration. Thus, with the responsibilities distributed among several *mayordomos* each with his "corporals," the people of Vicos indulged in the only community activities which they were permitted to organize. Even here, nevertheless, the Patron or the administrator would be asked to lend money, make gifts, and perhaps decide certain questions.

The parish priest from Marcará was normally contracted for these occasions and so made his only appearances in Vicos at these times. Wearing his "duster" coverall and sunglasses, the aging priest would arrive on horseback to celebrate the Mass. The roughly constructed chapel was barren except for the statues of the three Saints housed there, and the crosses, embroidered banners, and tall, waxen standards brought in by the Vicosinos for the festival. The Saints, like the people, were humbly dressed. In keeping with this milieu, the priest would usually bring his oldest vestments.

The feasts of St. Andrew and of Our Lady of Ransom attracted virtually all of the people of the manor as well as those from the surrounding area. The small, native flutes (*rayan, pinkullu,* and *chiska*), and drums *(tiuya),* locally made violins, and the "Youth of Marcará" brass band (or a similar group from Huaraz) played the huaynos by which people of every age danced, drank, ate, talked, and argued—all to excess. The festivals of Vicos were locally famous as drunken orgies and the Vicosinos, both men and women, engaged in great brawls on these occasions. The festival was a time for the expression of hostility and aggressive emotion not vented when one is sober. On Easter Sunday a dummy representing Judas Iscariot (and dressed as a Mestizo) was placed on a horse or donkey and driven about the plaza of Vicos. The people shouted the most scurrilous insults at it, pelted the figure with stones and kicked it until it disintegrated.(29) This was a joke and brought no reprisals. Such psychologically satisfying events as fiestas balanced the depressing effects of the manor society and undoubtedly were of enormous value in maintaining the very hacienda system itself.

The other Vicosinos who wielded power were the *mayorales* or straw bosses, whose power and position were derived and controlled from Mestizo sources. Chosen by the manor operator, the *mayorales* received special favors and concessions which tended to set them apart and against the interests of other Vicosinos. Consequently, although they came to possess certain wealth, the *mayorales* did not enjoy the respect which otherwise might have been theirs.

With these events the full cycle is described. Vicosinos, denied even a modicum of respect, affection, or moral stature in the larger society, were set against themselves within their own closed society. Whatever pride that existed was seriously and unrectifiably compromised by the absence of any effective means or power to alter the situation. The ultimate step in degradation was the realization of one's impotence as a Vicosino. This was not simply a "culture of poverty" but rather, one of repression.(30)

THE RECOVERY OF SELF:
VICOS IN 1964

To initiate the study of Vicos it was necessary for project members to create roles which were substantially different from those normally assumed by outsiders—particularly Mestizos—in Vicos. The first investigator, Dr. Mario C. Vázquez, accomplished this by living with Vicosino families, an act which at once was a stunning departure from the normal Mestizo custom. His doing what anthropologists normally do in field situations was enough to set himself clearly apart from the norm. He established beyond question the fact that he chose to be with Vicosinos and that he respected them as people, declining to adopt a posture of superiority towards them. This pattern was continued by the others who followed. Records indicate that at least seventy-five investigators of various descriptions have worked under the aegis of the Cornell Peru Project at Vicos(31) and their total impact must be considered as having been enormous, although virtually beyond measure. The fifteen-odd Peace Corps volunteers who have worked at Vicos since 1962 have also made contributions.

The "anthropological" behavior did more than break the stereotype of the outsider. It created difficulties in Marcará and Huaraz, the departmental capital—where the Mestizo upper class was at first puzzled and then resentful and suspicious of such happenings. It was disturbing that newcomers insisted on breaking the traditions by allowing Indians to ride in their vehicles, paying them the going daily wage for labor and services rendered, or by taking them to the hospital. Quite aside from the humanitarian and egalitarian values held by the researchers, this first "intervention" was in part prompted by the practical necessity of obtaining the confidence and cooperation of the Vicosinos in order to do the field work at all.

As mentioned previously, the first changes introduced were directed at the most overtly degrading aspects of the manorial system according to the people. Obligatory servitude was abolished. Wages were paid.(32) The new management informed the Vicosinos that they could not be forced to perform public labor at the whim of the district mayor, this being unconstitutional. The near absolute power of the Patron was more than enough to initiate radical changes in the patterns of respect, as well as of the economy. The power of the Patron was used to encourage Vicosinos to break the traditional patterns of subservience and to support those who did so. These provisions meant the end of the conspicuous consumption of Vicos labor in the district capital.

Vicosinos and Mestizos alike required time and encouragement to adjust to this innovation, a process which continues to the present. The change did not please all of the Indians who had enjoyed favored positions and it certainly provoked disfavor among Mestizos.(33) Placing a real value on the labor of the Vicosinos was not only a practical step towards economic independence but also an important symbolic step in aiding the former serfs to achieve a feeling of personal dignity and worth. One consequence of this is that Vicosinos have gradually substituted the use of burros and horses for many of the laborious, "brutalizing" tasks which they once performed, thus demonstrating that they did not behave as "animals" out of preference.(34)

A major task of the Cornell Peru Project was to introduce a dynamic concept of leadership and a new structure capable of handling community affairs. Chief among the problems encountered was one centered around what may be termed the "servant syndrome." Vicosinos were accustomed to showing extreme deference to the Mestizo superior, bowing, hurrying to get out of his path, removing his hat, and above all, obeying orders without comment. Thus it was extremely difficult at first—and for many adults this difficulty still continues—to take initiatives, generate new ideas, or express them in the presence of Mestizos, Cornell staff, or other outsiders. They were, after all, working under a severe handicap: the notion that their ideas, beliefs, and opinions might be worth something was novel, to say the least.

The kind of personality manorial conditions fostered among Vicosinos was a self-denigrating one, and not a matter of "humility" deriving from an inner sense of respect. In his intensive analysis of ten men who were over fifteen years old when the Cornell Peru Project began at Vicos, Klein(35) found that their self images contained a common theme of pacification of authority figures. In varying ways all these men saw themselves as weak and vulnerable appeasers finding safety in distance, or oppressed and overlooked at the bottom of the heap, as unnoticed as a "dead toad." One perceived himself as resembling a predatory animal who steals to survive, while several sought to ingratiate themselves with the authorities through complete compliance to orders and with subsequent attempts to evoke the pity of the Patron. Representing an extreme on this one-sided psychological continuum, probably, was the individual who felt that everyone else would be better off without him.

Despite the handicaps of such psychological burdens upon individuals, a corps of community leaders was formed with patient counselling and prodding. The Vicos community now annually elects a council *(junta de delegados)*, president, and business manager to manage their affairs. The elected officers have gradually acquired prestige which at present far surpasses that of the *varayoc* although the latter organization continues to function albeit on an increasingly limited scale. Its members have virtually no political or judicial functions, these having been assumed by the council and a legally appointed judicial representative, the lieutenant governor *(teniente gobernador)*, who is also a Vicosino.

The *varayoc* have called upon the elected community officers to resolve their own internal disputes on several occasions. The creation of the community council and general administrative positions (president, manager, secretary, and treasurer) has given capable young men the opportunity to participate in community affairs. Under the manorial system, only the old men with the conservative mandate of the Patron had been permitted this role. The new community by-laws, in fact, require that the administrative officers be literate so as to handle the corporate business effectively. Most of the potential candidates for these offices, therefore, range in a group between twenty and forty years of age. Untainted by patronal obligations, the elected members of the community organization may consequently lay legitimate claim to public respect which can, in turn, be given without compromise of dignity.

Many of the new leaders have come from the group of returned army draftees who have used this experience to acquire greater prestige and respect than their peers who remained home. These young men have learned Spanish and achieved an accepted status—albeit lowly—in the national society. In 1963 the first Vicosino in history (a former army sergeant) was a candidate for district councilman in Marcará. He was not elected but he was placed on the ticket. In the subsequent 1966 election a young Vicosino highschool graduate was actually elected to the District Council.

The increasingly important role of the younger men is of course not unusual in gerontocentric societies where some new element upsets the traditional means by which one may acquire prestige, respect, and power.(36) The young men have new avenues of mobility open to them—such as joining the army or attending school—which are not accessible to the older men. With their wider outside experience being greatly valued, the young men have regularly been elected to community offices; and so they speak where formerly they had remained silent. Intergenerational conflict has been thus far tempered through the annual voting process, providing the opportunity to reassess electoral choices. It would be incorrect, however, to conclude that the *yayas* have ceased to exercise power and influence in community affairs. Now, they work through their sons and grandsons, who are office holders. At public meetings deference is shown to the *yayas,* who have no reluctance in speaking out or attempting to silence younger men with whom they disagree. Their support is necessary in the conduct of community affairs.

With the exercise of power come the necessary problems of decision-making (and of making the wrong decisions), and discovering power limits. To date, the community and its elected representatives have demanded the recognition of their new status by forcing various external agencies to deal directly with them as a free community, instead of through surrogates such as the government agency that is responsible for the conduct of the development program. The council, for example, on one occasion locked the school director and the teachers out of the school because of their poor performance and attitudes towards the community. With padlock key in hand, a commission of Vicosinos traveled to the Ministry of Education in Lima to request that new personnel be appointed (which was done). Other members of the Peruvian government program have also been forced to leave for similar reasons, as indeed were several Peace Corps volunteers. In each case, the Vicosinos sought to make the outsiders respect their wishes, and their vitalized self respect and feelings of importance have thus produced results which are both understandable as well as predictable.(37)

The annual installation of the new members of the community council has also been the occasion for gaining additional respectability and acceptance. It has become the practice over the last five years to invite prominent regional and departmental officials to this event which constitutes an important festive— but sober—manifestation of Vicos autonomy. By their presence the visiting dignitaries bestow a legitimacy on the proceedings and recognition of the new community status.

The new possessions such as the former manor house, now the community meeting room, the clinic, teacher's apartments, the warehouses, and particularly the large primary school and the Ford-600 truck are the source of much community pride as products of their own work. The school is one of the best in the rural regions of the department.

One of the first acts of the community, upon purchasing the manor in 1962, was to buy the six-ton truck for transporting the potato crop to market in Lima. While the truck did serve this purpose, it was also evident that the people took enormous pride in its possession, painting on the front of the vehicle

"Vicos Communal Property" and "Cry of Reform." The people delighted in boasting of the truck to Mestizo acquaintances since vehicle ownership is most prestigeful in the Andes. Whenever the truck was idle at Vicos the people would have the hired driver take them to Huaraz or Marcará, largely for the ride and the impression it would make. One remembers with no small satisfaction, the mixture of pride, gaiety, and independence reflected in the faces of the riders. The Vicosino attachment to this symbol eventually reached the point where the community—outside advice notwithstanding—refused to sell it despite the fact that it was economically unprofitable to maintain. In psychological and cultural terms of course, it was another matter. The truck was particularly significant since its acquisition forced many local Mestizos to recognize the community and its potential, if not the individual Vicosino himself.

Recognition of Vicos on national and international levels has also affected the local status of the community. In recent years, the Vicos project has been a point of discussion in Peruvian magazines and newspapers.(38) Individual Vicosinos have appeared twice on Lima television programs, the community manager addressed official gatherings in Lima, and three Vicosinos (and two members of the teaching staff) traveled to the United States as participants in a rural leadership training program sponsored by the United States Agency for International Development and the National Farmers' Union. The Vicos project and the changes on the manor are approvingly discussed in "civic education" chapters of required highschool text books, and the case has been publicized by the Peruvian agricultural extension service (SIPA) and the United States Information Service in three educational films. The friendships resulting from Vicosino experiences in the United States led members of the National Farmers' Union in North Dakota to donate a John Deere tractor to the community in 1964. The cumulative effect of these honors and experiences has served to increment immeasurably the sense of collective self respect, pride, and regional social stature of the community.

Just as community pride has materialized, so too with respect to the individual. Vicosinos have begun to discover that they are endowed with the same abilities and basic human qualities as

Mestizos and even foreigners. This most fundamental change was dramatically conveyed to us in 1960. At that time it was rumored about the community, thwarted in its attempt to purchase the manor, that the manor owner (the Public Benefit Society of Huaraz) might again seek to rent out the property as before. During a discussion of the crisis a Vicosino grasped me firmly by the arm and with unmistakable conviction said, "I, my wife and my sons, we are all ready to die, but never again will we be peons."

The sum of these nascent personality changes has given the Vicosinos a growing reputation as aggressive and insubordinate in the traditional Mestizo view. "You are ruining the Indians," we were told. "They are becoming very pretentious." Four years ago a Peruvian congressman on an "inspection" tour of Vicos insultingly remarked that he was surprised to see many Vicosinos still chewing coca even though it was such a dirty habit. The Vicosino to whom the comment was directed coolly replied by asking the congressman why he was smoking a cigarette when he certainly must know that according to a Reader's Digest (Selecciones) article this was a cause of cancer. The congressman retreated. In 1952 such an exchange would not only have been impossible but inconceivable.

Vicosinos no longer constitute an undifferentiated mass of peasant laborers and may now seek new opportunities on their own merits. This became a possibility after many men had learned trades during the construction of the school and other buildings. Several men have in fact earned the title of respect, *maestro,* indicating that they are considered master of their specialty.

The most potent force for decisive change over the long term, despite its multiple deficiencies, is the school. The illiterate community has sent its children to primary school in relatively large numbers, although greatly weighted on the masculine side. The first Vicosinos have entered highschools in the provincial capitals of Carhuaz and Caraz, and, in a special teacher-training secondary school in Cajamarca. In December, 1964, the first Vicosino was graduated from highschool (fifth in his class of 27) and, a few months later, became the first Vicosino to pursue higher education by enrolling at the regional normal school with hopes of becoming a teacher. Because the highschool was attended primarily by Mestizo children, Vicosinos had doubted the ability of their children to compete with Mestizos and feared that some harm might befall the child who entered this alien domain. They have been proved wrong on both counts. School excursions gave further proof of this, especially as Vicos boys repeatedly demonstrated their aptitude for successfully playing the Mestizo game of soccer.

The school has also helped create a special status for many children. On one hand it has greatly amplified the social activity of children by opening the doors to new experiences and wider friendships (and hostilities) developing beyond the *casta*. School attendance has also relieved much of the drudgery of menial chores. School-acquired knowledge is also precipitating some significant changes within the family, where the children now possess skills which few adults mastered. They can read, write, add and subtract, and handle rudimentary Spanish. Skill in simple arithmetic and Spanish is of special importance to the family economy, for it enables one to expand commercial activity and avoid being short-changed by slick storekeepers who had made this a habit when dealing with the illiterate Indians. Consequently, the "learned child" *(leido)* is often placed upon a pedestal, consulted by his parents, and given special tasks and responsibility. Children have earned more respect, if not more affection, from their parents and in the community as a whole.

Women have not moved apace with the men in these developments. Few girls have been sent to school although their numbers gradually increase each year. More valuable insofar as the women are concerned has been the opportunity to learn the operation of sewing machines, a much admired skill in Vicos for both sexes. Girls who have this knowledge are considered as being potentially better homemakers than the others.

The modest degree of relative prosperity brought about by the development project has been reflected in festival activity. The parish priest, now a decade older, continued the pattern of infrequent visits to Vicos, usually only for the feast days, and the religious and moral aspects of Vicos life have remained in the care of the *varayoc*. Their role in these events appears to have become less secure, and certainly less obvious than it had been. Many more now actively participate as *mayordomos*.

Uniformed army veterans presently assume the responsibility for managing much of the feast of Our Lady of Ransom (patroness of Peru's armed forces) and carry the litter themselves in procession around the plaza.

The church has undergone some improvement over the past decade, but in essence, just like the cemetery, remains the same as before. In other respects, religious behavior in Vicos is animated by greater doses of music, rockets, new clothing, and generally through the consumption of newly gained wealth. Many people can now afford to make and carry the intricate, two- and three-meter-high waxen standards *(velones)*. New clothing for the occasion is noticeable, in large part made in the sewing shop by the women or even some of the men. Those who own them, wear shoes. Vicosinos have become increasingly fond of the music of the brass bands of the region and those *mayordomos* who can afford to hire them do so. As many as eight bands have performed in the plaza, in addition to the Vicos musicians playing their traditional flutes, drums, and violins. The formation of the St. Andrew's band of Vicos, and the fact that many young men now have learned to play a type of drum and flute (*caja* and *roncadora*) which has recently diffused into the area, has apparently increased the number of festival roles open to enterprising individuals.

In all of these respects the festival pattern has drawn closer to that of regional Mestizo styles of celebration, without, it should be noted, prompting either by the parish priest or Cornell Project personnel. The changes in musicians and their instruments is indicative of this. In 1964 one Vicosino even acquired a portable phonograph which he rented for family celebrations. The consumption of alcohol and *chicha* (maize beer) is as high as before (as it is in Mestizo festivals of the region). There are, nevertheless, far fewer fights, indicating a decrease in levels of unexpressed hostility, and the "annual" destruction of Judas Iscariot has been overlooked most of the past decade.

CONCLUSIONS

The face of Vicos has noticeably changed since 1952. The people are, as a whole, far better clothed and housed than ever in their history, although the Vicos level of living is but a few degrees above what many would consider minimal. Gone, however, are the hordes of gleaners who scavenged the Patron's fields and the degrading experience that this constituted. Around the plaza of Vicos, near the refurbished manor house, are the community buildings; several families have constructed homes adjacent to them, forming an "urban" nucleus so important to community status in Peru.

These changes have taken place without prompting from Project personnel. That these developments have spontaneously accompanied the enormously increased feelings of personal worth and dignity is no accident.

The original broad goals of the project from a practical standpoint were to improve the levels of living and the quality of life in the society.(39) The psychological and symbolic foundations upon which any significant socio-cultural changes of this nature could take place have been laid. The attainment of a degree of self and community respect where virtually none had existed, the increased stature of the individual both publicly and within the family, and the fluorescence of Vicos culture generally have highlighted these changes. The concepts concerning one's responsibility to himself and to others, especially the community, are being redefined. Finally, the stiff barriers to social mobility and cultural change, although still present, are now beginning to be scaled by Vicosinos who have the confidence to do so.

NOTES

1. M. Saenz, *Sobre el Indio Peruano y su Incorporación al Medio Nacional.* Mexico: Secretaria de Educación Publica, 1933, p. 172.

2. H. Ghersi B., "El Indigena y el Mestizo en la Comunidad de Marcará," Revista del Museo Nacional (Lima), vol. XXVIII (1959), pp. 118-188; vol. XXIX (1960), pp. 48-128; vol. XXX (1961), pp. 95-176.

3. M. C. Vázquez Varela, "La Antropologia Cultural y Nuestra Problema del Indio," Perú Indígena, vol. II, nos. 3 and 6 (1952), pp. 7-157.

4. J. O. Alers, *Population and Development in a Peruvian Community,* Ithaca: Cornell University Comparative Studies of Cultural Change, 1964, mimeo, p. 29.

5. Status as Indian, Mestizo, "white," or "yellow" was recorded in the civil registry of vital statistics in Marcará.

6. A. R. Holmberg, H. F. Dobyns, and M. C. Vázquez. "Methods for the Analysis of Cultural Change," Anthropology Quarterly, vol. 34, no. 2 (1960), pp.

Peasants, Power, and Applied Social Change

37-40. The general socio-cultural situation found here is not unlike that facing many minority groups in the United States and the problem of discrimination as it existed. See, for example, R. M. Williams, Jr., *Strangers Next Door*, Englewood Cliffs, N.J.: Prentice-Hall, 1964.

7. H. Martinez, "Vicos: Las Fiestas en la Integración y Desintegración Cultural," Revista del Museo Nacional, vol. XXVII (1959), pp. 204-205.

8. H. Ghersi B., 1960, op. cit., pp. 56-69.

9. Vázquez, 1952, op. cit., p. 32.

10. R. Price, "Trial Marriage in the Andes," Ethnology, vol. 4, no. 3 (1965), pp. 317-318.

11. A. R. Holmberg and M. C. Vázquez, "The Castas: Unilineal Kin Groups in Vicos, Peru," Ethnology, vol. 5, no. 3 (1966), pp. 294-295, 297-298.

12. Price, op. cit., pp. 315, 317, 319.

13. Vázquez, 1952, op. cit., pp. 31-33.

14. A. R. Holmberg, "Land Tenure and Planned Social Change: A Case from Vicos, Peru," Human Organization, vol. 18, no. 1 (1959), p. 9.

15. N. I. Fine, "Coca Chewing: A Social Versus a Nutritional Interpretation," Columbia University, 1960, mimeo.

16. Vázquez, 1952, op. cit., pp. 93, 103.

17. Ibid., pp. 47-50, 101-103.

18. M. C. Vázquez "The 'Castas': Unilinear Kin Groups in Vicos, Peru," Cornell University Comparative Studies of Cultural Change, 1964, mimeo.

19. This pattern of vocal tension extends to female singing as well, where it is particularly marked. This pattern would seem to give credence to the hypothesis put forth by Lomax that there is a close relationship between female exploitation and subordination and the pitch of the singing voice. A. Lomax, "Folk Song Style," American Anthropologist, vol. 61, no. 6 (1959), pp. 944-950.

20. Vázquez, 1952, op. cit., pp. 47-49. For a more recent description of "trial" marriage at Vicos and its relationship to pre-Columbian practices, see R. Price, "Trial Marriage in the Andes," Ethnology, vol. LV, no. 3 (1965), pp. 310-322.

21. A. R. Holmberg, "Child Training in Vicos, Peru," Delphian Quarterly, no. 34 (1951), pp. 3-8.

22. Vázquez, 1952, op. cit., p. 54.

23. Vázquez, 1952, op. cit., p. 52.

24. R. Patch, "Life in a Peruvian Indian Community," American Universities Field Staff, Reports Service, "West Coast of South America Series," vol. IX, no. 1 (Peru), p. 25.

25. M. C. Vázquez, "The Varayoc System in Vicos." Cornell University, Comparative Studies of Cultural Change, 1964, mimeo.

26. Ghersi, 1960, op. cit., pp. 113-123; Ghersi, 1961, op. cit., pp. 130-151; P. Doughty, *Huaylas: An Andean District in Search of Progress*, Ithaca: Cornell University Press, 1968, pp. 208-235.

27. G. Kubler, "The Colonial Quechua," in J. Steward (Ed.), *Handbook of South American Indians*, Washington, D.C., Bureau of American Ethnology Bulletin, no. 143, p. 146.

28. A more complete description of the manorial religious celebrations of Vicos is found in W. P. Mangin, "The Cultural Significancy of the Fiesta Complex in an Indian Hacienda in Peru," Ph.D. dissertation, Yale University, 1954.

29. H. Martinez, 1959, op. cit. p. 211.

30. A. R. Holmberg, "The Frightful World of the Manor Serf: An Examination of Some Relationships Between Psychobiological Deprivation and Culture." In press.

31. H. F. Dobyns, and M. C. Vázquez, *The Cornell Peru Project, Bibliography and Personnel.* Cornell Peru Project Pamphlet No. 2, Ithaca, 1964.

32. A. R. Holmberg, "Informa del Dr. Allan R. Holmberg sobre el Desarrollo del Proyecto Peru-Cornell," Perú Indígena, vol. 3, nos. 7 and 8 (1952), pp. 239-241.

33. H. F. Dobyns, C. Monge M., and M. C. Vázquez, "Summary of Technical Organizational Progress and Reactions to It," Human Organization, vol. 21, no. 2 (1962), pp. 109-115. More for the benefit of visitors than the Vicosinos were the signs painted on the walls of the community buildings. Two of these, Articles I and IV of the "Declaration of Human Rights" (UNESCO), frequently elicited Mestizo comment to the effect that the ideas expressed were revolutionary, if not immoral and Communist-inspired.

34. The number of families owning burros in Vicos has increased from 38 in 1951 to 113 in 1963, an increment of 297 percent. The number of families owning horses increased from 40 to 62, or 155 percent, over the same period (Alers, op. cit., p. 33).

35. R. Klein, "The Self Image of Adult Males in an Andean Culture." New York University Ph.D. dissertation, 1963, pp. 56, 63, 73, 79, 84, 90, 96-97, 103-104, 109.

36. L. Sharp, "Steel Axes for Stone Age Australians," in E. Spicer (Ed.), *Human Problems in Technological Change,* New York: Russell Sage Foundation, 1952, pp. 69-90.

37. P. L. Doughty, "Pitfalls and Progress of Volunteers in Peru," in R. B. Textor (Ed.), *The Cultural Frontiers of the Peace Corps.* Cambridge: MIT Press, 1965; and R. W. Patch, "Vicos and the Peace Corps," American Universities Field Staff, Reports Service, *West Coast of South America Series,* vol. 11, no. 2.

38. Dobyns and Vázquez, 1964, op. cit.

39. A. R. Holmberg, "Proyecto Peru-Cornell en las Ciencias Sociales Aplicadas," Perú Indígena, vol. 3, nos. 5 and 6 (1952), pp. 158-166.

Chapter V

WELL-BEING

J. Oscar Alers

For the Vicosinos the natural environment holds many potentially threatening factors which are technologically beyond their control as a subordinate population in an underdeveloped area. The physical environment of the Vicosino is one of rocky and sloping terrain, of dry spells alternating with torrential rains, of cold nights, of hidden parasitic and epidemic agents, narrow resources, and of a not unrelated history of interpersonal conflict. It has presented a continuing challenge to his health, safety, and comfort.

CLOTHING

When the Cornell Peru Project began its operation early in 1952, the Vicosinos were found to have been very poorly protected against their rather harsh climate, with most people owning only one set of clothes. This was especially true of children under the age of 12 who were frequently dressed in little more than rags. Adult Vicosinos of both sexes typically wore costumes largely made in, and distinctive to, their

Author's Note: This chapter is a revision of a paper originally published in the American Behavioral Scientist. That article was prepared for the Comparative Studies of Cultural Change Project, Department of Anthropology, Cornell University, under Contract AID/csd-296 with the Office of Technical Cooperation and Research of the Agency for International Development. The data analyzed were collected under grants from the Carnegie Corporation of New York and an anonymous donor. The conclusions are those of the author and do not necessarily reflect opinions or policies of any supporting agency or organization.

community. For the men these consisted basically of a greyish-white hat with downturned brim, a white shirt, a navy-blue long-sleeved waistcoat, navy-blue, full-length trousers, and the inevitable black poncho. Women wore hats rather similar in color and design to those of the men, long-sleeved white blouses, several full-length skirts, usually red or yellow in color, and short red capes over their shoulders. The material used in the making of these clothes was almost invariably wool, and the cost of each such costume, including labor, materials, and the purchase of some finished items, was the equivalent of the annual wages of a Vicosino.(1)

By virtue of their increasing wealth, Vicosinos now possess many more items of clothing and a greater variety as well. By 1963, when the latest census was taken by the Cornell Peru Project, a total of 89 children owned school uniforms, whereas none did in 1952 when the first census was completed. A great many men now possess Western-style felt hats, shirts, vests, trousers, and suits purchased in nearby market towns, whereas such items were almost nonexistent in the community in 1952. Additional style change is noted in the Vicosinos' acquisition of "walnut-colored" ponchos, a regional Mestizo style. Women's clothing has not increased as greatly in variety, but the advent

Table I. NUMBER OF INDIVIDUALS POSSESSING SELECTED ITEMS OF CLOTHING, 1952 AND 1963

Item of Clothing	1952 (a)	1963 (b)	Index Number (1952 = 100) (b/a) 100
Walnut-colored poncho	88	220	250
Drill-cloth trousers	55	143	260
School uniform	–	89	–
Cotton shirt	199	569	286
Blouse	28	220	786
Felt hat	–	204	–
Vest	–	127	–
Suit	–	59	–
Shoes	76	218	287
Sandals	–	140	–
Total population	1,703	2,102	123

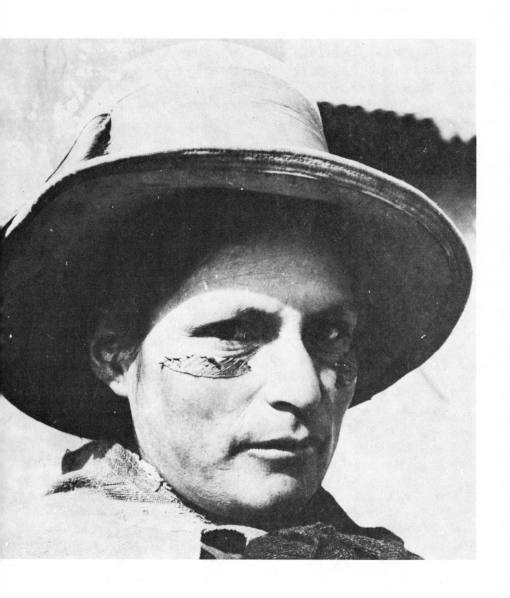

Well-being—A Vicos woman who feels aches and pains traditionally applied coca leaves to her cheeks for relief.

of sewing classes and the corresponding use of machines in Vicos have brought a substantial improvement in their quantity and quality. In addition, many persons now wear sandals, while most went barefoot prior to 1952, and the number of persons owning shoes has tripled, though the actual wearing of shoes is confined mostly to special occasions.

HOUSING

Similar changes have occurred in the field of housing. In 1952 the modal house in Vicos was square or rectangular in shape, had a tile roof, two rooms, and was constructed of adobe. There were, however, many circular, one-room houses with walls constructed of unmortared field stone and straw thatched roofs, these representing a survival of pre-Columbian housing style characteristic of high-altitude Indian dwellings in the Ancash region. The circular stone houses are regarded as inferior to the adobe and tile ones, and as such are exclusively identified with the Indian population. In Vicos, as elsewhere in the zone, it was common for a family to live in a cluster of tiny one- or two-room houses of either type, surrounding a small dirt patio, or corral.

All the houses had dirt floors, no windows, and very low roofs, barely high enough for a man (average Vicos height, 5 feet 3 inches) to stand erect. The prohibitive cost of windows, as well as the need for a snug house to hold the warmth of the hearth and to keep out the cold evening air and dampness of the rainy season, were good reasons for the continued maintenance of these dark and poorly ventilated houses. Piped water, gas, electricity, and sanitary facilities were, of course, completely lacking. Water was customarily drawn from one of the several small streams or irrigation ditches which criss-crossed the countryside as they descended from mountain glaciers. The elimination of bodily wastes took place in the hedge-rows at the end of the fields or in a secluded corner of the corral, usually at night.

Because of the small house size, living quarters appeared to be somewhat crowded: an average of almost five persons lived in each of these dwelling units. In most cases, the entire structure measured fifteen by twenty feet (exterior). Where two or more separate buildings comprised the dwelling unit, each section had a separate function: one edifice being used for sleeping and personal items, the others for storage of crops, etc. Cooking might be done either in the patio (on nice days) or inside one of the rooms. The crowding which could be attributed to these living conditions is mitigated by the fact that Vicosinos customarily spend most of their time out of doors tending to their various tasks, the houses serving principally for shelter at night and storage. Consequently, the function of the Vicos house is somewhat different from that of the Mestizo townsman or of a house in the United States, for example, where people may in fact spend much more of their time inside the home.

Though utilities are still lacking, in many respects the picture has changed considerably since 1952. Due to the increase in wealth and the development of building skills, the total number of houses in the community and the number of rooms per house have increased. Formerly, homes were widely dispersed throughout the estate, but many Vicosinos now have two houses, one located on the site of their farm plots and another on the main road; the community is thus gradually approaching an urban pattern of settlement. Relatively more houses now have tile roofs and plastered walls, and almost all now have wooden doors, rare in 1952. Buildings are now kept in a better state of repair and there has also been a substantial increase in the number and variety of household furnishings and utensils.

NUTRITION

As shown by several studies—part of the extensive research efforts undertaken in the community—the nutritional level of the people has also risen.

Over a ten-year period beginning in 1951, a team of investigators carried out a series of dietary surveys in 24 localities of Peru, selected in such a way as to be representative of the rural and urban zones of the three principal regions of the country, the coast, the sierra, and the jungle. The studies ultimately included more than 1,000 families comprising nearly

Table II. NUMBER OF HOUSEHOLDS POSSESSING SELECTED
FURNISHINGS AND UTENSILS, 1952 AND 1963

Item	1952 (a)	1963 (b)	Index Number (1952 = 100) (b/a) 100
Table	16	46	288
Chair	7	25	357
Cotton blanket*	348	455	131
Wool Blanket*	43	131	305
Kerosene lamp	–	116	–
Ceramic pot	359	452	126
Metal pot	–	136	–
Plate (enamel or china)	27	159	589
Metal spoon	352	441	125
Knife	358	428	120
Number of households	363	461	127

*Ponchos are also employed as blankets, and all men own these.

7,000 individuals, with the families to be studied selected
according to probability sampling techniques in most communities. In Vicos 519 persons in 98 families were studied in
four surveys, the first in July, 1952, the second in February,
1953, the third in May, 1956, and the fourth in July, 1961.(2)

It should be noted that, due to sampling and other
methodological weaknesses, a great deal of caution must be
exercised in evaluating the results of these surveys, some of
which tend to overestimate, and others to underestimate, the
actual nutritional level of the community. Thus, none of the
time samples was longer than a week, so that some of the
dietary fluctuations within a given year are not represented. All
four surveys missed the relatively lean December-January
months in Vicos, and all were taken in years when the harvest
was relatively abundant. The sample of subjects for the 1956
and 1961 surveys apparently over-represented the well-to-do
families of the community. In general, Vicosino families also
probably consumed less than what was actually weighed by the
nutritionist immediately prior to their meals and more by way
of snacks between meals. The nutritive benefits derived from
the school lunch program after 1953, and from the consumption of alcohol and coca, were not recorded.(3)

During the first two studies the survey team found that Vicosino families generally had two meals a day—a breakfast served between 6:00 and 9:00 a.m. and a supper between 4:00 and 6:30 p.m.—though some families enjoyed a noon meal as well. The two principal meals almost always consisted of a soup or stew, a side dish of parched corn, and when available, boiled potatoes. Parched corn was also carried by men working away from the home and consumed during rest hours.

The dietary habits of the Vicosinos were almost entirely dependent on what they produced in their fields, and their basic menu was therefore generally prepared from foods of vegetable origin: cereals (maize, wheat, and barley) and roots and tubers (potatoes, *ocas,* and *ollucos*), depending on the particular harvest season at hand. The mean weekly expenditure per family for food was about $1.25 in U.S. currency. The availability of food was thus closely linked to the success of the harvests; a poor harvest would lead to malnutrition, to migrant labor in exchange for food, and to stealing from the hacienda or neighbors. Indeed, theft from the Patron was highly institutionalized.

In neither of the two initial surveys was food of animal origin included in 25 percent or more of the family menus. Most of the families possessed domestic animals, but only rarely did they personally consume meat, eggs, or milk, since these were generally sold to provide one of the few sources of cash needed to purchase items such as sugar, salt, kerosene, tools, and clothing. Overall, then, out of economic necessity the Vicosinos were largely vegetarians.

The chewing of coca leaves has been a long-established practice among the men of the community, initially serving in each case as a rite de passage between the statuses of adolescence and manhood. The use of coca is most frequent during work breaks, since the Vicosinos believe that it gives them strength and deadens the sense of hunger they experience when working between meals. Most recently, however, some Vicosinos hired as laborers in the new forestation program have been prohibited the use of coca during working hours, and its consumption generally appears to have declined, especially among the younger men of the community.

With this picture of general consumption habits, it is not surprising that the Vicosinos were deficient in their nutrition.

Table III. RELATIVE FREQUENCY OF COCA CHEWING
AMONG MALE HEADS OF HOUSEHOLD, BY AGE AND YEAR

Would you say that you chew coca more frequently than most
Vicosinos, less frequently, or about the same?

Age Group	Percent, 1953			Total n
	More	Same	Less	
29 or less	8	33	59	(87)
30-39	12	40	48	(50)
40-49	15	44	41	(54)
50-59	28	48	24	(25)
60 or more	39	32	29	(31)
	Percent, 1963			
29 or less	4	47	49	(75)
30-39	11	43	46	(109)
40-49	11	47	42	(62)
50-59	18	47	35	(45)
60 or more	26	47	26	(34)

When average daily nutrient intakes per capita were compared
with the average daily recommended intakes, it was found that
intakes of calories and proteins were 76 percent or less of the
daily recommendations. The foods consumed were able to
supply the needs for iron, niacin, thiamine, and vitamin C, with
their average intake exceeding the recommended amounts, but
the intake of calcium, riboflavin, and vitamin A was 66 percent
or less of average daily recommendations. Though of small
consolation, it should be added that for the latter three
nutrients the deficiency was national in scope and not limited
to Vicos. Yet it is also true that with respect to the nine
principal nutrients studied, the number of families that consumed less than 75 percent of the recommended amount was
almost invariably higher in the rural than in the urban zones of
the country.

Medical examinations of Vicosino children and adolescents
revealed a number of clinical symptoms that were probably
related to the nutritive deficiencies of their diet. They were
found to be below average in height and weight, most had a
mild xerosis of the skin, and many showed modifications of the

tongue, lips, and ears such as to suggest a deficiency of riboflavin or other B vitamins. Also, an eye pigmentation found in many of the subjects may have been related to progressive vitamin A deficiency. Two-thirds of the adolescents had poor muscular development and more than half had a subnormal accumulation of subcutaneous tissue. The poor bodily development was probably a reflection of inadequate intakes of protein and calories. Again, however, this was not limited to the Vicosinos, but was characteristic of the entire valley in which Vicos is located.(4)

By the time of the third survey, completed in 1956 and followed by a separate study of food habits,(5) though they still are mainly the products of their harvests, the Vicosinos consumed a somewhat larger quantity of foods of animal origin, especially during the annual festivals and among the wealthier families of the community. Potatoes were found to be consumed during six months of the year instead of during one month only. As a result, between the first two surveys and the third only the per capita intake of thiamine had declined. The intake of proteins, calcium, iron, and riboflavin remained at about the earlier level, and the per capita consumption of calories, vitamin A, niacin, and vitamin C all increased. The increase in the daily intake of calories per capita was of a magnitude sufficient to raise the level of Vicos to that of Peru as a whole in 1956.(6) However, these increases occurred apparently not primarily because of the inclusion of new foods in the diet, but rather because of a higher intake of the same foods as in the early surveys; thus many of the same physical effects associated with poor nutrition were still found to be present in the community.

The Vicosino diet was still predominantly vegetarian at the time of the fourth survey in 1961, but relatively more families were partaking of a greater variety and quantity of foods than in any previous year, a development that was extended to include foods of animal origin.(7) Thus, while 36 percent of the families in the 1956 survey consumed a daily average of 20 grams of animal protein, in 1961 an average of 28 grams was consumed by 90 percent of the families, primarily in the form of meat and eggs. As a consequence of these dietary changes, only the intake of calcium and vitamin A had remained below standards. The average daily consumption of calories, proteins, iron, thiamine, riboflavin, niacin, and vitamin C all exceeded the recommended amounts, and it was found that many families had surplus foods in stock.

The nutritive gains registered in the community between 1952 and 1961, especially in the rise of daily caloric intake per capita, were largely the result of changes brought about by the Cornell Peru Project in areas related to nutrition. Beginning in 1952, the Project introduced several agricultural innovations, including a new seed potato and the use of chemical fertilizers and insecticides.(8) By 1958 the diffusion of these innovations had resulted in a tripling of potato production per acre in the community and in large gains in the production of other staple crops. These increases had the effect not only of directly placing more food in the hands of Vicosino families but, by making possible the large-scale cultivation of commercial crops, provided them with the income necessary to supplement their traditional diet, especially through the purchase of animal products and packaged foods. The products of the communal lands were also made available to the Vicosinos at prices lower than what previously could be obtained in nearby market towns.

In addition to this, in 1953 the Cornell Peru Project instituted a school lunch program in the community whereby a balanced meal, including milk, was provided for all school children. This program has continued to the present, supported by the community itself. The cultivation of family vegetable gardens and the raising of small domestic animals for personal consumption have also been encouraged. These efforts were accelerated after the last dietary survey of 1956 and have all been continued to the present. The people of Vicos now eat the equivalent of three full meals a day instead of two sparse ones.

PHYSICAL HEALTH

Aside from the previously noted consequences of poor nutrition, the physical health of the Vicosinos was threatened by several additional factors in their total environment. In 1952 an intestinal parasite survey was carried out in the Callejon de Huaylas, the intermontane valley in which Vicos is located.(9) The survey was based on the collection of stool specimens for over 1,000 persons in five predominantly Mestizo communities, and for 200 Indians in Vicos.

The findings showed that the overall incidence of the 16 types of intestinal parasites reported was much higher for Vicos than for the five Mestizo communities. Of the five most common intestinal parasites found in Vicos, 50 percent of the inhabitants were discovered to be hosting at least one and possibly all five. When the investigators conducted a series of studies to test for any possible resulting interference with the liver function, they found that very few subjects were thus afflicted and concluded that "apparently the residents of this valley have lived so many years with their parasites that their physiology is adjusted to accommodate the infections." Parasitosis has nevertheless been the number one health problem in the community.

Parasitic infestation, however, undoubtedly elevates the nutrient needs of the people, increases the incidence of intestinal ulcers, and contributes to the prevalence of respiratory disorders. Very little change in the incidence of intestinal parasites has probably occurred in Vicos since the 1952 survey, but with the improvement in the level of personal hygiene the incidence of lice and other bodily parasites has been reduced.

According to one report,(10) Vicosino patients in 1955 were most frequently diagnosed as suffering from gastro-intestinal or specifically parasitic disorders (over 21 percent, respiratory disorders 19 percent), and skin and eye disorders (13 percent). The last are also related to the very intense ultraviolet radiation of the environment and to the dryness of the atmosphere, combined with a very low fat diet. Disease epidemics such as measles, influenza, and whooping cough have also repeatedly struck the community and have been a frequent cause of death, especially among the very young (see Appendix A). The difficulties in controlling such events are acute in Vicos due to the usual unavailability of modern medicines or trained persons to apply them.

The results of such circumstances are not difficult to predict or to discover in the historic demographic record where it is available, nor, indeed, in the behavior of the people. Epidemics due to such causes mentioned above left population gaps in the community's demographic structure five times since 1905, the most recent occurring in 1964 when whooping cough swept unchecked through the area leaving behind an estimated 70 dead under 5 years of age out of approximately 300 in this age group (see Appendix A).

The helplessness of the Vicosinos before such onslaughts has led to the elaboration of various "empirical" methods of curing and home remedies. In the attempt to thwart illness the people utilize a variety of herbal teas and concoctions of home or local manufacture. A common sight is someone with a coca leaf pasted with saliva to the temple, cheek, or forehead to diminish headache symptoms. Foods are classified as being either "hot" or "cold" *(cálido* or *fresca)* according to the local interpretation of the ancient Greek system of "humors." Certain combinations of foods then are thought to provoke physiological disruptions of sickness of specified sorts.

Through their centuries of rural agricultural life without benefit of specialized medical personnel, the Vicosinos developed at least four models or theories of disease. That of thermal opposition is the model most commonly employed. The Vicosinos regard heat and cold as natural components of nature, and Montalvo(11) reports it is very rare that a person does not attribute an illness to an excess of one or the other quality, or both. Medicines are also classified as either hot or cold; warm therapy is employed to treat a cold illness, while cold therapy is applied against a warm cause.

A second "transcendent power model" again relates to Vicosino perception of nature. The Vicosinos view the immanent power of the earth, termed *patsa,* as transcending that of mere humans. So powerful that no one is immune to it, *patsa* can, however, enter a body only while an individual is sleeping or frightened.

Closely related to the transcendent power model is what Montalvo calls "the harmonic model." Vicosinos try to keep themselves in harmony with supernatural beings. They try to avoid offending supernatural persons, and petition them for health. The Indians perceive an element of reciprocity in this relationship, so they feel obligated to do something (such as sponsor a religious festival celebration) in order to receive the gift of health from the supernatural agency. The supernaturals, within the ken of the Vicosinos, include the spirits of prehistoric ancients below ground at sites of prehistoric occupation. More important, on the other hand, are Roman Catholic saints, which allow illness to lay low those who care not for God or the saints themselves. Therapy, therefore, also includes pleas to the saints to restore one's health.

A fourth Vicos model of illness Montalvo labels the "good-evil model." This derives from the Vicos view of innate human nature and its many intrafamilial and interfamilial conflicts. The Indians extol good neighborly behavior—respecting the property of others, not feeling envy for the success of others, etc.—but, since the Vicosinos do not believe man always to be good, evil behavior is anticipated. The milder forms of illness stemming from this model are those caused by rage, resentment, or sadness.

For illnesses whose causes are not readily apparent, the sick person or his family may well consult an expert to divine by means of a guinea pig. In this process, called *shoqma,* a guinea pig (male for men, female for women) is rubbed over the sick person's body and then killed and autopsied. The human ailment is purportedly to be discovered in the corresponding organ of the animal, and from this diagnosis, remedy is prescribed. Where the symptoms are diffuse and difficult to define, the causal agent may be determined as *susto* (fright) contracted by the patient when he passed some spot thought to be suspect or dangerous.

Death comes with capricious frequency in Vicos and the ritual surrounding it is considerable. The funeral ceremony for an adult is of five days' duration and marked by dancing, drunkenness, and appreciable sadness. During the course of each year Vicosinos remind themselves of the deceased during the celebration of All Souls' Day lasting three days.

Thus it is not surprising that the Vicosinos should manifest a profound preoccupation with death and illness. Klein reports that all the people interviewed in his study of Vicos personality expressed this. Among ten adult males reared under normal manorial conditions and intensively studied by Klein(12), no less than seven directly expressed preoccupation with death.

These individuals feared each illness as possibly leading to death. More psychologically significant for economic enterprise, perhaps, was the fear shared by several of them that every move placed them in danger, and as inferior and vulnerable beings, they tried to keep physically still. This general perception of the human body as weak, defenseless, even damaged, was shared as well by the three men in the sample who did not perceive themselves as directly preoccupied with death.

MENTAL HEALTH

The psychological set of fearful contact with the natural and social worlds, manifested in Vicosino preoccupation with death, appeared in other forms also. In the realm of sensation, the same pattern of personal withdrawal was apparent in the self images of men reared under manorial conditions. To half these men, a human touch was painful or interpreted as aggressive or bringing injury or death; hence pleasure was regarded as immoral and a luxury. The other five men shared this basic perceptual act in less acute form, regarding satisfaction as only a remote possibility, forbidden food as tasteless, and life as a constant struggle for survival by weak, hemmed-in beings.

Probably the outstanding emotional consequence of this pyschological set for the Cornell Peru Project's efforts to stimulate local social and economic development was individual alienation perceived as "loneliness." No less than eight of the ten intensively analyzed men perceived themselves as lonely, with overtones of constant fear, sadness, and anger shared with the other two men in this sample. Since rage, resentment, and sadness were viewed as causes of certain kinds of illness in Vicos, the incidence of such self images is not without its significance in gauging the availability of labor for developmental purposes.

The consequences of this psychological set for the Vicosino's perception of his own capacity for independent action were rather serious. One self image among adult males was that independent action was inconceivable. A very parallel perception viewed man as placed by God and necessarily obedient;

it limited a son to his father's precedent; it visualized a boy uncomfortable in a man's shoes—and, at the extreme, saw him as a baby wrapped in an umbilicus. This self image generated the conviction that one who struck out for freedom outcasted himself, so he obeyed and was free only when alone. One might venture to conclude that development occurred in Vicos in spite of the inhibitory personal psychology evidently induced by the manorial social system. The Cornell Peru Project changes which have occurred, however, began as modifications of the social and economic structure of the manor and not with direct attempts to alter individual personalities per se as a precondition to the development process.

It should also be noted that a preliminary analysis of data bearing on the mental health of the Vicosinos suggests there has been an increase in the level of anxiety in the community. Questionnaire surveys of virtually all male heads of households in 1953 and again in 1963 indicate a substantial increase in the reported incidence of trembling hands, palpitations of the heart, nightmares, headaches, loss of appetite, and difficulty in falling asleep. These items are components of a longer instrument— from which a total score is calculated for each respondent— developed by the Cornell Program in Social Psychiatry. The use of these scores as a device for screening psychoneurotic individuals from a general population has previously been validated on a hospitalized psychoneurotic group for use in a rural area of Canada.(13)

Factors that may be responsible for the increase in anxiety are now under study. A working hypothesis is that the shift has resulted from value conflicts engendered during the transition from a traditional to a modern society. When placed in context with figures obtained by Whyte and Williams for some of the same questionnaire items in over 20 localities throughout Peru,(14) Vicos has since 1953 shifted from a pattern of low anxiety, presently characteristic of the relatively developed coast localities, to the higher levels of some of the transitional communities of the sierra.

Several findings are also available on what may conveniently be termed the level of "social pathology" in the community. Although very few cases were involved in either year, the rate of divorce and separation per 1,000 persons in Vicos has been cut

Table IV. INCIDENCE OF ANXIETY SYMPTOMS AMONG MALE HEADS OF HOUSEHOLD, 1953 AND 1963

Item	Percent (n = 275 and 325)		
	Many Times	Sometimes	Never, or Almost Never
Does it happen some- times that your hands shake until it disturbs you?			
1953	5	38	57
1963	21	38	41
Does it happen some- times that your heart palpitates until it bothers you?			
1953	6	58	36
1963	22	46	33
Have you had any dif- ficulty in falling asleep and staying asleep?			
1953	4	47	49
1963	19	53	27
Does it happen some- times that you are bothered by night- mares?			
1953	5	60	35
1963	29	46	26
Do you suffer from headaches?			
1953	12	72	16
1963	34	46	20
Have you sometimes lost your appetite?			
1953	3	65	32
1963	25	53	22

almost in half between 1952 and 1963. In the early years of the Project pilferage of livestock, crops, and other items of property was rather high in the community, especially when the harvest was poor. This has declined considerably with the improvement of the economy and with the introduction by the Project of the practice of branding livestock.

Mutual assault, also commonly associated with accusations of pilferage, has declined for the same reasons. However, the incidence of assault in connection with disputes over land ownership has apparently risen. The increase has a direct relationship with the increased fractionalization of land holdings and some changes in inheritance since women now demand and receive greater equity as heirs.

Suicide, homicide, and infanticide have occurred and still occur in the community, but generally not frequently enough to warrant the collection of systematic data on the incidence of these crimes.

PERSPECTIVES ON DEVELOPMENT

Since its inception, the Cornell Peru Project has explicitly sought to improve the health standards of Vicos and has therefore given special attention to Vicosino health problems.(15) In addition to the school lunch program, already mentioned, arrangements starting in 1954 were made for at least weekly visits by a doctor and nurse under the auspices of a unit of the Peruvian Ministry of Public Health. By the end of that year, some member of almost half the total number of families in Vicos had received medical care, and by the end of 1955 a regular attendance of 40 to 50 Vicosinos had been established.(16) With the stimulus provided by these results, a clinic was constructed in the community in 1957. After 1961 clinical services had to be discontinued when the medical team was shifted elsewhere by the Peruvian government, but they were resumed to some degree by the assignment to Vicos by the United States Peace Corps of a practical nurse from October, 1962, to June, 1964. Despite these efforts, there have been four epidemics in the community since 1951, the last occurring early in 1964.(17) The disease agents in the most recent case were whooping cough and measles, causing the death of about 70 children, mostly under one year of age.

Such mortality cannot be attributed to a complete rejection of modern medicine on the part of the Vicosinos. On the contrary, the Indians have tended to accept such medical treatment as has been made available to them. A rather dramatic shift in Vicosino perception of the ability of medical doctors to cure illnesses stemming from various locally defined causes was found by Montalvo.(18) Whereas no one he interviewed in 1956 believed medical doctors could cure anger-caused illness, by 1966 no less than 59 percent of those interviewed did so believe.

The next largest shift concerned sickness attributed to heat, cold, or malevolent winds. Half those Montalvo interviewed in 1966 thought doctors could cure such illness compared to only 3 percent a decade earlier. A less dramatic but significant shift occurred with regard to illness caused by fright. No one interviewed in 1956 felt a doctor could cure such an illness, but 29 percent did by 1966. Less impressive was the increasing faith that doctors could cure illness caused by *patsa,* up from zero to 18 percent. More resistant was witchcraft. No one thought a doctor could cure bewitchment in 1956, and only 5 percent did in 1966.

All these specific changes together indicate the marked trend toward accepting modern medical practice in Vicos, as does the adoption of preventive innoculation of livestock against hoof-and-mouth disease as well as preventive innoculation of poultry.(19)

It should be noted that medical personnel are in very scarce supply throughout the Peruvian highlands, especially in the rural areas. This is due to the relatively poor financial rewards and living conditions available to doctors practicing outside Lima—where the vast majority of them are concentrated—and to their simple unwillingness to minister to Indians. The imbalance is much the same with respect to medical equipment and facilities. The only hospital in Huaraz, the capital city of the Department of Ancash, did not have a microscope in 1963.

Although the Vicosinos are now better clothed, better housed, and better fed, when the incidence of epidemics is combined with the evidence of parasitic infestation and retarded physical development, it would appear that the achievements of the Cornell Peru Project in the field of health have lagged behind the major successes attained in the fields of educational and economic development. This is perhaps most concisely summed up in the fact that there was an increase in the death rate between 1952 and 1963.

But there is another side to this picture. Between 1940 and 1952, prior to Project intervention, the population of Vicos had been increasing at a rate of slightly more than 1 percent per year. Since 1952 the death rate has risen in the community, but the birth rate has gone up at a faster pace, so that the rate of natural increase has resulted in a substantial net addition to the population of the community. But the annual rate of growth of the population has remained virtually constant between 1952 and 1963. The importance of this result can be appreciated from the fact that as early as 1952 there were already 284 persons per square mile of arable land on the estate, and by 1963 there were 350. The relative stability of the rate of growth in the face of a rising birth rate is accounted for almost entirely by the rise in the death rate and by a net loss to the community through migration. The latter loss resulted by lifting barriers to migration that had been imposed by the former hacienda system; losses were most pronounced up to 1956.(20) In that year, however, Vicos became self-governing and many of the migrant Vicosinos began to return to their developing community. This has contributed to the increasing pressure of the population on the land. Some of the more recent in-migrants have also begun to return for the purpose of convalescing from illnesses, thus contributing to a decline in the general health standards of the community.

Even at the current rate of population growth, by 1975 there will be approximately 429 Vicosinos per square mile of arable land on the estate. But evidence indicates that the rate of growth will actually increase in the near future, thus threatening the gains to well-being that have been achieved with Cornell Peru Project help over the past 14 years. Should the health standards of the community be considerably improved and the effects of recurrent epidemics be strongly mitigated, this would be a foregone conclusion.

Good health is like motherhood: no one is against it. But at what cost is it to be reached? Almost everyone would like the Vicosinos to be healthy, wealthy, and wise, but the enjoyment of such a state is a rare achievement in any human society. A population that is healthy to the point of overcrowding is one that threatens its wealth and its wisdom by straining the capacity of its economic and educational systems. To circumvent this paradox, four basic strategies may be followed:

The first is to develop the economy and educational system so rapidly that the rate of population growth pales by comparison and can be ignored. As shown by the case of Vicos, this can be an effective short-run option, but it is one that can hardly be sustained over the long range in the modern world.

The second is to encourage out-migration and discourage returnees. This strategy is a two-edged sword in that it shifts the problem elsewhere and, through the loss of younger and more forward-looking members, deprives the community of an important part of its human resources for development. The return of only an optimum number of healthy migrants over the years would stimulate the process of development through the application of talents and attitudes gained by experience in more developed areas. Too few out-migrants (or too many returnees) will increase population pressure and the rate of growth; too many out-migrants (with few returnees) will deprive the community of experience that could well be used at home.

A third strategy is to lower the birth rate. This option was not available in Vicos (as in many areas of the world), but it is ultimately a disservice to satisfy the demand for reducing deaths without being allowed the concomitant opportunity of reducing births.

Fourth, and generally not as well recognized, is the strategy of placing the major available resources into the development of education and the economy, while allocating to the lowest priority those health improvements that tend to lower the death rate. Though not by design, this is in effect what has occurred in Vicos.

The achievements of the Cornell Peru Project in education, economics, and health were attained in the first instance by the exercise of its political power within the community, with the most progressive Vicosinos encouraged to assume position of leadership, and also by the persistent application of its political influence at the highest levels of Peruvian national government. The prospects for an accelerated rate of future development in Vicos would be greatly enhanced if the Vicosinos themselves were able to employ the same methods. In order to do this, however, they would have to develop their literacy rate to the point where they would become an effective voting bloc, and develop their wealth to the point where they could afford to organize themselves, and similar Peruvian communities, into pressure groups with the resources to carry out effective lobbying activities, locally and nationally. To achieve this the first need is for the development of politically productive educational and economic means—at the expense, if necessary, of immediate consumption in the form of health improvements. It cannot be accomplished if the people of Vicos increase at a rate such that they compromise the educational and economic means of their future political effectiveness.

NOTES

1. M. C. Vázquez, "La Antropología Cultural y Nuestro Problema del Indio: Vicos, un Caso de Antropología Aplicada," Perú Indígena, vol. II, nos. 5 and 6 (1952), p. 129.

2. C. Collazos Ch., et al., "Dietary Surveys in Peru—Chacan and Vicos: Rural Communities in the Peruvian Andes," Journal of American Dietetic Association, vol. 30 (1954); and C. Collazos Ch., et al., La Alimentación y el Estado de Nutrición en el Perú. Lima: Anales de la Facultad de Medicina, 1960. Also C. Caceres de Fuentes, "Encuesta Alimentaria en Diez Familias de Vicos, Julio 1961," Servicio Cooperativo Inter-Americano de Salud Publica, Lima, typescript, n.d.

3. M. Newman, "Nutrition, Disease, and Physical Status of the Indians of the Peruvian Sierra, Based Largely on Data from Vicos," dittoed, 1960; and H. H. Martinez A., "Vicos: Los Habitos Alimenticios," Revista del Museo Nacional, vol. XXIV (1960).

4. Newman, op. cit.

5. Martinez, op. cit.

6. Collazos, 1960, op. cit. pp. 11, 140.

7. Caceres de Fuentes, op. cit.

8. R. K. Goldsen, and W. W. Stein, "The Introduction of New Seed Potatoes in Vicos: The Store Line." dittoed, 1956.

9. E. H. Payne, L. Gonzalez Magaburu, and F. M. Schleicher, "An Intestinal Parasite Survey in the High Cordilleras of Peru," American Journal of Tropical Medicine and Hygiene, vol. 5, no. 4, (1956).

10. Newman, op. cit.

Peasants, Power, and Applied Social Change

11. Abner Montalvo, "Sociocultural Change and Differentiation in a Rural Peruvian Community—An Analysis in Health Culture." Ithaca: Cornell University Latin American Studies Program Dissertation Series, No. 5, 1967, pp. 83-89.

12. Ralph Klein, "The Self Image of Adult Males in an Andean Culture." New York University Ph.D. Dissertation, 1963, pp. 53-55, 59, 64-65, 70-71, 75-76, 81-82, 87-88, 92-93, 99-100, 105-106.

13. A. Macmillan, "The Health Opinion Survey: Technique for Estimating Prevalance of Psychoneurotic and Related Types of Disorder in Communities," Psychological Reports, vol. 3, (1957), monograph supplement 7; and A. Macmillan, "A Survey Technique for Estimating the Prevalence of Psychoneurotic and Related Types of Disorders in Communities," in B. Pasamanick (Ed.), Epidemiology of Mental Disorder, Washington: American Association for the Advancement of Science, 1959.

14. W. F. Whyte, and L. K. Williams, "The Use of Questionnaire Surveys for Community Studies of Culture Change and Economic Development," a paper read at the Annual Meetings of the American Anthropological Association, 1964, mimeo.

15. A. R. Holmberg, "Changing Community Attitudes and Values in Peru: A Case Study in Guided Change," in Social Change in Latin America Today. New York: Vintage Books, 1961.

16. W. C. Blanchard, "Informe del Proyecto Peru Cornell: 1954," Boletín Indigenista, vol. XV, no. 3 (1955), p. 276; and W. C. Blanchard, "Informe del Proyecto Peru-Cornell: 1955," Boletín Indigenista, vol. XVI, nos. 2 and 3 (1956), p. 204.

17. J. O. Alers, "Population and Development in a Peruvian Community," Journal of Inter-American Studies, vol. VII, no. 4 (1965).

18. Montalvo, op. cit., pp. 110-117.

19. Luis Negrón, Tesis, Universidad de San Antonio del Abad del Cuzco, 196 ,

20. J. O. Alers, M. C. Vázquez, A. R. Holmberg, and H. F. Dobyns, "Human Freedom and Geographic Mobility," Current Anthropology, vol. 6, no. 3 (1965).

Chapter VI

ENLIGHTENMENT AND

SKILL FOUNDATIONS OF POWER

Henry F. Dobyns

Many changes in the lives of Vicos Indians since 1952 highlight the strategic effects of increasing enlightenment and skill upon their sharing of power in Peru. A complete exposition of the many and complex relationships among skill, enlightenment, and power lies outside the scope of a single chapter. Still, a summary of post-1952 Vicos experience illustrates both the theoretical and practical significance of numerous gains in power achieved by this rural ethnic group. Formerly socially and politically subordinate to an astonishing degree, Vicosinos increased their share of power by employing newly acquired skills and enhanced enlightenment to interact in new ways with other citizens of Peru.

Enlightenment and skill were always strategic for wielding power under the traditional and tenure system in the central Andean region. Analysis of that social structure with its clearcut social dominance of a few individuals over many others gains in

Author's Note: This chapter has been expanded from an American Behavioral Scientist article originally prepared for the Comparative Studies of Cultural Change, Department of Anthropology, Cornell University, under Contract AID/csd-296 with the Office of Technical Cooperation and Research of the U.S. Agency for International Development. The data analyzed were collected for the most part under the direction of the late Allan R. Holmberg with financial assistance from the Carnegie Corporation of New York, an anonymous donor, and a contract with the U.S. Peace Corps. This chapter could not have been written without Mario C. Vázquez's contributions. Conclusions are the author's sole responsibility and do not imply endorsement by any agency or donor which supported the research.

clarity by comparison to pre-industrial European social and economic history.(1)

In the first place, the traditional manor system of the Andes cuts off serf populations from sources of knowledge and innovation.(2) Each manor is maintained as more or less a spatial, social, and psychological isolate with respect to modern Western civilization.(3) Each manor resembles rather closely those independent landholding peasant communities Wolf(4) labels "corporate," except that manor serfs lack "jurisdiction over the free disposal of land" which the manor owner or his representative controls, and the fact that manors typically occupy relatively good rather than marginal land.

Each manor serf population is reduced to dependence upon its own store of traditional knowledge and typically displays the same "defensive ignorance" or "active denial of outside alternative" that characterizes the corporate peasant community.(5) Parents resist sending children—useful field hands and shepherds—to school, especially when prejudiced Mestizo teachers discipline them with corporal punishment and assign them menial tasks. This means that the society of manor serfs remains quite small in scale,(6) and with little chance to accumulate ideas it necessarily remains relatively stable.(7) Serf knowledge is augmented only occasionally by such small increments as the overlord may decide to force upon the closed society of the manor. Serf farming is customary husbandry as it was historically in Europe. Land is exploited, as in the corporate peasant community, by means of a traditional technology requiring much manual labor, and serf plots are typically assigned on the more marginally productive steeper slopes within any given manor. Hard work and thrift and conformity to local "Indian" patterns of dress and behavior are extolled, while sloth and greed are viewed as vices,(8) just as in the corporate peasant community. "Institutionalized envy" constitutes, moreover, an important mechanism of social control in the manor population as in the peasant populace.

The exception to this description is the patronal institution that dominates the manor serfs. The overlord, as part of his role as the most powerful single individual connected with a traditional Andean manor, is the person in this interaction

Enlightenment—Marcela Cruz, a Vicos girl educated in the local school system, working as a teaching aide with young beginning pupils in a district school.

system who enjoys the greatest access to national educational facilities outside the manor. Historic Andean society is one in which acquiring knowledge is the privilege of a few persons selected either formally, or indirectly for economic reasons, or by inheritance in terms of a fundamental assumption that Indians are different in kind from Europeans.(9)

After the overlord, his Mestizo overseers are those individuals connected with the traditional manor who enjoy greatest access to formal education, although they cannot expect the same quality education as that obtained by the typical overlord.

The serfs are in general excluded from the formal education system unless and until the overlord decides to permit them access to it. It bears repeating that the introduction of a government-financed public school into Vicos originally occurred more to provide a paid job for a relative than to furnish effective education to serf children. Between its foundation in 1940 and 1951, this school enrolled a total of thirty-nine students, or 3 percent of the Vicos population aged seven and over at the beginning of 1952. Only five inhabitants of Vicos could read or write in 1951—and that very poorly. Only 2 percent could even speak the major trade language of Peru, Spanish.(10) Only 4 percent of the school-age children in 1952 attended school in 1951.

Thus the overlord and sometimes his overseers are the only persons connected with the traditional manor whose exposure to world culture is usually sufficient to permit any one of them to achieve that concentration of ideas that Barnett(11) sees necessary for innovation. The superior enlightenment of the overlord has been directed historically, however, not toward innovation, but toward maintaining the power domain(12) of each overlord over his particular serfs.

Such small amounts of power as are not held by the overlord are tied into a political-religious system involving adult males who achieve power in it by group decision, as in the corporate peasant community. In the manor, as in the corporate peasant community, this traditional political-religious system based on medieval Spanish models defines the boundaries of the manor population and serves as a symbol of such unity as may exist among the serfs.

PARTICIPANT
INTERVENTION

When the Cornell Peru Project undertook to dismantle the patronal institution and distribute among the serfs of Vicos the control of its power domain, the strategic importance of enlightenment for power was amply and repeatedly demonstrated. The Project staff explicitly took into account the proposition that cultural freedom exists only for those citizens who can elect one or another cultural alternative on a basis of adequate knowledge and comprehension of them. Observing that such understanding is obtained largely by a process of formal education in contemporary Western civilization(13) Cornell personnel set out effectively to introduce the national formal education system to Vicos with the goal of achieving eventual complete literacy.

The formal structuring of the Cornell Peru Project itself reflected the enlightenment and skill in human relations of its founders. They correctly predicted that the Vicos power domain could be materially altered only by bringing it within a larger power domain. In this case, the national government approved the formation of a bi-national power domain constituted by Cornell University and the Peruvian Indian Institute. The Director and Co-Director turned their personal knowledge, and the respect accorded to them for it, to wider account(14) in incorporating provincial power domains, such as those of Mestizo trading-town merchants, into the larger power domain. The Cornell Peru Project and the Peruvian Indian Institute (from 1959 to 1965 the Peruvian National Plan for Integrating the Aboriginal Population) thereby coordinated the local efforts of numerous government entities.(15) In the process of assisting Vicos toward "a position of relative independence and freedom within the larger framework of Peruvian national life,"(16) the Project established a spatially large, although relatively weak, power domain in the Peruvian nation through mass media diffusion of reports of its practical successes.

The series of specific innovations the Cornell Peru Project introduced to the Vicos population was drawn simply from the wide range of intellectual and technical knowledge at the command of the members of the Project that had hitherto not been communicated in any way to the serfs of the former manor. When Dr. Vázquez undertook to convey, to seventeen Indian near-subsistence farmers, technical agricultural ideas that enabled sixteen of them to raise large potato crops, he and other members of the Project drew these technological concepts from the great fund of experimentally accumulated knowledge available to them. They were not experienced farmers at all.

They were, however, consciously determined to teach Vicos Indian serfs farm practices that would enable them to grow food crops more successfully than they had been doing. The first year's instruction involved daily visits by Vázquez to each participating farmer, to discuss with each one his potato gardening activities during that day. These daily discussions meant that Vázquez repeated the technical instructions over and over again during the growing season, from planting to harvest. He repeated them with all the authority of a man the serfs took to be a Patron, or at least an employee of the Patron, albeit a strange one, and the authority of the Patron who had advanced seed and fertilizer under a sharecropping agreement. In contrast to all previous Patron representatives in Vicosino experience, Vázquez used his authority to drive home the lessons of how to raise more and bigger potatoes, rather than to seize a larger share of the little the serfs already knew how to produce. He achieved the first significant increase in Indian mastery of the natural environment since the introduction of Old World cereals, livestock, and short-term fallowing customs early in colonial times.(17)

POTATO
POWER

If a man's power consists of his ability to influence others, the Vicos Indians acquired "potato power" with the farming skills they learned from Vázquez and his successors in the farm practice change program. Potato power provoked many changes in dominant group behavior toward Vicos Indians:

1. Increased potato production provided Vicosinos greater equality with nearby Mestizo trading-town merchants in their complex commercial-ceremonial kinship relations. The Indians

produced more farm surplus for sale, and by growing more needed to purchase less, thus freeing themselves to a considerable degree from merchant exploitation.

2. Potato production increases permitted Vicosinos to escape the local market to sell produce on the regional and national markets for cash, with no ceremonial relationships affecting prices. Significantly augmented cash income allowed the Indians to strengthen their position relative to local merchants by enabling them to withdraw from the local labor market where their unskilled surplus formerly depressed wages. Simultaneously they were enabled to spend more cash than before.

At the same time, commercial sales proceeds gained from the regional and national market attracted regional merchants pursuing profits. Alert urban businessmen in the department (i.e., state) capital began to dispatch truckloads of merchandise directly to Vicos, by-passing local merchants. They also offered Vicos farmers manufactured goods such as sewing machines on credit, facilitating in ways not previously open to these Indians their integration into the world industrial economy.

3. Commercial potato production placed Vicos Indians in the cabs of "tramp" trucks plying the highways to the nation's capital. By social custom, reinforced by economic differentials, dominant group individuals rode inside, Indians on the truck bed or on top of its cargo. As large-scale potato shippers, the Vicosinos could demand cabin space for Indian representatives accompanying community cargo to market. The Vicosino potato production community purchased a truck in 1962, as mentioned elsewhere in these pages, and the Indian farmers became employers by hiring a driver.

4. Even though Vicos later sold its truck, the skilled potato producers continue to exercise economic power that has materially altered—if not entirely reversed—their former dependence on ill-paid unskilled labor. They hire skilled Mestizo workers when needed. For years the community farm enterprise employed a Mestizo accountant. Not long ago the community hired a team of blacksmiths to repair metal tools in Vicos. Thus, potato power converted Vicos from a large exporter of unskilled labor to a steady small hirer of skilled labor while it cut local labor outflow to a comparative trickle.

An important point about these consequences of potato power is that they flowed from skills the Cornell Peru Project imparted to Indian serfs who hardly qualified for the label "farmers," skills later reinforced by representatives of the Peruvian Agricultural Development Bank and the Supervised Agricultureal Credit Program of the Interamerican Cooperative Food Production Service.(18) A conventional economic analysis of classical production factors would show that the natural resources remained the same. Manpower actually decreased in community commercial farming compared to manorial levels, although it increased on family gardens. Monetary capital investment in Vicos agriculture indeed increased markedly following 1952, especially in purchases of improved seed varieties, fertilizers, and pesticides. Yet all of the spiraling capital investment depended upon the Indians acquiring the skills to use it in terms of rational farming techniques. Macro-economic analysis finds "rise in general level of training and education" to be an important factor in national product growth, but a difficult one to measure.(19) Microanalysis of potato power at Vicos at least illustrates that acquiring production skills is basic to all economic development in marginally subsistence gardening society. The degree of ignorance of effective crop production techniques in Vicos in 1951 may appear inconceivable to the reader in the United States more than a century after the land-grant college system began systematically to spread knowledge of crop production techniques. That ignorance was, however, so great that, combined with a repressive social structure, it kept the Vicos serfs on the verge of starvation. The extreme unskillfulness of the Vicos serf made his contribution to the market economy so small it illustrated that conventional economic analysis can begin to measure the contribution to economic growth of various classical factors of production only *after* the process begins. The Vicos data indicate that the process of growth begins with learning new skills—how to employ the factors of production to increase yields. Classical economics developed, after all, long after European farmers had acquired these basic production skills, so it is perhaps understandable that such a level of farm production skill might be taken for granted. The Vicos gardeners illustrate that the farmer's knowledge of how to employ factors of production is indeed a critical skill that cannot be assumed in non-European societies. The unskilled gardening formerly carried on by the Vicos serfs very likely represents the crop production capability of a large part of the world's peasantry today.

The Cornell Peru Project investment in "human capital" showed that instilling new crop production methods in an unskilled gardening population dependent on its own production and sale of labor to subsist, can bring the classical factors of production into operation. To be sure, the monetary cost of teaching new production skills could be measured, but the present analysis focuses instead on the point that Vicos potato power derives from a quantum jump in level of crop production skill.

When Professor Holmberg undertook to create full-time artisans in Vicos where no full-time non-farming specialists had existed prior to 1952, he hired journeymen building trades specialists to instruct their Indian helpers while erecting new buildings to house Project personnel and activities, school pupils, and teachers.

The journeymen were themselves Mestizos. Although the Director of the Cornell Peru Project established novel conditions of employment on its building projects at Vicos—teaching Indian serfs building trades skills, for example—the Mestizo journeymen accepted those conditions. They conveyed their skills to their serf helpers in a rapid on-the-job training program established deliberately by the Project.

When Dr. Vázquez and the author undertook to interest Vicos women—nearly completely shut off from the formal educational process by local values(20)—in household-oriented formal instruction, they recruited a bilingual seamstress to begin teaching sewing in 1960. This Mestizo seamstress already held the trust of many Vicos women because she had long sewn their dresses for them. Her dressmaking skills had in part been learned from her mother, who worked as a seamstress before her, and in part learned during a brief period of training in a seamstress school. She turned out to be an enthusiastic teacher. Provided with a new sewing machine by the Project, she also turned out to be an effective teacher, cheerfully communicating to former serf women the sewing skills on which she and other

Mestizo seamstresses had long enjoyed a local monopoly, in return for a regular salary of small proportions.

Vicos women responded so enthusiastically to this instruction that the Peruvian government added it to the on-going integration program. By 1962 three classes enrolled 134 women who made over 2,000 items—and studied Spanish too. Twenty-seven women learned to read(21) during sewing class, which served the dual function of craft and academic instruction. In 1963 no less than 167 women enrolled in three sections and produced nearly 2,500 articles of clothing.(22) By 1964 this program had imparted basic sewing skills to so many women enrollment and classroom production began to decline.(23)

Each of these Cornell Peru Project actions, based upon the concentrated knowledge of the accumulated store of cultural traits termed Western civilization, created a temporary power domain of greater or lesser duration under the control of the designated instructor. It must be emphasized that in no case was Indian attendance at public school or adult education classes compulsory. Even army service has been voluntary, at least in the sense that Vicos youths were persuaded by Dr. Vázquez not only to cease fleeing, but actually to present themselves to draft authorities. Each power domain established by an outside instructor came into temporary being because the enlightenment of the instructor attracted would-be emulators from among the Indian population. Thus each instructional power domain resulted directly from elightenment and skill, which commanded the respect of potential and actual students. Since no severe deprivations could be employed by teachers against their potential pupils (except in the army) the power wielded by them appears to be the influencing type envisioned by Russell, Tawney, Parsons, and Cartwright.(24)

The Cornell Peru Project did establish other power domains from its pinnacle of authority as temporary overlord. While all forms of extra, unpaid serf labor *(pongaje)* were promptly abolished as the most irksome manor exactions discovered by scientific interviewing, the basic three-day work week field labor obligation was retained during the transitional period. Thus field hands who learned the elements of modern potato growing on the manor's commercial fields under the supervision of the overseers did not do so voluntarily. Nor did the workers who erected the first new school buildings volunteer for the task: it was assigned to them as part of their obligatory labor. Most important of all, the local Indian field bosses *(mayorales)* who were trained in democratic discussion and decision-making in weekly seminars conducted by Project staff did not voluntarily attend those seminars in the beginning, even though a very high proportion of the Project field director's time and skill was devoted to converting them into enlightening sessions focusing attention, in Lasswell's words, on "all versions of reality, all value demands and all the identifications" relevant to the social process.

During the first year of Cornell Peru Project operations under Holmberg's personal direction, he adapted the university seminar to teaching Indian serfs how to think about Vicos as a whole, to consider issues in terms of a common good as well as individual and family interest, and how to arrive at group decisions upon a basis of open discussion. On Monday of each week Holmberg presided over a research seminar attended by the anthropologists studying Vicos while they intervened in its affairs, and by those studying neighboring Recuayhuanca,(25) and nearby Marcará(26) and Hualcán(27) in order to provide comparative perspective. Each week's intervention strategy was hammered out during the research seminar meetings.

Holmberg then presided over a meeting of the *mayorales* of the manor on Tuesday of each week. Transferring seminar techniques to these meetings, Holmberg gradually drew the timid and fearful Indian foremen into discussions of manorial activities and eventually of manorial policy, through the fluent Quechua of overseer Enrique Luna and anthropologist Mario C. Vázquez. The decisions reached on Tuesday were then announced at the labor shape-up held every Wednesday. Traditionally, the overseer had always announced the specific three-day labor assignments of each serf during the Vicos-wide gathering of workers representing each family.

Slowly the serfs learned to discuss manorial activities in the shape-up meetings until they learned to make community-wide decisions in what became a sort of town meeting.

The seminar-style meetings with the Indian leaders constituted a key institutional transition from the very authoritarian manorial system to the present Vicos community farm enterprise. This was a critical change because the manorial system, and Mestizo-Indian relations in general, provided only one model for decison-making by the serf population—that of dominance-subordinance. The Vicos Indians knew only how to give orders or to take them, since their prior experience consisted entirely of issuing or obeying orders in a dyadic social relationship. They were as culturally limited in this repect as those Australian aborigines whose entire social system is based on dyadic relationships of dominance and subordinance, with all participants in the social structure being either dominant or subordinate in relation to the other members.(28)

Starting from the clearly dominant position of manor Patron, Holmberg proved his genius as a teacher by showing unlettered, horny-handed Indian sons of toil the elements of open democratic discussion, and rational decision-making by majority rule in open voting. In these latter cases, teaching farm-practice changes on manor fields, initiating school building construction, and starting training in peer discussion and decision-making, the power wielded by the Cornell Peru Project was the type backed up by severe deprivations for non-conformity as discussed by Lasswell and Kaplan and Bierstedt.(29)

Holmberg's greatest achievement at Vicos was to devolve his patronal decision-making power to Indian leaders trained in his and later seminar discussions led by William P. Mangin and William C. Blanchard. These anthropologists with Vázquez's aid achieved an orderly devolution of power by deliberately not exercising it. Thus they forced Indian leaders to take over patronal power as it was gradually withdrawn from active use. Although the prospect of severe deprivations for non-conformity was always present, Holmberg and his successors as field director managed to transfer that mantle of power smoothly from their shoulders to those of the several Indian leaders produced in the training seminars. So in 1956 an orderly transition to self-government by an all-Indian Council of Delegates from ten electoral zones could and did occur.

This greatest single shift of power in Vicos, and the immediate key transfer of patronal power to the Indians, built a community council upon the base of leaders trained in the Project seminars. As the termination of the Project sublease on the manor approached, at the end of 1956, the serfs organized for self-government under additional Project research stimulus. From May to September the residents of the manor were consulted as to the future they wanted for Vicos after the Cornell Peru Project sublease expired. Project personnel consulted the Indians in personal interviews, small group discussions in which neighbors and relatives participated, in zone assemblies, and in one general assembly. The majority of the Indians favored purchasing the manor. In order to reach this goal the local leaders suggested that the Indians work the manorial lands cooperatively and pay for the property out of profits. A cooperative farming enterprise would necessitate organizing the Indian labor to conduct it. The development of skills relating to decision-making, administration, and government in general was absolutely vital to the achievement of long-term goals.

The Vicosinos decided to divide the manor into ten geographic zones defined according to more or less traditional areas of population concentration and manorial lineage distribution. Each zone became an electoral district sending an elected representative to an estate-wide Council of Delegates, which in turn selected its administrative officers. Later, the council president was elected by the voters.

The Council of Delegates convenes once each week to conduct the business of the community farm enterprise. It functions with an ideal of full representation of all ten zones at each session. Since it would be humanly impossible for every zone delegate to attend every meeting without fail, the former serfs have set up a substitute system reminiscent of the system of presidential succession originally established by the Constitution of the United States. In each electoral zone the candidate receiving the second highest number of votes in each annual election becomes the substitute for the zone delegate in his absence. The delegate and his alternate now bear responsibility for administrative enforcement of council decisions. When community farm enterprise work assignments are made to a given zone, the delegate from that zone becomes responsible for turning out his constituents on the assigned dates to accomplish the work that needs to be done.

In Vicos one can examine in microcosm the operation of factors contributing to economic development with a precision not yet achieved in comparative analysis at the national level. Some correlation between per capita income and portion of national income invested in classroom education has been found in comparing nations.(30) Economic growth and increasing investment in classroom education were correlated at Vicos from 1952 to 1959. The proportion of literates and primary school graduates, and persons who have attended school, rose, and continued to rise after 1959, although investment in classroom education leveled off and economic productivity may actually have declined somewhat. The correlation between increasing investment in formal education and increasing economic productivity between 1952 and 1959 was, in fact, a correlation between two independent processes that happened to be occurring concurrently without being causally connected.

The increasing investment in formal education came in large part from the government of Peru (for teachers' salaries), and in part from the expanding Vicos economy which paid for new classrooms, a hot lunch program, desks, and so forth, out of community farming profits, and purchased texts and uniforms out of family farming profits. Formal classroom educational expansion benefited from and was made possible by the economic expansion of Vicos—potato power—and national government revenues. It did not in any way set in motion the increase in farm productivity.

The increase in Vicos farm production was started by direct enlightenment of farmers outdoors, in their fields, by anthropologist Mario C. Vázquez explaining in Quechua the principles and practices of scientific potato production. He demonstrated as many of the skills involved as he could. The burst of economic productivity achieved in Vicos resulted from practical enlightenment of adults who made immediate decisions about farming practices. Thus, the time lag between enlightenment and increases in farm production was very short.

The initial increase in economic production in Vicos was accomplished, moreover, before the formal classroom educational process had significantly increased the level of literacy and other formal knowledge in the population. Impressive improvement in economic productivity was achieved by illiterate Indian serfs on the basis of enlightenment in their own language and with practical demonstration to impart simple skills. Enlightenment was sometimes as simple as a stick, pre-cut by the Cornell Peru Project staff and later by the government's agricultural technician attached to the rural nuclear school, to measure the proper planting interval between seed potatoes. The author has heard of comparable efforts to teach Indian farmers exactly the same concept of seed spacing in another Indo-American country that failed to enlighten. The agricultural technicians there reiterated the proper planting interval, in centimeters, in Spanish rather than the Indian language of the farmers, and employed no device such as the pre-cut stick to demonstrate physically what the interval actually should be.

After the Vicos Indians assumed the management of their own affairs, literacy and writing skills assumed more importance in connection with the community farm enterprise. Still, nearly all the councilmen continued to be illiterate farmers with almost no classroom exposure up until the middle 1960s. Ten years of agricultural development occurred under the leadership of a small handful of literates—less than 1 percent of the total population.

These events raise some questions, at least, about the standards various writers have urged for the level of classroom instruction required for rapid economic development. Vicos achieved significant economic development years before 6 percent of its population was so enrolled, even though Peaslee(31) found that no sustained national economic growth began, in all cases he examined, before at least 5 percent of the total population was enrolled in primary schools. Certainly Vicos obtained significant economic improvement before 10 percent of its population was enrolled in primary school, the level Peaslee urges for national progress.

Economic gains that began in Vicos in 1952 helped to finance the classroom construction, lunch program, uniform purchases, and school-book buying that got 10 percent of the local population into primary classrooms approximately one decade later. This is not to assert that the "crust of custom" in traditional Vicos society was not broken by introducing "a more systematic means of obtaining and disseminating information about the production and distribution of goods."(32) The Cornell Peru Project sharecropping system was precisely a systematic means for disseminating information about production. The important point is this "systematic means" occurs not only in the school classroom.

Even when Vicos achieved a primary school enrollment of 10 percent of its population, it still fell short of having 2 percent of its population enrolled in secondary school. McClelland(33) arrived at the proportion of 20 secondary school students per 1,000 population and one secondary school teacher per 1,000 population as an approximate ratio for rapid economic development. McClelland also concluded that rapid development could be accomplished in the decade when Vicos began formal education with 200 third-level enrollments per 100,000 population. Instead of two-tenths of 1 percent of its population enrolled in collegiate institutions, Vicos by 1965 had one student at this level who completed normal school at the end of 1968.(34)

While this discussion focuses on Vicos, a single community, rather than the nation as the unit of analysis, the demonstration of the temporal order of connection between economic development and increased classroom enrollment appears relevant to the discussion of whether investment in classroom education fosters economic development, or whether increasing education instead results from economic development.

LITERACY AND
FAMILY POWER

The research findings on the long-range consequences of strategic intervention in Vicos by the Cornell Peru Project are not entirely assimilated yet, nor are they likely to be for some time. At least another full generation of Vicosinos must be observed before final conclusions can be reached concerning many important questions. One of these questions is the impact of classroom education in fostering sustained, long-range economic development. There is an inevitable time lag between classroom instruction and occasions when a former student can put into effect his formal learning.(35) In the program for transforming Vicos formal classroom instruction was included right from the beginning, yet this unavoidable time lag between stimulus and response severely limits what may yet be concluded about the impact of classroom instruction on Vicos development.

The Cornell Peru Project goal of building the national school system of Peru into the emerging Vicos community in such a way as to insure its functioning as an effective contact institution(36) has been achieved. This is not to say that the Vicos population has already all gone through the public-school classroom. Far from it. By 1963 only 18 percent of the Vicos population aged seven or more had ever attended school. Only 17 percent in this age category spoke Spanish. Only 35 percent of the school-age population was enrolled in school in 1959 (70 percent of school-age boys but only 6 percent of school-age girls).(20) Although the process of formal education must continue for many years in order to make all Vicos inhabitants literate, the public-school institution has been firmly established as a principal contact institution. The integration of formal enlightenment in Vicos was signalized by a parental lockout in 1961 aimed at forcing an improvement in the teaching staff. The incident demonstrated the internalization in Vicos of the enlightenment value.(37)

As the Cornell Peru Project provided opportunities for the acquisition of skills and for enlightenment not formerly possible for Vicos residents, those who voluntarily became more skilled or more enlightened promptly began structuring new power domains of their own that clearly rest upon the foundation of their relatively greater skill or enlightenment. That such enlightenment brings power over the unenlightened has, of course, been postulated by political analysts from Bacon to Bakunin and Machajski and more recent Marxists.(38) Many Vicos examples might be given, but a few illustrations must suffice here.

The diffusion of literacy, and the ability to speak Spanish, through the public school and adult literacy classes greatly enlarged by the Cornell Peru Project (with regard to physical plant), and the Ministry of Education (with regard to teaching staff), has led to establishment of new power domains of several sorts.

One consequence of such enlightenment is a considerable alteration of roles within the power domain of the family. Vicos families' newly acquired literate, Spanish-speaking sons, have been assigned new responsibilities. With the passage of time and observance of many demonstrations of social and economic advantages educated boys enjoy, family after family in Vicos has come to place more and more confidence in its educated representatives.

Wealthy stock-owning or potato-growing grandfathers, whose decisions were absolute under traditional manor conditions, now make no significant economic moves without consulting their educated grandsons—frequently following their advice. Mere striplings find themselves with heady decision-making power. For, quite naturally, the formally educated bilingual youths have not been slow to realize their command of Quechua and Spanish gives them tremendous advantage over their own kinsmen, and particularly over their own parents and grandparents who remain monolingual and frightened of the still-strange Mestizo world. While 17 percent of the Vicos population could speak Spanish by 1963, this skill is still largely restricted to younger men and boys who have attended local primary school or adult literacy classes or served in the Peruvian army.

Thus a stable system of interpersonal relationships in a family structure—formally ruled by male elders for at least 400 years—has been turned topsy-turvy within little more than one decade. This singular situation supports Mead's observation(39) that rapid change is possible, and Beaglehole's proposition(40) that social change can occur with great rapidity when new procedures "offer a welcome release from a crippling traditional system." The kind of Indian personality produced by the manor system leaves little doubt that the traditional social system of manorial Vicos was a psychologically crippling one. The existing condition of interpersonal relations within Vicos families calls into question a Wallace(41) claim that a cultural form that is not congenial to the personality structure of a group cannot be introduced to its members within a single generation. If the modal Vicos personality was as despairing as it appears to have been, then the present fairly ebullient, optimistic community leaders and dominant young family members, born and weaned under the traditional manor system, certainly seem to disprove the Wallace dictum.

The rapid rise to power by comparative youngsters in Vicos families under the special circumstances of differential enlightenment also helps us to see that many of the attributes of power assigned to family heads are not inherent.(42) The powers of the Vicos parent appear to have derived from a relatively greater degree of enlightenment and skill in a simply organized social system in which learning comes from experience rather than instruction. Present-day flux in Vicos society shows that the power of parents under the traditional manorial system derived from cumulative knowledge about how the system worked, and from skill in playing upon the emotions of the overlord in order to gain competitive advantages over other serfs. With the abolition of the traditional system in Vicos and the increasing integration of its former serf population into Peruvian national society, the functional utility of the traditional form of enlightenment and the traditional skills diminished. In their stead the new skills of literacy, democratic discussion, and decision-making have acquired such great functional value that possessors of them have come to dominate their families. In many cases this was true regardless of relatively tender age, lack of traditional attributes of maturity (such as spouses and offspring), and traditional norms of respect by youths toward elders.

There exists, then, what should be a temporary situation in Vicos, assuming the entire adult population becomes literate at some future date. The present Vicos condition approximates the customary state of affairs in a number of simply organized social systems in which power clearly does not reside in the oldest family member, but in the most efficient economic producer. This is usually the most enlightened and skilled individual in terms of the particular requirements of the group's economic system.(43)

NEW POWER DOMAINS

Other power domains that newly literate Vicos youths are establishing affect individuals outside their immediate families in ways unknown under the traditional manor system.

After the Cornell Peru Project's five-year period of direct responsibility for administering the Vicos estate terminated and the former serfs took over responsibility for directing their own affairs, they decided to conduct a community farm enterprise. This business venture is carried out on the same fields that once were farmed by serf labor to the profit of the overlord. It is sustained by a labor tax that resembles the obligatory labor system of the traditional manor. One fundamental principle of collecting this labor tax is that it must be equitable. That is to say, no individual is to be taxed more nor less than any other.

Achieving this ideal in practice has led to the establishment of a kind of power domain based entirely on the literacy of key individuals rather than upon traditional criteria of power.

The Vicos community council soon decided to make each councilman responsible for supervising the workers from the zone which elected him. This made the delegates responsible for administering the labor tax equally among their own constituents. The latter were quick to point out to their elected delegates, if the latter did not already realize it, that carrying out the ideal of equal taxation in the fields over the period of an agricultural season required the keeping of accurate records of the days worked by each individual. The delegates were, however, generally illiterate, having grown to maturity under the traditional manor system with no opportunity for literacy. Over the seven years ending in 1964-65, the delegates ranged around 42 years of age and without schooling at all to an average of a few months. Illiterate delegates took the only course open to them: they began to recruit the services of newly literate schoolboys (termed *leídos* = learned) to accompany them to the fields to serve as timekeepers.

Since the *leídos* kept records which no one else in the work group could read—including the delegates, they immediately acquired considerable power over both delegates and zone residents. The *leído* necessarily become the final arbiter of disputes over labor tax payment, citing his work records as authority for saying that a person did or did not still owe labor time. Schoolboys thus attained a kind of power in the fledgling community that would have been impossible for youths of comparable age under the traditional manor system. It is not unknown, as a matter of fact, for the Vicos *leído,* who is also genetically related to a delegate, to assume—to an extent embarrassing to other members of the community council—that he may sit in the council's deliberations in the absence of the delegate himself.

One of the more striking new power domains at Vicos involves the first natives to take teaching roles in the formal enlightenment process there. Vicos did not have to wait for local students to complete normal school, nor even secondary school, to begin having classroom-educated individuals served as teachers of younger children.

Despite the small proportion of girls attending school in Vicos, the first local teacher was a teenage girl. A Peace Corps volunteer who opened a new sectional school in the Wiash Zone in 1963 employed a local bilingual, literate helper. Since the volunteer was female, she chose a female assistant, the best-educated Vicos girl. The latter attended the local primary school for three years on a scholarship provided by a scientist who carried out studies at Vicos in 1960. This young lady is not a native of the zone where the new school operates, so that when she began assisting the volunteer in charge of the new school she acceded immediately to a position of authority over school children from families other than her own in a zone other than her own. This was the first time such an event occurred in Vicos.

A further extension of this type of teacher-student power domain occurred in 1963. A Vicos boy with a fourth-grade education opened another new sectional school in Ullmey Zone with a Peace Corps volunteer as his helper. The latter eventually succeeded in integrating his pupils into the central prevocational school, and volunteer teachers ended their Vicos assignments in 1965. Such assistant teachers with only primary education are cut off from other than temporary employment in Peru's national public school system by rising qualification standards. Stricter teacher training standards herald a stage in national development when classroom education at higher and higher levels is required to obtain employment in educational institutions. If the exchange economy of Peru does not expand employment opportunities for primary school graduates as fast as its primary educational system produces them, unemployment and discontent will result, just as has occurred in Ghana, Kenya, Uganda,(44) and elsewhere.

The establishment of even temporary teacher-pupil power domains involving Vicos natives as teachers portends a sweeping change of interpersonal relations within the community as more and more enlightened youths return from normal school to teach Vicos children. The first Vicos graduate of a secondary normal school for rural teachers returned home to teach in the Vicos school in 1965. He joined several secondary school graduates who have returned to Vicos to farm, but who make the Holmberg Memorial Library, in the old manor house, their "club," where they meet, talk, read, and write. These Vicos "intellectuals" confirm the proposition that the amount of cultural change produced in a cross-cultural situation is proportional to the amount of personal interaction.(45) For the most modernized and most changed persons in Vicos are the very youngsters who have spent the most time in the formal educational system. Their principal impacts on their native community still lie in the future as they reach ages of effective decision-making, and take over the day-to-day operation of community affairs.

A second type of new power domain stems from artisan skills. The handful of artisans who really learned basic building trades during the Cornell Peru Project's construction period carried the Vicos population a long step down the road toward a social system based upon social contract rather than ascribed statuses. Contracts had existed in Vicos prior to 1951, to be sure. Individuals who needed the local style poncho contracted with a part-time weaving specialist to make the garment. Agricultural tasks and house construction were carried out by many persons collaborating in the reciprocal labor-exchange institution called the *minka* (work "bee"). One good reason for erecting houses with large gangs of unskilled laborers, provisioned with food and drink by the house-builder, was that no one was any more proficient than anyone else and in such circumstances many heads were better than one.

The construction situation changed with the training of a number of specialists on Project building programs. Masons and carpenters with a considerable degree of technical competence emerged, although they continued to farm and performed their specialties only part-time. The difference between their technical competence and their efficiency as a result of it became readily apparent to their peers. As a consequence, when community authorities had to build new or repair existing structures, they began to contract with these specialists instead of organizing a *minka*. They found that the specialist-constructed building cost less than one put up by less-skilled, often intoxicated *minka* laborers; it also endured better and was more esthetically pleasing—the walls did not lean. Thus the new artisans built small power domains in the building construction field in Vicos. As they practiced their trades, these men perfected their skills and acquired reputation. One native Vicos plasterer has in recent years worked on buildings in neighboring Chancos and the Mestizo towns of Pariahuanca and Carhuaz as well as the capital city of the department, Huaraz. A Vicos carpenter goes to work for months at a time in towns on the Andean western slope, taking two sons as helpers.

In the building trades, as in family gardening, Cornell Peru Project training taught Vicosinos new skills which enabled them greatly to augment their productivity. The Vicosino artisans who now gain employment in the general economy are clearly trained workers producing more for themselves and for the Peruvian nation than the same individuals did as unskilled less-than-subsistence gardeners. Conventional economic analysis which "considers the individual as an interchangeable unit, without regard to his qualifications,"(46) simply does not apply to this kind of development situation. No amount of capital investment could have drawn into artisan industry Vicosinos who lacked any marketable skills. The investment that made them productive was Project investment in "human capital," in teaching them skills. Once Vicosinos acquired artisanry skills they began to market them in response to already existing demands. Only when equipped with skills *could* these Indians begin to behave as economic theory postulates men act. Only when equipped with artisanry skills could they establish a new power domain in Vicos and in the region based on their new-found productivity. And only then, indeed, would their contributions begin to register even slightly on the Gross National Product scales of national development.

The growth of the artisan power domain can be measured not only in the increasing level of skills of particular individuals, but also in the more conventional terms of numerical and proportional increase of specialists in the Vicos population, as indicated in Table I.

Viewing Vicos in the framework of national development, its rate of human resource development since 1952 appears startling. A few indicators of such development used for national comparisons also allows us to measure at least approximately the degree of change in Vicos. In 1952 the single rural school teacher working at Vicos meant the population had 5.9 teachers per 10,000 population. By 1959 Ministry of Education assignments raised this figure to about 42.8 primary school teachers per 10,000 population. Estimating the 1968

Table I. ARTISANS AGED 15 AND OVER IN VICOS IN 1951 AND 1963

Specialty	1951	1963	Percentage Increase
Mason[a]	0	15	–
Flavored ice dealer[a]	0	12	–
Midwife	3	30	900
Carpenter	3	11	266
Firewood dealer	12	42	250
Iceman (cutting glacial ice)	5	15	200
Charcoal-maker	16	40	150
Vendor	21	48	129
Weaver	58	106	83
Dyer	10	17	70
Muleteer	31	52	68
Basketmaker	32	51	59
Cantor	4	6	50
Tailor or seamstress	12	14	17
Musician[b]	67	55	22
Healer[b]	5	3	40
Number of specialists	177	297	68%
Number of persons 15 and over	1,010	1,260	25%

Note: Only two specialties declined in absolute numbers, and two were created entirely between 1951 and 1963.(47) Declining specialties are marked by (a) and new specialties by (b) above.

Vicos population as about 2,300, this figure was perhaps 52 per 10,000. Significantly, by 1965, when the first native Vicos teacher returned to teach in the local primary school, Vicos acquired an approximate rate of four native primary school teachers per 10,000 population and began to diminish its dependency upon external specialists in formal education.

The proportion of school-age children enrolled in classes also measures the rate of human resource development. Using the age group seven to sixteen instead of the more usual five to fourteen (because of the relatively advanced age at which Vicosinos enter school), Vicos put only 4 percent in a very ineffective school in 1952. By 1959 Vicos enrolled 35 percent of its children in this age group in primary school.(48)

Vicos did not enroll any student at the secondary level until 1960. Two years later three Vicos youths attended this second educational level, or about 1.4 percent of the population aged 15-19 in 1963.(49) Measured by proportion of population enrolled in secondary and higher education, Vicos was still "underdeveloped" in 1962, roughly in the same range, there-fore, as countries such as Afghanistan, Saudi Arabia, Nyasaland, and far below Peru as a whole, which ranked as a "partially developed" country.(50) It was moving rapidly, however, doubling its percentage of the 15-19 age group enrolled in 1963—with two boys in Carhuaz secondary school, three in Caraz Agricultural Institute, and one in Jaén Rural Normal School.(51) Vicos reached an estimated composite index of over 6 by 1965 when the first Vicos student entered college-level normal school. While still far below the Peruvian national average, this placed Vicos in the approximate range of human resource development of countries such as Kenya, Nigeria, Haiti, Senegal, Uganda, and the Sudan.

Another indicator of Vicos human resource development provides both a quantitative and qualitative measurement of progress. In 1963 parents of small children in two zones of Vicos some distance from the central school built or rehabili-tated existing structures to house new sectional schools.(52) As mentioned earlier in this chapter, the Cornell Peru Project initiated central school construction with obligatory serf labor in order to create the physical plant which would prompt central government response in the form of additional teachers.

A decade later adult Vicosinos applied the lesson learned under the Project in order to bring formal classroom instruction to their neighborhoods so timid younger school-age children would not have to walk to the distant central school and suffer the bullying of older students.

The Wiash and Ullmey sectional schools have been mentioned in discussing new power domains of educated Vicos youths. Qualitatively, these schools demonstrated parental participation in the process of school construction to pressure the central government to provide teachers that goes on all over rural Peru.(53) Quantitatively, these two projects added two neighborhood schools which enrolled pupils who would not have walked to the central school—further increasing the rate of human resource development in Vicos. The Ullmey school reported enrolling forty students in 1965 and claimed perfect attendance.(54) That was 16.6 percent of the enrollment in the Vicos Central School, and a significant increase in total teaching.

Building a school plant to obtain additional teachers from the national government marked one kind of Vicosino participation in the Peruvian political process. Direct political participation appears to be one form of power that lags behind formal education, at least in countries which impose both age and literacy qualifications upon voters. Illiteracy barred the Vicos population from exercising electoral power until some years after the formal education process began producing youths who could qualify as literate. They still had to wait to reach voting age. By 1962 Vicos had twenty-five registered voters among 380 in the Marcará District, or about 6.6 percent. Several were disqualified in the purge of electoral lists conducted under the military junta ruling the country before the 1963 national election. Vicos then counted twelve of 295 registered voters in Marcará District, or 4 percent of that electorate.

Finally, the fundamental new power domain of Vicos itself bears emphasis. Some may view Indian acquisition of potato power as basic to all later change in Vicos. The near-subsistence gardeners learned neotechnic potato growing from Dr. Vázquez and later from technicians of the Peruvian government's supervised credit program. By producing large quantities of commercial potatoes they provided the economic potential needed for development and political parity with Mestizos. This chapter shows, however, the strong functional linkages between changes in (1) economics and technology, (2) education, (3) nutrition and health, and, especially, (4) social organization. Holmberg(55) defined these as the four "major areas of development" he started at Vicos. The full potential of potato economic power almost surely would have been dissipated by Vicos family production-consumption units behaving in traditional "tragedy of the commons" manner,(56) in competition with hostile Mestizo socio-political power domains.

Holmberg's seminar training for Indian leaders provided Vicos with the social structure pattern to permit realization of the economic potential of potato power. Coupled with Vázquez's explanation of the socio-political advantages of cooperation, that pattern enabled the Indians to organize to meet Mestizo competition. Vicos created a community production enterprise that unified family marketing of increased production and institutionalized community economic enterprise. This transformed the newly self-governing community into a functional power domain in Peru. Augmented production obtained by applying skills learned from outsiders indeed brought Vicosinos considerable economic independence. Thus potato power laid the foundations for a Vicos power domain. Only Indian social organization on the democratic lines laid out by Holmberg and Vázquez enabled the Vicosinos actually to build a local power domain on those foundations. The domain allowed them a measure of political liberty and even brought them growing political power. It achieved a measure of social freedom from traditional restrictions, and diminution in customary discriminations. These shifts in power stem directly from multiple key increases in skills and enlightenment that has gone beyond a shift in degree to convert Vicos into a different kind of social unit than it was in 1951.

NOTES

1. M. Bloch, *Feudal Society.* Chicago: University of Chicago Phoenix Books, 1964, Vol. I, pp. 241ff. See also G. C. Homans, *English Villagers of the Thirteenth Century.* Cambridge: Harvard University Press, 1941, pp. 340-349. G. Dalton,

Peasants, Power, and Applied Social Change

"Theoretical Issues in Economic Anthropology," Current Anthropology, 10:1 (Feb. 1969) 64 urges the relevance of such historical analyses to economic anthropology.

2. A. R. Holmberg, "Changing Community Attitudes and Values in Peru: A Case Study in Guided Change," in *Social Change in Latin America Today*. New York: Council on Foreign Relations, 1960, p. 89.

3. A. R. Holmberg and H. F. Dobyns, "The Process of Accelerating Community Change," Human Organization, vol. 21, no. 2 (1962), p. 107.

4. E. Wolf, "Types of Latin American Peasantry: A Preliminary Discussion," American Anthropologist, vol. 57, no. 3 (1965), p. 456.

5. Ibid., pp. 457-459. Something of what "defensive ignorance" meant in Vicos may be gleaned from the self-images of adult men reared under the manorial system, ten of whom have been intensively analyzed by psychologists. Every one of the ten feared others would turn against him whatever he might say. Every one viewed himself as secretive, lonely; he feared conversation as dangerous, using language as a defensive tool. Ralph Klein, "The Self-Image of Adult Males in an Andean Culture." New York University Ph.D. Dissertation, 1963, pp. 56, 62, 68, 73, 78-79, 83-84, 95, 102, 108-109.

6. G. Wilson and M. Wilson, *The Analysis of Social Change*. Cambridge: Cambridge University Press, 1945, p. 25.

7. H. G. Barnett, *Innovation*. New York: McGraw-Hill, 1953, p. 40.

8. H. F. Dobyns, C. Monge M., and M. C. Vázquez, "Summary of Technical-Organizational Progress and Reactions to It," Human Organization vol. 21, no. 2 (1962) p. 111.

9. Holmberg, op. cit., 1960, p. 68.

10. J. O. Alers, "Population and Development in a Peruvian Community." Journal of Inter-American Studies, vol. 7, no. 4 (1965), p. 442, Table 19.

11. Barnett, op cit., p. 41

12. H. D. Lasswell and A. Kaplan, *Power and Society*. New Haven: Yale University Press, 1950, p. 95.

13. A. R. Holmberg, H. F. Dobyns, and M. C. Vázquez, "Methods for the Analysis of Cultural Change," Anthropology Quarterly, vol. 34, no. 2 (1961), p. 43.

14. H. D. Lasswell, "Integrating Communities Into More Inclusive Systems," Human Organization, vol. 21, no. 2 (1962), p. 116.

15. W. F. Whyte, "Discussion," of "Community and Regional Development: The Joint Cornell Peru Experiment," Human Organization vol. 21, no. 2 (1962), p. 122. See also H. F. Dobyns, "Discussion," ibid. C. Monge M., "Discussion," ibid.

16. A. R. Holmberg, "Participant Intervention in the Field," Human Organization, vol. 14, no. 1 (1955), p. 23.

17. Vicos Paleotechnic cultivation belonged to the "Mediterranean Ecotype" in terms of Eric R. Wolf's scheme. *Peasants*. Englewood Cliffs: Prentice-Hall, 1966, pp. 19-21, 32-33.

18. This organization is described in J. C. Sandelman, "Agricultural Extension Work Through the *Servicio* in Peru," in H. M. Teaf and P. G. Franck (Eds.), *Hands Across Frontiers: Case Studies in Technical Cooperation*. Ithaca: Cornell University Press, 1955, pp. 217-263.

19. M. Debeauvais, "The concept of human capital," *UNESCO International Social Science Journal*, vol. 14, no. 4 (1962), p. 660.

20. M. C. Vázquez, *Educacion Rural en el Callejon de Huaylas: Vicos*. Lima: Editorial Estudios Andinos, 1965, p. 90.

21. P. Roman U., "Informe de Actividades del Plan Nacional de Integracion de la Poblacion Aborigen en el Periodo del lo de Enero de 1962 al 30 de Junio de 1963," Perú Indígena, vol. 10, nos. 24 and 25 (1963), p. 114.

22. P. Roman U., *Plan Nacional de Integracion de la Poblacion Aborigen: Informe, Actividades Enero 1963-Junio 1964.* Lima: Ministerio de Trabajo y Asuntos Indigenas, 1964, p. 116.

23. P. Roman U., *Plan Nacional de Integracion de la Poblacion Aborigen: Informe Actividades Julio 1964-Junio 1965.* Lima: Ministerio de Trabajo y Asuntos Indigenas, 1965, p. 44.

24. B. Russell, *Power.* London: Allen & Unwin, 1938, pp. 38ff; R. H. Tawney, *Equality.* New York: Harcourt, Brace, 1931, p. 229; T. Parsons, *Essays in Sociological Theory,* (rev. ed.). New York: Free Press, 1954, p. 391; D. Cartwright, "A Field Theoretical Conception of Power," in D. Cartwright (Ed.), *Studies in Social Power.* Ann Arbor: University of Michigan, 1939, pp. 187-211.

25. A government-recognized Indigenous Community across the Marcará River from Vicos. See J. C. Snyder, "The Changing Context of an Andean Community," in *Cultural Stability and Cultural Change.* Proceedings of the 1957 Annual Spring Meeting of the American Ethnological Society, pp. 20-29.

26. A Mestizo trading town six kilometers down-canyon from the Vicos plaza. See H. Ghersi B., "El Indígena y el Mestizo en la Comunidad de Marcará," Revista del Museo Nacional, 28: 118-188; 29: 48-128; 30: 95-176.

27. An Indian settlement partly of freeholders and partly of serfs with large-scale labor migration on the same slope of the *Cordillera Blanca* as Vicos, a few miles farther north. See W. W. Stein. *Hualcan: Life in the Highlands of Peru.* Ithaca: Cornell University Press, 1961.

28. R. L. Sharp, "People without Politics," in *Systems of Political Control and Bureaucracy in Human Societies,* Proceedings of the 1958 Annual Spring Meeting of the American Ethnological Society, pp. 5-7.

29. R. Bierstedt, "An Analysis of Social Power," American Sociological Review vol. 15, no. 6 (1950) p. 733. See also note 16.

30. Debeauvais, op. cit., pp. 663-664; M. J. Bowman, "Perspectives on Education and Development," International Development Review, vol. 6, no. 3 (1964), pp. 3-4.

31. A. L. Peaslee, "Elementary Education as a Prerequisite for Economic Growth," International Development Review, vol. 7, no. 3 (1965), p. 20.

32. Ibid., p. 19.

33. D. C. McClelland, "Does Education Accelerate Economic Growth?" *Economic Development and Cultural Change,* vol. 14, no. 3 (1966), p. 278.

34. H. F. Dobyns, A. R. Holmberg, M. E. Opler and L. Sharp, *Methods for Analyzing Cultural Change.* Ithaca: Cornell University Department of Anthropology, 1967, p. 147, and F. U. Sanchez, personal communication.

35. Populations like that in Vicos in possessing only incomplete school systems face a schooling delay before feedback begins from students who attend secondary school or college. For example, the Vicos youth who first entered secondary school spent the period 1960 to the end of 1968 in secondary school and college. Since he was not then assigned to the Vicos primary school, there has been a further delay before his knowledge can be brought directly to bear on Vicos affairs, although it will benefit the Peruvian nation.

36. B. Malinowski, *The Dynamics of Culture Change.* New Haven: Yale University Press, 1945.

37. Holmberg and Dobyns, op. cit., p. 109.

38. M. Nomad, *Apostles of Revolution* (rev. ed.). New York: Collier Books, 1961, pp. 203-204.

39. M. Mead, *New Lives for Old.* New York: William Morrow, 1956, pp. 445-446.

40. E. Beaglehole, "Evaluation Techniques for Induced Technological Change," International Social Science Bulletin, vol. 7, no. 3, p. 384.

Peasants, Power, and Applied Social Change

41. A. F. C. Wallace, "Some Psychological Determinants of Culture Change in an Iroquoian Community," in W. N. Fenton (Ed.), Symposium on Local Diversity in Iroquois Culture," Bureau of American Ethnology Bulletin 149, 1951, p. 75.

42. The traditional Vicos family resembled the Navajo and Mormon (as described by F. L. Strodtbeck, "Husband-Wife Interaction Over Revealed Differences," American Sociological Review, vol. 16, no. 4 (1951), p. 472 and Detroit urban family as described by D. M. Wolfe, "Power and Authority in the Family," in Studies in Social Power, pp. 107-116 in that wives and husbands made decisions.

43. Among the Siriono, for example, such power as is wielded gravitates to those individuals whose enlightenment as to the habits of Amazon Basin wildlife, and skills in making and using native weapons and tools permit them consistently to provide more food than other individuals. A. R. Holmberg, "Nomads of the Long Bow." Smithsonian Institution, Institute of Social Anthropology Pub. no. 10, 1950, pp. 58-60.

44. Philip Foster, Education and Social Change in Ghana. University of Chicago Press, 1965, pp. 296-297.

45. H. F. Dobyns, "Blunders with Bolsas," Human Organization, vol. 10, no. 3 (1951), p. 32.

46. Debeauvais, op. cit., p. 661.

47. J. O. Alers, op. cit., p. 446, Table 22.

48. Ibid., p. 441.

49. H. F. Dobyns, A. R. Holmberg, M. E. Opler, and L. Sharp. Methods for Analyzing Cultural Change. Ithaca: Cornell University Department of Anthropology, 1967, p. 146.

50. Indicators mentioned in this paragraph are drawn from F. Harbison and C. A. Myers, Education, Manpower and Economic Growth. New York: McGraw-Hill, 1964, pp. 27-33.

51. Roman, 1964, op. cit., p. 111.

52. Ullmey, ibid., p. 110; Wiash, H. F. Dobyns, P. L. Doughty, and A. R. Holmberg, Measurement of Peace Corps Program Impact in the Peruvian Andes: Final Report. Ithaca: Cornell University Department of Anthropology, 1965, p. 71.

53. H. F. Dobyns, The Social Matrix of Peruvian Indigenous Communities. Ithaca: Cornell University Department of Anthropology, 1964, pp. 51-58.

54. Roman, 1965, op. cit., p. 46.

55. Holmberg, 1960, op. cit., pp. 82-83. In other words, Holmberg identified what J. H. Steward (Theory of Culture Change. Urbana: University of Illinois Press, 1955, pp. 93-94) termed the "cultural core" of Vicos subculture, as consisting of conventional understandings in a wider range of culture than technology, at least for purposes of rapid guided social and economic change.

56. G. Hardin, "The Tragedy of the Commons," Science, vol. 162, no. 3859 (1968), pp. 1243-1248.

Chapter VII

THE TRANSFERABILITY

OF VICOS STRATEGY

Harold D. Lasswell

A question often raised about the Vicos experience is how significant is its example for the enormous task of bringing peasant communities into the modern world? After all, the objection runs, only two thousand villagers are involved, while the number of peasant hamlets and villages on the face of the earth is in the millions. Part of the reply is this:

The program as a whole is transferable with little change to many social and physical environments.

Vicos resembles many peasant communities in the experience they have had in taking collective action in pursuit of a wide range of important common interests, no matter how many barriers have been put in their way by outside power groups. Peasants are often accustomed to a dual system of agriculture in which the joint production of some commodities is combined with family (or individual) production of others. Further, in spite of some discrepancies among families and individuals in the degree of effective access to wealth, power, and other value outcomes, the broad pattern of distribution is relatively egalitarian, and a measure of responsibility is accepted for providing at least minimal security for all who are traditionally identified as members of the community. Institutional practices are in harmony with one another, and hence maintain continuity in the basic pattern of value shaping and sharing.

Given these predispositions it is feasible to initiate and partially stabilize practices that incorporate leading features of the world pattern of techno-scientific civilization. Modern civilization exploits non-human sources of energy on an unprecedented scale, and fosters a world-wide division of labor that is largely implemented by the price system, rather than by barter or the long-term reciprocities characteristic of a traditional society.

The Vicos program of encouraging the peasants to own their land, and to combine the dual method of production with money crops that depend on scientific knowledge (of soils and pesticides, for example) is a transferable project.

In many agricultural villages there is little doubt about how to raise the crop that produces a money income; or, if there is uncertainty, enough agricultural specialists exist in the region to give convincing demonstrations and to advise the peasants during the first periods of transition. For many Indian villages in the Peruvian Andes potatoes will be the potential money crop; and the success of Vicos provides the necessary demonstration of both technical and economic strategies. The United Nations, the agricultural departments of the nation states, and the universities of many countries have the knowledge and knowhow pertinent to the task. Once the channels of communication and collaboration have been consolidated among peasants, scientists, and officials, it will be feasible for peasant communities to formulate their future policies in the light of changing knowledge and circumstances. Further, the concept of diversification applies to commercial and industrial facilities as well as to animals and crops. Hence agriculture can be discreetly combined with industry.

The Vicos program is much more than a strategy affecting power and wealth, crucial as these values are in the life of any community. More fundamental in the long-run, perhaps, are innovations that allow a community to obtain access to the contemporary stock of empirical knowledge. Enlightenment generates skill; it contributes to changing levels of well-being and to the readjustment of norms pertaining to affection, rectitude, and respect. These additional components of the total program are likewise transferable to thousands of peasant contexts.

Rectitude—the Bishop of Huaraz (center, in black cassock) leaves the Vicos chapel following confirmation ceremonies held there for the first time in many years.

Many specific techniques are transferable to environments where the whole program cannot be applied.

Many elements of the "Vicos package" are common features of many if not all programs of development, and can be utilized in mixes suitable to different conditions. Some technical devices are as common as the modern school; others are often less frequent, such as the use of credit arrangements.

The modern school is perhaps the most drastic innovation of all, since it builds into the local community an enduring escalator of change. In Vicos the school quickly made its influence felt, as indeed it has in countless places over the globe. More pupils were able to attain a level that prepared them to receive higher instruction outside the village. In future years it is to be expected that some of them will continue to settle permanently in Vicos as job opportunities expand and living standards rise.

One tactic in strategies of innovation is to look for unplanned solutions to emerging problems, and to encourage their diffusion to appropriate situations. Use of credit by the Vicosinos affords a striking instance of the appearance of a technique that was unanticipated by outsiders. When the villagers had an opportunity to buy the estate, they drew on the money assets of some Indian communities in return for promises to deliver high-quality seed potatoes. It had not been anticipated that the decision-makers would adopt this sophisticated method of assembling some of the capital assets required. Yet the use of the credit mechanism in this way is obviously adaptable to the needs and opportunities of peasants who live in many different situations.

A prototype that trains scientists and politicians can have an escalator effect on development.

The participation of highly trained scientists in the Cornell-Vicos Project had an important influence on the tempo of change over a fifteen-year period. If the initiative had been taken by a less well-recognized anthropologist, or by a less well-established university, the impact would have been much less. We have no convenient way of knowing how many school teachers or faculty members of obscure institutions of higher learning have been inspired by a vision similar to that of Holmberg and his associates. It is highly probable that similar aspirations have occurred to many dedicated persons. Yet they made little immediate imprint on the life of those in any locality beyond their own, and it is unlikely that they were successful in bringing about sufficiently drastic alterations in the local peasant village to mobilize the assets of others.

An elite social scientist like Holmberg and an elite school like Cornell could readily work in harmony with a world-renowned physician, and with other top figures in science and public affairs. Vicos was a training center for young scientists, teachers, and leaders from Peru as well as Cornell; and the unfolding significance of the Project affected the careers of many qualified persons who joined in both expediting and learning from the development process.

Given the culture of an academic elite, it was predictable that a flow of publications would intensify the impact of the Vicos approach. The scientific, administrative, and popular stream of presentation began early and countinues to date, as this volume demonstrates.

More significantly transferable than the particular program or the specific techniques of the Vicos Project is the fundamental strategy.

It would be possible to itemize scores of specific techniques that were employed at one time or another by the directors of the Project. However, such an enumeration would miss the creative implications of the entire enterprise either for the task of development as a whole, or for the future of the social sciences.

The fundamental strategy recognized the decisiveness of power, together with the interdependence of power and all other values in the social process.

Holmberg was intensely aware of the crucial character of power for the future of Vicos. Dedicated as he was to the dignity of man, and understanding, as he did, the indispensability of power-sharing to the realization of man's dignity in theory and fact, Holmberg perceived the project as one focused on authority and control. It was plain from an early time that the object of the exercise was not to consolidate a caste of anthropologists as successors to the patrons of the tradition society. The aim was to contribute to the internal decision-making and applying process of Vicos by emphasizing its *democratic* and *realistic* dimensions. To be democratic the polity of the community must share power widely, not narrowly. To survive in the Peruvian and the world environment democracy must be *enlightened*. Its devotees must be able to comprehend the social and natural environment—not perfectly, but better than when they perpetuate the self-preoccupied images of a primitive society. In a world whose inescapable characteristic is interdependence, Holmberg believed that it was morally irresponsible for those who are nurtured in an "interfering" culture to deny the young people of Vicos (or of any peasant community) an opportunity for access to the knowledge available to the "interferer."

Holmberg was also aware of the fact that, at first, peasant power is no bootstrapping operation. The isolated peasant is more an object than an initiator of history. He may, like insects, multiply bodies, and like every species of life search far and wide for a favoring habitat. Yet population pressure is not the peasant's only contribution to history. He can transform his established ways and become a contributing member of the world search for knowledge and diversity of expression. His early steps depend on outside help; and this depends on outside as well as inside forces operating cumulatively through time.

When we think of change on a wider scale than a single peasant community, the basic strategy can combine simultaneity with cumulation.

The recommended strategy (a) selects villages for proto-typical projects in a given region, such as the habitable valleys and plateaus of the Peruvian Andes; (b) plans an orderly sequence of advice and assistance; and (c) encourages diffusion and cooperation at all levels (neighborhood, regional, national, transnational).

Strategy requires the choice of relevant criteria of development and of appropriate indicators of change.

If a strategy is to be clearly formulated and adequately appraised, the choice of evaluative criteria is critical. These criteria call for specific indicators to supplement information obtained from case studies and experienced judgment.

As Holmberg was fond of saying, the visitors who confused development with buildings were disappointed when they dropped in to take a cursory look at Vicos. The familiar marks of a suburban real-estate subdivision were missing. There was no smooth road flanked by stately trees leading to the Plaza. At first the cluster of one- or two-story buildings around the embryonic plaza had no impressive eye-catcher, save the Catholic church, which spoke more eloquently of yesterday than of today. The peasants of Vicos had inherited no grand appurtenances of an estate: there was no great manor house, and no parade ground for cattle or horses. During the early fifties the human urgencies of health, of modestly improved agricultural technique, of patient debate and discussion were too pressing for project energies to be diverted into "showcase" monument building.

It is, of course, debatable whether the project should have made earlier and more numerous concessions to conventional criteria of judgment. Visitors kept coming to Vicos, and more support for projected changes might have been forthcoming if an ingenious means of dramatizing the "New Vicos" had been discovered early. As it was, the first building that seemed to confirm the vigor of the community was the school, which did indeed provide a focus of identity and pride for young and old.

The intellectual challenge of finding satisfactory "indicators" of the past, present, and future of a community like Vicos led ultimately to several sharable techniques, especially as the significance of the "decision seminar technique" and the "social planetarium" were tentatively evolved and haltingly adapted to the problem in hand.

Crucial to development is a strategy of inner and outer (trans-boundary) coalition.

The Vicos story verifies the comparative hopelessness of structural change in villages that must depend exclusively on their own initiative. In terms of their social environment, peasants are relatively powerless; and their powerlessness is both a consequence and a further condition of their continuing lack of power. Hence it is imperative for ambitious programs of change to evolve a strategy that brings participants in the larger environment into an effective coalition with local groups.

The principal Vicos coalition included the elders who were originally available, the Patron (Holmberg) and the manager (who lived near the hacienda). In Lima the key figure was the internationally famous physician (Carlos Monge Medrano, M.D.) and his friends in official and private circles. At home in Ithaca the Department of Anthropology could count on university administration backing. The money came principally from the Carnegie Corporation of New York.

The Vicos Project demonstrates that peasant liberation is often possible by strategies of mini-violence.

Despite the dramatic examples of violent revolution, it is of more than local importance to emphasize that more peaceful means of structural change can in fact occur. This is encouraging from the point of view of all who abhor violence and admire persuasion, or who take note of the disappointing consequences of many revolutionary movements (European, Asian, Latin American) in which peasants have played a conspicuous part.

The romantic axis: peasants and intellectuals.

We note that one of the great traditions of political change dramatizes a possible coalition of urban intellectuals and the peasantry. Historically the peasant-intellectual axis has expressed several value priorities. Some initiatives have come from moral pity or righteous indignation, fortified by theological doctrines about the equality of man in the eye of God. These rectitude movements are not altogether dead. On the contrary, it is obvious that during the last two decades disaffected members of the lesser clergy have repeatedly joined with students from relatively privileged backgrounds in migrations to the countryside. The hope has been to establish direct connection with the peasantry. Parallel initiatives are found in 18th-century Europe; or, for that matter, in earlier years.

A more glamorous set of initiatives has been the coalition between agitational or conspirative intellectuals and peasants. Often the intellectuals have been based on factory workers (or other members of the urban proletariat) and have also included dissident students and dropouts. Such combinations have played a major part in radical revolutionary movements whose chief ideological source has been Marxist. In resource-rich but science-poor regions workers in mines or on plantations have been the principal proletarians recruited.(1)

The power coalition at Vicos successfully brought peasants and scientists together.

Vicos suggests that a new type of intellectual is effective in contemporary politics. The older symbols of reference to an "intellectual" carry connotations that are poorly adapted to the task of identifying the new elements involved. Holmberg and his associates were not primarily recruited from among journalists, or teachers with broken careers, as was so often true of professional revolutionaries of the old school. On the contrary the careers of the Holmberg circle had been launched by successfully meeting the tests imposed by top universities and by competent faculties of the social and behavioral sciences. Principally they were recruited from the anthropological division of the field as a whole.

Instead of characterizing the Vicos-type coalition as a peasant-intellectual axis, it is more descriptive to refer to it as a coalition of peasants and scientists. The striking fact is that the decisive initiative came, not from the former, but from the latter. Instead of exemplifying an agitational, marginally professional approach, the Vicos strategy was originated and executed by dedicated and accepted scientists who saw themselves as extending—not circumscribing or abandoning—their fields of primary competence.

They were exemplifiers of an approach that cuts across all the specialties collectively called the social or behavioral sciences; and, indeed, all the fields of knowledge (physical and biological as well as cultural). The latter category, the cultural, includes the traditional scholars of the "humanities" as well as of the more recently christened social and behavioral sciences. I prefer the term "policy sciences" to characterize this point of view, but other terms are often used equivalently.(2)

The triple powers: peasants, scientists, politicians.

A third member of the Vicos-type coalition is, no doubt, of sufficient importance to justify separate billing. Politicians were directly and indirectly involved, even though the nature of the association differed from one time to another. Not every official, general, or party leader was eligible, any more than every scientist was a suitable participant. Eligibility depended primarily on the value-institution orientation of the person concerned. Only those with self-commitment to human dignity were relevant; and it was necessary for their conceptions of human dignity to harmonize with one another. Hence the participants in the Vicos were self-selected on an informal basis. If it were discovered that they misunderstood one another, they were under self-pressure to withdraw. Politicians differ greatly in the degree to which they are committed to the use of authoritative control as a means of realizing wide or narrow participation in the sharing of power or of other values.

The same point applies to scientists. They, too, were fully eligible for the Vicos coalition when they combined their commitments to the advancement of scientific enlightenment with concern for the sharing of power (and of other values). And ultimately the same point also applies to the peasants. Only those who were willing to clarify and execute a program compatible with human dignity could be full coalition mates of the scientists and politicians who molded the new Vicos.

The skill struggle in contemporary politics.

The Vicos coalition is widely significant as an indicator of the changing character of the group participants in the political process of our time. A well-established mode of identifying these participants speaks in terms of "class," and analyzes politics as a perpetual class struggle that continues until a class society produces its opposite, a class-less society. Class analysis is a useful intellectual tool in situations where a few large landholders confront a mass of peasants or serfs, and where they utilize institutions that perpetuate their monopoly of power, wealth, and other assets. The picture is complicated in societies where political power is disassociated from private wealth, but where a self-perpetuating elite of officials (civil, military, police) is able to impose itself and its successors on the body politic by monopolizing the means and instruments of selection. The picture is also complicated in societies with a science-based technology where an enormous number of groups are in shifting coalitions.

In these circumstances a more complex model than the traditional class image is needed. For example, the struggle for skill may be more significant than class analysis, since it emphasizes the differentiations that follow in a world in which a science-based technology is encompassing the globe. The specialists on scientific knowledge are divisible into many professional, vocation, and artistic fields; and they create new careers that cross-reference with the traditional specialists on violence, production, symbol manipulation, and diplomatic negotiation. Claims of social class or caste lose their efficacy as means of evoking the support required to wield power in our techno-scientific age.

NOTES

1. The writer characterized the world revolution of our time as "the permanent revolution of modernizing intellectuals" in H. D. Lasswell and Daniel Lerner (Eds.), *World Revolutionary Elites: Studies in Coercive Ideological Movements* Cambridge: MIT Press, 1965, pp. 80ff. The present distinction between earlier and contemporary intellectuals—contrasting scientists with more romantic or power-centered types—is a refinement of the fundamental construct.

2. See the writer's "Policy Sciences" in *The New International Encyclopedia of the Social Sciences.*

Chapter VIII

THE SIGNIFICANCE OF VICOS FOR

THE EMERGING POLICY SCIENCES

Harold D. Lasswell

INTRODUCTION

The Vicos experience is important for the strategy of acquiring and utilizing knowledge in modern civilization. Hence it goes much beyond the theory and practice of "modernization" or "development" and is to be understood as a step in elucidating the scope and method of the emerging policy sciences.

The term "policy sciences" was invented at about the same time that Holmberg and his original associates were becoming involved with the future of Vicos. The expression "the policy sciences" was a deliberate coinage designed to assist in identifying and fostering a change of emphasis, not only in the social and behavior sciences, but in the place of knowledge in the decision processes of society. The years between World War I and World War II had witnessed a rapid expansion of the social sciences in the United States, a development that was exemplified and facilitated by the establishment of the Social Science Research Council (SSRC) which provided a common instrument for the independent associations professionally engaged in anthropology, political science, economics, sociology, psychology and related disciplines. Funds for research and training programs were forthcoming from private foundations, notably the Rockefeller Foundation, and local councils were organized at several universities to strengthen work in the social sciences.

One of the principal aims of the founding fathers of the SSRC was to contribute to the policy forming and executing process at all levels of government. In order to accomplish this task it was obvious that the reputation of the disciplines in question must be improved. In turn this seemed to depend on raising the level of methodological competence and sophistication in every field. Some disciplines were further advanced than others in both reputation and competence in specific matters. Hence the principal immediate task of the SSRC seemed to be the upgrading of the social sciences as a whole by encouraging the diffusion of successful techniques from one field to another.

The economists and psychologists were the professional groups with the greatest degree of acceptance, and this appeared to depend on the synthesis of theory and empirical data. Anthropologists, though well-recognized by natural scientists, were poorly established as observers of culture. During the nineteen-twenties and thirties, however, they became influential among fellow students of society, partly for their techniques of field work, partly for a functionalist theory. Sociology, political science, and social psychology rapidly expanded their preoccupation with "empirical theory"—meaning a body of conceptual formulations that could guide experimental and field research. Many dynamic conceptions were generalized from psychiatry, especially psychoanalysis, and from the psychologist's theories of learning.

The upshot of these inter-war changes was a methodologically improved level of training and investigation by the scientists of man and society. Yet, in many respects, the evolution was disappointing. Somehow or other, the social sciences failed to connect with the policy-forming process of governmental or private organizations. The physical and biological sciences seemed to expand in acknowledged relevance as a simple function of their methodological improvement and quantitative growth. Thus engineering schools flourished side by side with graduate schools whose primary dedication was to "pure" science. Although schools of business, social work, or public administration multiplied in number, they were less than satisfactory in public or academic standing.

Policy Science Research Results—Hon. Edward M. Kennedy expressed respect for the accomplishments of the people of Vicos during his 1961 visit, presenting Vicos elected officials with John F. Kennedy inaugural medallions.

Evidently something was amiss about the way in which social scientists were conceiving their role. As might be predicted, the current interpretation took two different directions. For convenience we distinguish between the interpretation that advocated more of the same—more support for theory, training, and research of the previous period—and emphasis on policy. The principal point of the latter was far from the simple-minded demand that scientists ought to concern themselves with currently recognized problems of public policy. The policy sciences approach held that the scientific aspirations of social scientists at least were frustrated by their failure to think contextually and to apply a comprehensive problem-oriented methodology to the study of man. It was suggested that social scientists had partially emasculated themselves by seeking to apply an inappropriate version of natural science techniques to their mission.

As usual among intellectual movements, the policy science viewpoint was paralleled by many convergent formulations. In sociology as early as 1939 a set of lectures by Robert S. Lynd bore the title "Knowledge for What?" In economics there were calls for a restoration of the "political" in "political economy." In social psychology an early expression of dissatisfaction coupled with positive action was "The Society for the Psychological Study of Social Issues" (SPSSI). In anthropology the "applied anthropology" movement mobilized many "action-oriented" members of the profession.

The policy sciences approach was congenial to Holmberg because it offered a comprehensive theoretical and operational system; it stimulated him to go forward with his own efforts to find satisfactory ways of articulating the vision that inspired his professional career.(1) In turn the experience of working with Holmberg and his colleagues in connection with Vicos helped to clarify and advance the emerging theory and practice of the policy sciences. It may be useful to underline a few points in more detail.

THE DUAL SCOPE OF THE POLICY SCIENCES

Holmberg was acutely aware of the fact that current conceptions of the policy process were unsatisfactory. Hence one objective of the Vicos project was to increase our knowledge of decision processes in general, and of Vicos-type operations in particular. If the decision-makers of the community were to be more effective in post-Cornell years it would be necessary to achieve "intelligence" and "appraisal" functions that would keep Vicos in realistic touch with the larger environment. The policy scientist ought to possess enough knowledge *of* such a decision process to provide the guidance required to achieve the requisite level. Moreover, the policy scientist should be able to judge the type and source of knowledge that would be helpful *in* such a decision process. Although interconnected, the two tasks are separable, and call for the development of different social institutions.

For example, the task of evaluating the social consequences and policy implications of society's stock of knowledge at any given time calls for close cooperation with specialists on every field of physical, biological, and cultural science and art. It makes necessary the continuing projection of future lines of probable change, and the consideration of these developments in the light of postulated value goals relating to the social context. Given maps of the expected future it is feasible to examine the policy problems of a specific organization or individual in reference to these disciplined visions of reality. Obvious the map of the future (whether possible, probable, or preferred) must be disciplined by critical methods of procedure. Clearly, the policy orientation implies a set of methodological procedures that were unavailable when Holmberg initiated the Vicos project.

The dual requirement of the policy science approach point to the need for data gathering and interpreting procedures of a novel kind. Before we touch on these issues, let us summarize the theoretical dimensions of the policy sciences approach that found an answering resonance in Holmberg's experience and outlook.

CONTEXTUALITY, PROBLEM-ORIENTATION, MULTI-METHODOLOGY

Three terms are useful in describing the policy science (or dynamically functional) approach. The first term—contextuality—emphasizes the importance of locating any specific detail (or problem) in reference to the social process as a whole. The context comes into view in connection with every feature of problem-orientation.

Five intellectual tasks become explicitly relevant: the clarification of goal; the description of trend; the analysis of conditions; the projection of future developments; the invention, evaluation, and selection of policy alternatives. When formalized, these questions lead to complementary models for the guidance of inquiry. There are "preference models" (postulating general goals for the transformers of society); "historical models" (displaying the sequence of movement toward or away from goals); "analytic models" (identifying the factors in development and the patterns of inter-determination among the components of the changing system); "projective models" (giving estimates of the probable sequence of future events in the absence of further policy intervention); "action models" (exhibiting the strategies, and the net results of policy options). Before a generalized preference model can be applied, it is necessary to obtain information about trends, conditions and projections; and to select goal maximizing (optimalizing) options in the light of changing information.

By the expression "multi-methodology" is meant the pertinence to every problem of considering the possible contribution of *every* technique of theory formation, and of data gathering and processing. The study of Vicos called for every technique known to the cultural sciences: surveys, depth interviews, participant observation, and so on. The Vicos study also drew upon every pertinent procedure of the physical and biological sciences: blood-cell counts, bacterial tests, and so on.

VALUES AND
INSTITUTIONS

An intellectual consequence of the contextual orientation is to underline the importance of drawing a conceptual distinction between values and institutions. Among social scientists the economists are most experienced in handling these categories; hence when problems of development gained importance, economists were relatively well equipped to participate. As a rule they were unacquainted with the institutional details of tribal societies, of reviving ancient civilizations or of non-industrial nations. Yet the conception of wealth-shaping and sharing (of economic value and valuation) provided an abstract model of what to look for. However novel the institutional practices of a specific society might be, a search instrument was available with which to scan patterns, and to identify production, distribution, investment and consumption phases of the value process.

The categories of value and institution were helpful in stating theories of economic growth. Growth was conceptualized as a sequence of levels or stages, a mode of analysis that made it possible to think of development as progress toward a self-sustaining process of value accumulation. Some institutional assumptions were included in the model, since it was taken for granted that rapid value accumulation presupposes such important institutional changes as the introduction of technologies for assembling and processing the factors of production that rely on non-human sources of energy (like electricity). It was recognized that the choice of growth (in preference to non-growth) depends on changes of value demand and expectation that presently become stabilized as institutions. Economic institutions are patterns of practice relatively specialized to the shaping and sharing of wealth. Each practice is a relatively stable pattern of subjective events (perspectives) and of operations (behaviors). Conceived in the aggregate, the perspectives are the economic "myth" of society; the operations are the economic "technique" of managing men and resources in the value process.

Faced with the policy task of relating a single value-institution model to the social context, some economists of development began to be more explicit about the surrounding cultural situation. Thus W. W. Rostow introduced various "propensities": to develop fundamental science (physical and social); to apply science to economic ends; to accept innovation; to seek material advances; to consume; to have children.

The challenge of development caught political scientists in the midst of clarifying the distinction between the power value and the institutions of government, law, and politics. One result has been to accelerate the explicit use of these distinctions, and to identify the significant interconnections with the inclusive social context. Sociologists, like anthropologists, include general theorists of society and social process. The specialists on particular value-institution sectors (like the family or skill groups) tend to divide into social psychologists or social psychiatrists who study perspectives; and structural social scientists who investigate operational technique. Specialists on the small community—often rural sociologists—are trained to a configurative approach, and frequently contribute policy-oriented persons to the tasks of development.

Though some demographers, social biologists, and public health professionals have been involved in projects of modernization for years, they have not invariably considered health and safety in the context of all values. It is relatively rare to find a chemist, physicist, or geologist who sees his activities in an explicitly social frame of reference. Individual soil chemists, civil and electrical engineers, and mineralogists, for example, perform some of the roles of a policy scientist, such as suggesting knowledgeable personnel to advise, teach or execute. They do not, however, usually add much to the principal intellectual task of the policy scientists, that of understanding the process of decision.

From an early date the Vicos project offered data gathering facilities to any qualified scientist and attempted to fit every new fragment to the contextual map. Improved knowledge of the dynamics of decision depended mainly on policy-oriented social and behavioral scientists.

VALUE SHAPING AND SHARING
(A GENERALIZED MODEL)

The generalized model outlined here can be applied to a small social context like Vicos, to a national context like Peru, or to a trans-national configuration (regional or universal).(2) It begins by conceiving any social process, whatever the scale, as "man seeking to maximize value outcomes through institutions utilizing resources." During any period the flow of interaction is characterized as value shaping and sharing. Hence it is possible to summarize the aggregate result in terms of gross value outcome and of net; and therefore it is possible to arrive at a figure for net value accumulation (or disaccumulation). The pattern of aggregate value participation can be described as general or narrow. This mode of analysis can be applied to any social process. The model is contextualized in terms of eight possible value shaping and sharing sectors, with their specialized institutions.

The inclusive model:

VALUE SHAPING AND SHARING

Initial base values	Gross value outcome (less value inputs equal) Net value outcome	Net value accumulation (initial base values less depreciation plus net income less value enjoyment) and value participation (general, narrow)

Note: Values are power, enlightenment, wealth, well-being, skill, affection, respect, rectitude.

A few comments are offered here to suggest how this model relates to Vicos. A power outcome is defined as the act of giving or receiving (or withholding, rejecting) support in a decision (e.g. an election; in general, in community commitments sustained by severe sanctions, actual or potential). Political growth at Vicos was understood to be movement toward a stable decision process in which participation was widely shared, and in which the institutional practices involved characteristically led to realistic results. The main problem of the Vicos Project was to consolidate effective support for a decision process in harmony with these specifications.

The Project was not unconcerned with growth in terms of all other values and institutions at Vicos. These were viewed, however, as factors mainly affecting the power process. If a realistic decision capability could be attained, other changes could be left to the Vicosinos after the withdrawal of the Cornell personnel.

THE STRATEGY OF
PROTOTYPING

A policy-oriented approach is open to all the methods that have been invented to observe and process data. It also calls for somewhat distinctive ways of exploring a social context. The Vicos Project is of general interest in this connection, since it represents a somewhat distinctive methodology that is transferable to many other communities. The reference is to prototyping, whose characteristics can be clarified in terms of Vicos.

Prototyping is an active method of "manipulation." Hence it has more in common with experimentation or intervention than with the study of historical records or the making of spectator notes on activities that the scientist does not influence.

Prototyping is distinguishable from experimentation in several ways. A prototype studies an institutional *practice* as a total pattern. Thus the strategies of power devolution employed at Vicos are available for diffusion elsewhere. Experiments, on the other hand, are typically concerned with *factors* that are deliberately isolated, for purposes of study, from one or more institutional practices. For example, symbols of self-identification ("Vicos" equivalents) are part of several patterns; it is possible to design experiments to discover the factors that condition the occurrence of such symbols. Small group experiences can be arranged in which individuals identified with "Vicos" are in the minority or majority. Does the intensity of identification with Vicos remain the same? Or is a larger identity adopted? At what rate?

Prototyping is distinguished from intervention by the fact that scientists control prototypes and politicians control interventions. In the perspective of Peruvian politics the Vicos Project did not begin as an intervention. It was launched quietly out of the glare of intense partisan controversy. Since the main goal was recognized to be the advancement of knowledge, scientists were left in charge. Presumably this is unusual among programs of development, since scientists are kept in advisory or spectator roles.

Experiments or interventions can usually be divided into rather clear-cut stages that separate the preparatory activities involved in "introducing" an innovation from the "results." The results or responses usually begin at the moment when the experimenter or the intervener changes the environment of the subjects. In prototyping, however, it is often difficult to distinguish between preparations and results. Hence it is problematic when a change is "introduced." The point is important because it is not helpful to learn that a project has failed because the scientific staff did not believe in the possibility of successful innovation anyhow; or that the staff contained too many misfits, persons whose character traits would not permit them to play the roles assigned. Or further, that the project was never supported by enough significant figures in the community to get off the ground. Since institutional practices are patterns of both perspectives and operations, a practice must be acceptable to effective decision-makers before it can be said to be introduced.

The criteria of "introduction" must not be so strict that only successful results are possible, thus giving the innovators a built-in alibi that anything short of success means that, "like Christianity, the proposal has never been tried." When we stipulate than an innovation must be acceptable to effective decision-makers (beyond the project staff), unanimous optimism is not implied. It is enough if an effective majority of leaders is willing to participate in a change and believes that some advantages, at least, may not unreasonably be expected. From an early date Holmberg was able to elicit from among the elders of Vicos an attitude of cautious willingness to enlarge the scope of their responsibilities.

Prototyping brings the scientific observer explicitly into the context of interaction. As the strategy of prototyping is refined, I predict that self-observation will be emphasized further. More is required than for a field investigator to take note of what he and others said and did, or even to describe in his diary his fluctuating moods and images about the undertaking. Investigators can profitably be encouraged to adapt free-association technique to the task of bringing covert as well as overt moods and images into the record. As a result the scientist will undoubtedly modify himself in the process, seeking to acquire more effective strategy for dealing with himself and others. Group self-observation (only incidentally for therapeutic purposes) is also indicated. Prototyping is part of the insight revolution that has been accelerated in our civilization by the techniques of free association (individual, group) for examining subjective events. Cultivation of the self calls ultimately for a continual strategy in which objectives and performance are subject to planned innovation, followed by appraisal and further innovation.

Prototyping is not identical with most of what is usually meant by the term "pilot study." Usually a pilot study is planned in detail. A creative feature of prototyping is that, although objectives are relatively explicit, many ambiguities remain. Hence an aim of any prototypical study is to devise a better strategic program.

The interplay between prototyping and other methods for the advancement of knowledge is complex. The Vicos prototype depended in part on transferring instruments and techniques from experimental situations to the field (e.g. psychological tests, blood typing). In turn, Vicos stimulated further experimentation. (One example is the search for simplified ways of studying "self-other" perceptions.)

It is understandable that prototypes stimulate programs of field study whose design is fully experimental (with "manipulated" and "control" groups). No scientific observer can fail to recognize that much is to be learned by adapting the strategy employed at Vicos to other communities. What would be the result in villages with less equal access to power, wealth, and other values? Or with most adults employed in distant jobs? Or with a different distribution of personality patterns?(3)

Although the Vicos Project has inspired other programs, it may not be possible in every case to adhere to a strict experimental design or even to explore new prototypes. Political considerations may gain the upper hand and interfere with the advancement of knowledge. (However, official interventions will undoubtedly continue to be influenced by the Vicos prototype.)

THE CONTINUING SEMINAR POLICY TECHNIQUE

The prototyping procedure has been greatly clarified in connection with Vicos. Another technique—the continuing policy (or decision) seminar—has also benefited from the experience of those involved at Vicos. One of the earliest explicit seminars was installed at Stanford in 1954-55 as a means of aiding Holmberg in his reassessment of the project as a whole. Cooperating with Holmberg were a political scientist, a psychologist, and an economist. They met regularly for the academic year in the same environment and developed a chart room to provide an auxiliary to recall and to effect the concept of systematic study.

The details of the continuing seminar technique have been described elsewhere and need not detain us here. It is relevant to point out that no specific pattern included in the technique is unique. As instruments of instruction seminars are supposed to invite original contributions by every member; and this feature is continued. Some seminars have continued for a long time, and have benefited by recalling their former active members. The present technique incorporates this feature and adds the requirement that everyone agree to continue actively for an indefinite (or at least an extended) future. Individuals may change, but the central focus does not; and the charts, maps and other material act cumulatively.(4)

The continuing policy seminar is concerned with working out the implications of the contextual, problem-oriented, multi-method approach. Thus the audio-visual, computer, or library features are not the most important. The chief aim is to affect judgment and imagination by controlling the focus of attention.

By referring to the continuing policy technique as an instructional instrument we are underplaying the versatile tasks to which it is adaptable. Research guidance, for example, is one significant function. Indeed the Vicos seminar at Stanford was itself a research, not an instructional, project. Holmberg was concerned with making up his mind how to act in the future toward Vicos, and this was conceived as a contribution to fundamental enlightenment in the growth of anthropology and related disciplines. The fundamental strategy was to guide the focus of attention of the participants by definite *procedures* and conceptions of relevant *content.* These were suggested by the contextual, problem-oriented, multiple method character of the inclusive approach.

The Vicos experience adds another dimension to the policy seminar technique by pointing the way to its incorporation in the decision process of any organization, governmental or private. Some features of the decision seminar technique were introduced at Vicos at various stages. Project directors were explicit in describing the decision process itself, hoping in this way to provide intellectual tools that would improve the problem-solving capability of the community. To a modest extent visual aids were incorporated into the proceedings of decision-making bodies and the setting in which they functioned. The experience gained has been helpful in devising prototypical interventions elsewhere.

We have referred to the use of the continuing policy seminar in value-institution activities specialized respectively to skill, enlightenment, and power. On reflection it is evident that the procedure is adapted to the policy process of every sector in the social process, hence to the institutions specialized to wealth, well-being, affection, respect, and rectitude.

TIMELINESS

Reference was made at the beginning of this volume to the restlessness of young people who are in search of relevance. We believe that the approach described here is especially pertinent to the aspirations of all who would innovate fundamental changes in the world community as a whole or in any component context. The aspiration toward relevance implies the will to grasp and change reality. Programs of this kind can be expedited by the spread of a technique that builds self-correction into its every application.

Such is the legacy of Holmberg and the early phases of the Vicos experience. Power reorientation is the message of dynamic functionalism in anthropology and of the general policy science approach to knowledge, man, and society. The coalition of peasants, scientists, and politicians is a sample of the coalitions that harness knowledge and power, and hopefully innovate or strengthen institutions that expedite the patterns of value shaping and sharing required by the conception of human dignity.

NOTES

1. See his essay on "Dynamic Functionalism" which was prepared in 1958 and distributed to his graduate students at Cornell, chapter 11 of A. A. Rogow (Ed.), *Politics, Personality and Social Science in the Twentieth Century.* Chicago: University of Chicago Press, 1969.

2. Holmberg critically evaluated this general model which is published by the writer and Holmberg as Chapter 8, "Toward a General Theory of Directed Value Accumulation and International Development" in R. Braibanti (Ed.), *Political and Administrative Development.* Durham, N.C.: Duke University Press, 1969. The original paper was to have been accompanied by a detailed empirical exemplification prepared by Holmberg utilizing data from Vicos. Illness prevented completion of the material.

3. A critical discussion of prototyping in reference to the context of a mental hospital is found in the last chapter of Robert Rubenstein and H. D. Lasswell, *The Sharing of Power in a Psychiatric Hospital.* New Haven: Yale University Press, 1966. Like the Vicos Project the innovations at the Yale Psychiatric Institute were concerned with the strategy of "devolution," or power sharing on a wider scale.

4. For more detail see the writer's treatment, "The Continuing Decision Seminar as a Technique of Instruction," Policy Sciences, vol. 2, no. 1 (1971), pp. 43-57.

APPENDICES

VICOS AREA AND

POPULATION GROWTH

J. Oscar Alers

Before purchasing Chancos, Vicos comprised a total area of about 43,750 acres.(1) Approximately 8,400 acres consisted of virtually uninhabited and unusable wasteland. Nearly 6,700 acres were high-altitude pastures. The inhabited and cultivated area of the estate consisted of 3,700 acres, or less than six square miles, of arable land—not even one-tenth of the entire estate. The area economically exploited by tree farming, grazing, and all forms of cultivation amounts to some 10,400 acres or 16.2 square miles.

The 1952 Cornell Peru Project census enumerated a total population of 1,703 Quechua-speaking Indians. They lived at altitudes above 9,500 feet above sea level on farmsteads scattered across the steeper portions of the economically exploited area of the hacienda at the rate of 105 persons per square mile (see Table 1). By 1963 the number of Vicosinos had increased to 2,102. This rise of 23 percent meant a growth rate of 1.5 percent per year occurred during the 1952-63 period. Since the land base remained constant, Vicos correspondingly rose to 129 persons per square mile in population density on the economically exploited area.

The mean number of individuals per Vicos household remained fairly constant between 1952 and 1963, even though the total population increased. This stability resulted from a 27

Editor's Note: This appendix has been adapted from J. O. Alers, "Population, Attitudes, and Development: The Case of Vicos." Cornell University Ph.D. Thesis, 1966, pp. 39-54.

Table 1. VICOS AREA OF ECONOMIC EXPLOITATION, POPU-
LATION, AND POPULATION DENSITY AT BEGINNING AND
END OF CORNELL PERU PROJECT

Year	Economically Exploited Area (Square Miles)	Enumerated Population	Persons per Square Mile
1952	16.2	1,703	105
1963	16.2	2,102	129

Table 2. MEAN NUMBER OF PERSONS PER VICOS HOUSEHOLD

Year	Enumerated Population	Number of Households	Persons per Household
1952	1,703	363	4.69
1963	2,102	461	4.56

Table 3. VICOS POPULATION ESTIMATES AND ANNUAL
RATES OF POPULATION GROWTH FROM 1593 TO 1963(2)

Year	Estimated Population	Annual Rate of Growth (percent)
1593	99	–
1774	301	0.6
1848	513	0.7
1876	682	1.2
1940	1,570	1.3
1952	1,785	1.1
1963	2,102	1.5

percent rise in the number of households between 1952 and 1963. Households were started, in other words, at a faster rate than the population increased—a demographic trend leading to a dearth of possessions in many households by 1963, reflected in some of the tables in this volume.

Five estimates of Vicos population before 1952 are presented in Table 3, with annual rates of growth that occurred between the dates for which estimates are available. Apparently the annual population growth rate rose rather slowly yet steadily from 1593 to 1848, then increased rapidly after that time, and declined slightly after 1940, only to rise again after 1952. Taking into account the population and territory annexed at Chancos, there will be 2,514 Vicosinos distributed over the economically exploited area at a rate of 153 persons per square mile by 1975, if the 1952-63 growth rate of 1.5 percent is sustained over the succeeding 11 years.

Whether the 1952-63 growth rate rises, declines, or remains about the same depends partly on fertility and mortality trends. The civil registry of the District of Marcará—of which Vicos is a political subdivision—yielded data on the number of births and deaths for the years 1952 and 1963 presented in Table 4. Projecting the enumerated census populations forward six months at the growth rate of 1.5 percent per year produced midyear population estimates for this calculation.

Table 4. CRUDE BIRTH RATES, DEATH RATES, AND RATES OF NATURAL POPULATION INCREASE AT VICOS

Year	Midyear Population Estimate (a)	Number of		Crude Rate		Rate of Natural Increase (b − c/a) 1,000
		Births (b)	Deaths (c)	Birth (b/a) 1,000	Death (c/a) 1,000	
1952	1,798	82	26	45.6	14.5	31.1
1963	2,118a	119	52	56.2	24.6	31.6

a. The 63 inhabitants gained by the acquisition of Chancos are excluded from this figure.

Table 5. RATE OF VICOS INFANT MORTALITY

Year	Number of Live Births (a)	Number of Deaths in First Year of Life (b)	Infant Mortality (b/a) 1,000
1952	82	10	122.0
1963	119	17	142.9

Table 6. VICOS CHILD-WOMAN RATIOS(3)

Year	Number of Children 0-4 Years of Age (a)	Number of Women 15-44 Years of Age (b)	Child-Woman Ratio (a/b) 1,000
1952	270	371	728
1963	312	485	643

Table 7. VICOS GENERAL FERTILITY RATES

Year	Number of Women 15-44 Years of Age (Midyear Estimate) (a)	Number of Live Births (b)	General Fertility Rate (b/a) 1,000
1952	375	82	219
1963	490	119	243

There were no serious epidemics in Vicos in either 1952 or 1963. The fact that Vicos has a very young population—as will be seen in the subsequent data—and the lack of epidemics probably account for the rather low death rates. Improved registration surely accounts for some of the increase in birth and death rates. Since it is not likely that there was a differential registration of births and deaths, the rise in the rate of natural increase is probably the most reliable index of the actual trend.

The Vicos infant mortality rate calculated in Table 5 is high compared to a rate of 103.4 for all Peru in 1960.(4)

Defining the Vicos fertility trend is complicated by the decline in fertility between 1952 and 1963 as measured by the child-woman ratio—that is, the ratio of children under five to women in the child-bearing years (see Table 6). This finding conflicts with the observed increase in the birth rate.

The Vicos child-woman ratio appears to be subject to extreme fluctuations caused by very large annual variations in the number of deaths in early childhood.

A birth rate of 56.2 and a child-woman ratio of 643 are both rather high rates compared to Peru as a whole with its 1960 birth rate of 32.5. The Vicos fertility prospect is for an increasing growth rate. This prediction is bolstered by two kinds of evidence. On the one hand, the number of Vicosino women of child-bearing age increased by 2.3 percent per year between 1952 and 1963, a faster rate than that of the whole population. Secondly, general fertility rate also increased between 1952 and 1963, as indicated in Table 7.(5) It is a more direct measure of fertility than either the crude birth rate or the child-woman ratio.

Most arable land in Vicos has been and still is divided into tiny subsistence gardening plots, so the rising population creates increased pressure on land resources. Recent changes in the mode of property inheritance have contributed to this problem. The prevailing custom under the traditional hacienda system was patrilineal ultimogeniture, whereby the landed property of a father went to his youngest son, although provision was made for the latter's elder brothers to assume control of the land in case their father died during the childhood of the youngest son. Since Cornell Peru Project intervention, Vicosinos are accept-

Table 8. MEDIAN AGE OF VICOS POPULATION BY SEX

Year	Male	Female	Total
1952	17.5	21.3	19.4
1963	18.0	20.7	18.3

Table 9. VICOS SEX RATIOS BY MAJOR AGE GROUPS

	1952			1963		
	Number of		Sex Ratio	Number of		Sex Ratio
Age Group	Males (a)	Females (b)	(a/b) 100	Males (a)	Females (b)	(a/b) 100
Total	804	898	89.5	990	1,107	89.4
0-14	351	341	102.9	421	416	101.2
15-44	347	371	90.9	448	485	92.4
44+	106	186	56.4	121	206	58.7

Table 10. VICOS DEPENDENCY RATIO

	Age Group				Dependency
Year	0-14 (a)	15-64 (b)	65+ (c)	Total (d)	Ratio (a = c/b) 100
1952	692	942	68	1,702	80.7
1963	838	1,178	81	2,097	77.6

ing—though not without considerable conflict—the principle that all adult sons have a right to a parcel of their father's land. This principle has been extended during the past few years to daughters as well.(6) In this context the Vicos community council is now often required to resolve interfamilial as well as intrafamilial disputes over land ownership.(7)

The changed authority over rules of inheritance in a settlement with a growing population may be expected to generate increased conflicts over property. One may anticipate that family-held plots will be even further fractionated.

AGE AND SEX COMPOSITION
OF THE POPULATION

An assessment of likely future Vicos population trends must take into account the age and sex structure of its population. Since population growth depends basically on the supply of children from whom future parents can be drawn, a young population is likely to grow at a faster rate than an old one. Where marriage is monogamous as it is in Vicos, a population with an equal number of men and women theoretically allows every woman to marry and bear children. Where women are overabundant relative to men, the reproductive potential of some portion of them will likely never be fully exploited. Vicos had a very young population in 1952, and by 1963 it had become even younger, as indicated in Table 8. The median age of Vicos females has remained consistently higher, however, than that of males.

On the other hand, a salient feature of the Vicos population is a dearth of males relative to females. The sex ratio remained virtually unaltered between 1952 and 1963, not only for the whole population, but also within the three major age groups, as shown in Table 9. This ratio steadily declines over the major age groups, so that there are almost twice as many Vicosino women as men over 45. The ratio of males to females is not quite so low during the child-bearing years (15 to 44), yet nearly one in every ten women in this age group will find it difficult if not impossible to acquire a mate in Vicos.

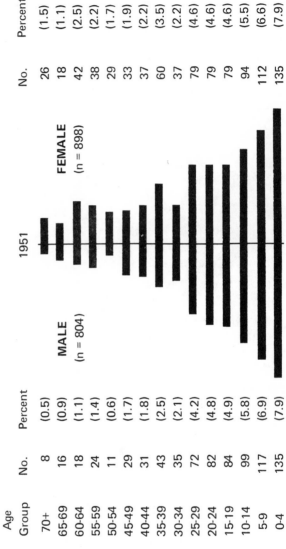

1951

MALE (n = 804)   **FEMALE** (n = 898)

Percent

Age Group	No.	Percent	No.	Percent
70+	8	(0.5)	26	(1.5)
65-69	16	(0.9)	18	(1.1)
60-64	18	(1.1)	42	(2.5)
55-59	24	(1.4)	38	(2.2)
50-54	11	(0.6)	29	(1.7)
45-49	29	(1.7)	33	(1.9)
40-44	31	(1.8)	37	(2.2)
35-39	43	(2.5)	60	(3.5)
30-34	35	(2.1)	37	(2.2)
25-29	72	(4.2)	79	(4.6)
20-24	82	(4.8)	79	(4.6)
15-19	84	(4.9)	79	(4.6)
10-14	99	(5.8)	94	(5.5)
5-9	117	(6.9)	112	(6.6)
0-4	135	(7.9)	135	(7.9)

Age Group	No.	Percent		No.	Percent
70+	11	(0.5)		26	(1.2)
65-69	18	(0.9)		26	(1.2)
60-64	8	(0.4)		29	(1.4)
55-59	22	(1.0)		36	(1.7)
50-54	25	(1.2)		36	(1.7)
45-49	38	(1.8)		53	(2.5)
40-44	30	(1.4)		40	(1.9)
35-39	74	(3.5)		61	(2.9)
30-34	57	(2.7)		72	(3.4)
25-29	84	(4.0)		85	(4.1)
20-24	98	(4.7)		117	(5.6)
15-19	104	(5.0)		109	(5.2)
10-14	124	(5.9)		119	(5.7)
5-9	148	(7.1)		135	(6.4)
0-4	150	(7.2)		162	(7.7)

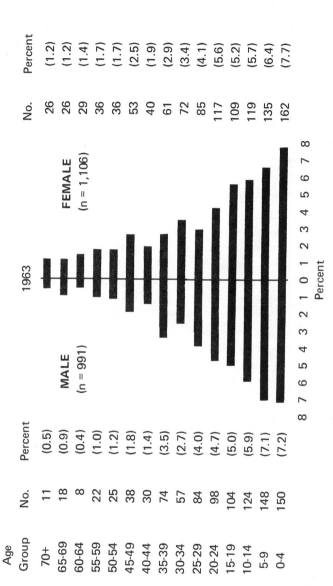

MALE (n = 991)

FEMALE (n = 1,106)

1963

Percent

8 7 6 5 4 3 2 1 0 1 2 3 4 5 6 7 8

Figure 1. FREQUENCY AND PERCENTAGE DISTRIBUTIONS OF THE POPULATION OF VICOS, BY AGE AND SEX, 1951 AND 1963

Such data demonstrate the existence of a major drain on the manpower supply, particularly for work on the community farm enterprise. Yet the burden of dependency borne by the active population remained almost constant between 1952 and 1963, as shown by a "dependency ratio" in Table 10—that is, the proportion of dependent children and dependent aged for each 100 persons in the most productive age-group.

The sex and age distribution of the Vicos population given in Figure 1 presents a detailed picture of the past history, the ᴄurrent structure, and possible future trends of this population. The most salient characteristic of the two pyramids is their general shape. This clearly portrays an expanding population, with its broad base made up of the youngest age groups from which future parents will be drawn.

Two particularly striking breaks in the regularity of the distributions occur which require explanation. One comes in the five-year age brackets from 40 to 54 in the 1952 pyramid— particularly in the upper five-year bracket of this category. The other irregularity appears in the five-year age group 30-34 for the same year. These two breaks should—and for the most part do—carry through into the 1963 pyramid in the age group corresponding to the eleven-year lapse in time between the two censuses.(8) In other words, the 1952 age group 50-54 moves up mostly into 1963 age group 60-64, while the 1952 age group 30-34 aged into the 1963 category of persons 40-44. These two groups include individuals born between 1899 and 1903, and between 1919 and 1923, respectively.

Age-specific losses of the magnitude shown by these two groups suggest that they were caused by past epidemics. Although mortality statistics for Vicos remain largely to be compiled, five specific epidemics stand out in the memory of informants.

First, and by all accounts the most severe, was a typhus epidemic that evidently occurred between 1905 and 1915. If 1910 be taken as the most likely date, losses in the 40-54 age group depicted in the 1952 pyramid are largely explained, as the epidemic would have primarily affected children under 15 years of age at that time.

Vicosinos appear not to recollect an epidemic during 1919 or immediately afterwards that might account for notable age-specific attribution rate in the 30-34 age group in the 1952 pyramid. Conceivably this loss stemmed from a famine during this period, or a natural disaster or forced mass migration at some later time. The world influenza epidemic of 1918-19(9) seems a much more likely cause for these losses.

The second epidemic recalled by Vicosinos is described as influenza. It occurred during 1951 and was confined mainly to children. This helps to account for the losses experienced by the 10-19 age group in the 1963 pyramid, but it does not explain why mortality was mostly confined to females. Some of that mortality can be attributed to the third remembered epidemic, identified as measles, which took place between 1955 and 1957. It did differentially affect female children. That epidemic also explains the attrition rate among females aged 5-9 in 1963.

The fourth remembered epidemic brought death to about 60 children, mostly under the age of five, in 1959. Whooping cough combined with measles in this double epidemic, accounting for the losses in the 0-4 age group in 1963. Again, one cannot explain why the loss was so great among males.

An additional irregularity in the 1963 pyramid appears in attrition of males in the 30-34 age group. Increased out-migration following the Cornell Peru Project leasing of the hacienda in December of 1951 probably best explains this phenomenon, since emigration had been suppressed until that time by the heavy labor obligations of the hacienda system.(10)

The effects of a fifth remembered epidemic do not appear in the two population pyramids since it occurred in January of 1964. The disease agents were whooping cough and measles, mainly affecting children under five years old. Estimates of mortality in this age group ran as high as 70 children. Almost no infants under one year survived. The effect of this epidemic episode on the growth rate of the Vicos population will be felt for the next forty-odd years.

NOTES

1. Gary S. Vescelius, "The Area of Vicos," 1965 (typescript), and H. F. Dobyns, "Monetary Credit and Transculturation." Cornell Peru Project Papers read before the American Anthropological Association 1961 Annual Meeting. Lima: Cornell Peru Project, 1962, p. 12.

Peasants, Power, and Applied Social Change

2. Population estimates derive from: 1593–Toribio A. de Mogroviejo, "Libro de Visitas, 1593," Revista del Archivo Nacional del Peru, Tomo 1, Entrega 1, 1920, pp. 64-65. Vázquez, "La Antropologia Cultural y Nuestro Problema del Indio: Vicos, un Caso de Antropologia Aplicada," Perú Indígena, vol. 2, nos. 5 and 6, 1952, p. 36. 1848–Peru, Ministerio de Hacienda y Comercio, "Matricula de Indigenas de la Provincia de Huaylas, Tomo I," Documento No. 367 Archivo del Ministerio, 1848. 1876–Peru, Ministerio de Gobierno, Resumen del Censo General de Habitantes del Peru Hecho en 1876. Lima: Imprenta del Estado, 1878, pp. 14-16. 1940–Peru, Ministerio de Hacienda y Comercio, Censo Nacional de Poblacion de 1940, Vol. III. Lima: Imprenta Torres Aguirre, 1944, p. 115. 1952–Cornell Peru Project census of Vicos, corrected 5 percent for underenumeration. 1963–Cornell Peru Project census of Vicos.

Annual rates of growth were calculated by fitting the population estimates to a logistic curve of growth as described, for example, in G. W. Barclay, Techniques of Population Analysis. New York: John Wiley, 1958, p. 207.

3. One female in 1952 and two males and three females in 1963 have been excluded for lack of age data from this and all subsequent tables where age appears as a variable.

4. Center of Latin American Studies, University of California, Los Angeles, Statistical Abstract of Latin America, 1962. Los Angeles: 1963, p. 17.

5. That Vicosino women are concerned about their frequent pregnancies is signalled by the fact that they frequently approach women visitors to seek information concerning modern birth control methods.

6. M. C. Vázquez, "The Castas: Unilinear Kin Groups in Vicos, Peru." Ithaca: Cornell University Department of Anthropology Comparative Studies of Cultural Change, 1964, p. 34.

7. A. R. Holmberg, and M. C. Vázquez, "The Castas: Unilineal Kin Groups in Vicos, Peru," Ethnology, vol. 5, no. 3, (1966), p. 300.

8. That they do increases the degree of confidence that may be placed in the consistency of the data.

9. A. H. Gale, Epidemic Diseases. London: Penguin Books, 1959, pp. 42-50.

10. M. C. Vázquez, "Proceso de migracion en la comunidad de Vicos, Ancash," in H. F. Dobyns and M. C. Vázquez (Eds.), Migracion e Integracion en el Peru. Lima: Editorial Estudios Andinos, 1963, pp. 95-96.

LOCAL AND NATIONAL POWER STRUCTURE

IN RELATION TO VICOS, 1951-1966:

AN EXPLANATORY NOTE

Paul L. Doughty

In order for the reader to conceptualize the various dimensions of the society which enveloped Vicos and how the structural relationships changed in the fifteen-year period described in this volume, three diagrams of power relationships have been constructed. These schematic presentations show a number of interrelationships in the form of structural characteristics involving Vicos and the process of change.

The power continuum is expressed in these diagrams by the wedge bearing upon the people of Vicos. The relative amount of power accessible to individuals and institutions is broadest at the top and diminishes to a point at the bottom. The position of the statuses and institutions illustrates the functional hierarchy relative to power: those positions which intersect the continuum exercise the greatest power, and those furthest away and not directly attached to it, the least. Strength and pervasiveness of power is represented by the hierarchical ordering of positions. In addition, the official, legal statuses and institutions are shown (on the left) in contrast to the extra-official and informal ones (on the right) in terms of their relative positions of dominance vis-à-vis the Vicosinos.

Local and National Power Structure from the Vicos Perspective, 1950

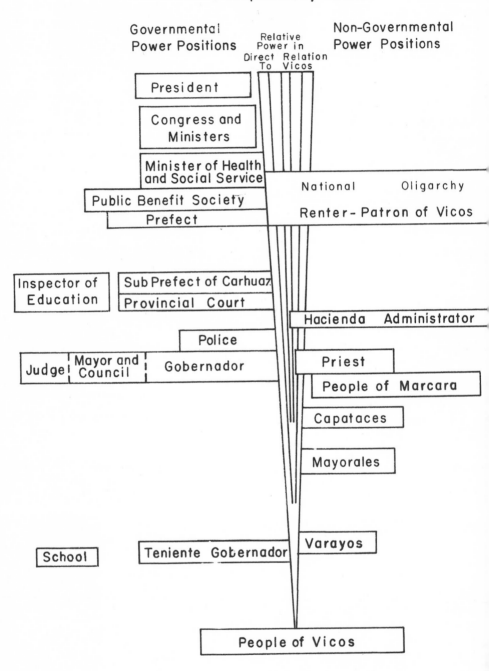

Governmental
Power Positions

Relative
Power in
Direct Relation
To Vicos

Non-Governmental
Power Positions

President

Congress and
Ministers

Minister of Health
and Social Service

Public Benefit Society

Prefect

National   Oligarchy

Renter- Patron of Vicos

Inspector of
Education

Sub Prefect of Carhuaz

Provincial Court

Hacienda   Administrator

Police

Judge | Mayor and
        Council

Gobernador

Priest

People of Marcara

Capataces

Mayorales

School

Teniente Gobernador

Varayos

People of Vicos

During Course of Cornell
Peru Project, 1952-1962

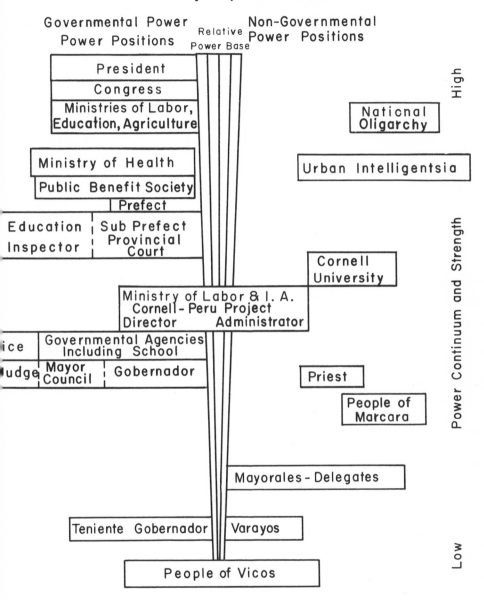

Local and National Power Structure and Strengt
from the Vicos Perspective,1966

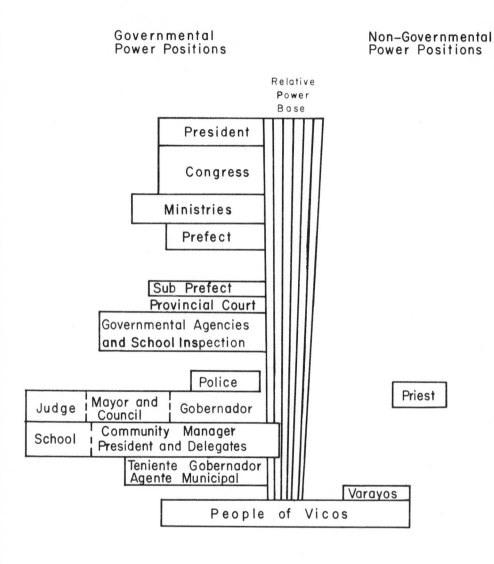

Governmental
Power Positions

Non-Governmental
Power Positions

Relative
Power
Base

President

Congress

Ministries

Prefect

Sub Prefect
Provincial Court

Governmental Agencies
and School Inspection

Police

Judge | Mayor and Council | Gobernador

School | Community Manager President and Delegates

Teniente Gobernador
Agente Municipal

Priest

Varayos

People of Vicos

By comparing the three figures, the reader will notice the changing juxtaposition of the various institutional variables and the process by which, through the intervention of the Cornell Peru Project "umbrella," some of these were realigned and others removed altogether from the picture. In the third figure the reader sees a representation of the situation in 1966. Particularly noteworthy at this stage is the shortening of the social distances between Vicos and the wielders of power affecting the community, the participation of Vicosinos in the exercise of power, and the removal or displacement of informal and non-governmental elements from positions of dominance over Vicos lives.

BIBLIOGRAPHY

In addition to references cited by chapter authors, this bibliography lists published scientific and Cornell Peru Project administrative reports concerning Vicos, shown by asterisk (*).

ALERS, J. OSCAR
1965a "The Quest for Well-Being." American Behavioral Scientist, 8 (March) 18-22.
1965b "Population and Development in a Peruvian Community." Journal of Inter-American Studies, 7 (October) 422-48.
*1965c "Población y Desarrollo en una Comunidad Peruana." Lima: Proyecto Perú-Cornell, Folleto 4.
1966 "Population, Attitudes, and Development: The Case of Vicos." Ithaca: Cornell University Ph.D. Thesis.
*1970a "Interviewer Effects on Survey Response in an Andean Estate." International Journal of Comparative Sociology, 11 (September) 208-19.
*1970b "Reliability of Survey Techniques in Highland Peru." Rural Sociology, 35 (December) 500-11.
ALERS, J. OSCAR, MARIO C. VAZQUEZ, ALLAN R. HOLMBERG and HENRY F. DOBYNS
1965 "Human Freedom and Geographic Mobility." Current Anthropology, 6 (June) 336.
ALLEN, FRED H., Jr.
*1958 "Inheritance of the Diego (Dia) Blood-Group Factor." American Journal of Human Genetics, 10 (March) 64-67.
BARCLAY, G. W.
1958 Techniques of Population Analysis. New York: John Wiley.
BARNETT, CLIFFORD R.
1960 "Indian Protest Movements in Callejón de Huaylas." Ithaca: Cornell University Ph.D. Thesis.
BARNETT, H. G.
1953 Innovation. New York: McGraw-Hill.

Peasants, Power, and Applied Social Change

BEAGLEHOLE, ERNEST
1955 "Evaluation Techniques for Induced Technological Change." International Social Science Bulletin, 7.
BIERSTEDT, R.
1950 "An Analysis of Social Power." American Sociological Review, 15.
BLANCHARD, WILLIAM C.
1953 "Tercer Informe del Proyecto Perú-Cornell." Perú Indígena, 5 (Diciembre) 153-59.
1954 "Estudio y Experimento Antropológico en la Hacienda Vicos." Revista del Museo Nacional, 23: 174-81.
1955 "Report of the Peru-Cornell Project 1954." Boletín Indigenista, 15 (Setiembre) 274-85.
1956 "Peru-Cornell Project Report, 1955." Boletín Indigenista, 16 (Agosto) 202-15.
BLOCH, MARC
1964 Feudal Society. Chicago: University of Chicago Press.
BOWMAN, M. J.
1964 "Perspectives on Education and Development." International Development Review, 6.
CACERES DE FUENTES, CARMEN
n.d. "Encuesta Alimentaria en Diez Familias de Vicos, Julio 1961." Lima: Servicio Cooperativo Inter-Americano de Salud Pública. Typescript.
CANCIAN, FRANK
1965 Economics and Prestige in a Mayan Community. Stanford: Stanford University Press.
CARTWRIGHT, DORWIN
1959 "A Field Theoretical Conception of Power," in D. Cartwright (ed.), Studies in Social Power. Ann Arbor: University of Michigan.
COLLAZOS CHIRIBOGA, CARLOS, HILDA S. WHITE, RUTH L. HUENEMANN, EMMA REY, PHILIP L. WHITE, AURORA CASTELLANOS, ROSA BENITES, YOLANDA BRAVO, ANGELICA LOO, IRMA MOSCOSO, CARMEN CACERES y AIDA DIESELDORFF
1954 "Dietary Surveys in Peru—Chacan and Vicos, Rural Communities in the Peruvian Andes." Journal of the American Dietetic Association, 30 (December).
COLLAZOS CHIRIBOGA, CARLOS, IRMA MOSCOSO F., YOLANDA BRAVO DE RUEDA, AURORA CASTELLANOS, CARMEN CACERES DE FUENTES, AMALIA ROCA y ROBERT C. BRADFIELD
1960 "La Alimentación y el Estado de Nutrición en el Perú." Lima: Anales de la Facultad de Medicina, 43.
COLLIER, JOHN and MARY
1957 "An Experiment in Applied Anthropology." Scientific American, 196 (January) 37-45.

CHUECA SOTOMAYOR, CARLOS
n.d. "Participación del SCIPA en la Comunidad de Vicos." Typescript.
1961 "La Comunidad de Vicos (Ancash), Su Integración á la Vida
Nacional." Typescript.
DALTON, GEORGE
1969 "Theoretical Issues in Economic Anthropology." Current Anthropology, 10 (February).
DEBEAUVAIS, M.
1962 "The Concept of Human Capital." UNESCO International Social
Science Journal, 14.
DIAZ LIRA, GUILLERMO, JUAN LEON, CATO LUBE y ABNER
MONTALVO
*1959 "Evaluación de una película en una población andina del Perú."
Boletín de la Oficina Sanitaria Panamericana, 42 (Diciembre)
520-25.
DOBYNS, HENRY F.
1951 "Blunders with Bolsas." Human Organization 10 (Fall) 25-32.
*1961 "El Proyecto Perú-Cornell." Perú Indígena, 9 (Enero-Junio)
125-30.
1962a "Monetary Credit and Transculturation." Paper Read before 1961
Annual Meeting, American Anthropological Association. Lima:
Proyecto Perú-Cornell. Mimeo.
1962b "Eleventh Report of the Cornell Peru Project." Ithaca: Cornell Peru
Project. Mimeo.
1964 The Social Matrix of Peruvian Indigenous Communities. Ithaca:
Cornell University Department of Anthropology, Cornell Peru
Project.
*1965 "The Strategic Importance of Enlightenment and Skill for Power."
American Behavioral Scientist, 8 (March) 23-27.
*1966 "The Struggle for Land in Peru: The Hacienda Vicos Case."
Ethnohistory, 13 (Summer-Fall) 97-122.
DOBYNS, HENRY F., PAUL L. DOUGHTY and ALLAN R. HOLMBERG
1965 Measurement of Peace Corps Program Impact in the Peruvian
Andes: Final Report. Ithaca: Cornell University Department of
Anthropology.
DOBYNS, HENRY F., ALLAN R. HOLMBERG, MORRIS E. OPLER and
LAURISTON SHARP
1968 Methods for Analyzing Cultural Change. Ithaca: Cornell Univer-
sity Department of Anthropology.
DOBYNS, HENRY F., CARLOS MONGE M., y MARIO C. VAZQUEZ
*1961 "Desarrollo Comunal y Regional. Experimento Conjunto del
Proyecto Perú-Cornell." Perú Indígena, 9 (Enero-Junio) 133-39.

DOBYNS, HENRY F., and MARIO C. VAZQUEZ
1964 "The Cornell Peru Project: Bibliography and Personnel." Ithaca: Cornell University Department of Anthropology, Cornell Peru Project Pamphlet 2.
DOUGHTY, PAUL L.
*1965a "The Inter-Relationship of Power, Respect, Affection, and Rectitude in Vicos." American Behavioral Scientist, 8 (March) 13-17.
1965b "Pitfalls and Progress in the Peruvian Sierra," in R. B. Textor (ed.), Cultural Frontiers of the Peace Corps. Cambridge: M.I.T. Press.
DOUGHTY, PAUL L. with the collaboration of MARY F. DOUGHTY
*1968 Huaylas, An Andean District in Search of Progress. Ithaca: Cornell University Press.
FARROMEQUE D., C. A.
1959 "Informe sobre el crédito agrícola supervisado, campaña 1957-58." Perú Indígena, 8 (Enero-Junio) 253 ff.
FINE, NORMAN L.
1960 "Coca Chewing: A Social versus a Nutritional Interpretation." New York: Columbia University Department of Anthropology. Mimeo.
FOSTER, PHILIP
1965 Education and Social Change in Ghana. Chicago: University of Chicago Press.
FRIED, JACOB
1960 "Enfermedad y Organización Social." Etnología y Arqueología (Lima) 38-49.
1962 "Social Organization and Personal Security in a Peruvian Hacienda Indian Community: Vicos." American Anthropologist, 64 (August) 771-80.
GALE, A. H.
1959 Epidemic Diseases. London: Penguin Books.
GHERSI BARRERA, HUMBERTO
1959, 1960, 1961 "El Indígena y el Mestizo en la Comunidad de Marcará." Revista del Museo Nacional (Lima) 28: 118-88; 29: 48-128; 30: 95-176.
*1963 "Características de la Migración en el Distrito de Marcará." in H. F. Dobyns y M. C. Vázquez (eds.), Migración e Integración en el Perú. Lima: Editorial Estudios Andinos.
GOLDSEN, ROSE and WILLIAM W. STEIN
1956 "The Introduction of New Seed Potatoes in Vicos: The Story Line." Ithaca: Cornell University Department of Sociology and Anthropology. Ditto, Mimeo.
HARBISON, F. and C. A. MYERS
1964 Education, Manpower and Economic Growth. New York: McGraw-Hill.

HARDIN, GARRETT
1968 "The Tragedy of the Commons." Science, 162 (13 December).
HOLMBERG, ALLAN R.
1950 *Nomads of the Long Bow*. Washington: Smithsonian Institution, Institute of Social Anthropology, Pub. No. 10. Anchor Books edition, (1969)
1951 "Child Training in Vicos, Peru." Delphian Quarterly, No. 34 (January).
1952a "La realización del Proyecto de Antropología Aplicada en la Zona de Vicos, Marcará, Ancash." Perú Indígena, 2 (Enero).
*1952b "Estudios de Aculturación en el Callejón de Huaylas." Perú Indígena, 2 (Enero).
*1952c "La universidad de Cornell y el Instituto Indigenista Nacional en un Plan Conjunto de Antropología Aplicada." Boletín Indigenista, 12 (Marzo) 58-69.
1952d "Proyecto Perú-Cornell en las Ciencias Sociales Aplicadas," Perú Indígena, 2 (Junio) 158-66.
1952e "Informe del Dr. Allan R. Holmberg sobre el desarrollo del Proyecto Perú-Cornell." Perú Indígena, 3 (Diciembre) 237-48.
*1953 "Segundo informe sobre el desarrollo del Proyecto Perú-Cornell." Perú Indígena, 4 (Setiembre) 162-65.
1955 "Participant Intervention in the Field." Human Organization, 14 (Spring) 23-26.
*1957 "Educational Intervention in Peru," Journal of Education, 89 (September) 381-84.
*1958 "The Research and Development Approach to the Study of Change." Human Organization, 17 (Spring) 12-16.
1959 "Land Tenure and Planned Social Change: A Case From Vicos, Peru." Human Organization, 18 (Spring) 7-10.
1960 "Changing Community Attitudes and Values in Peru: A Case Study in Guided Change," in *Social Change in Latin America Today*. New York: Harper, for the Council on Foreign Relations.
*1961 "Age in the Andes." in R. W. Kleemeier (ed.), *Aging and Leisure: A Research Perspective into the Meaningful Use of Time*. New York: Oxford University Press.
*1965 "The Changing Values and Institutions of Vicos in the Context of National Development." American Behavioral Scientist, 8 (March) 3-8.
*1966a "Intervención Participante en el Campo." *Vicos, Método y Práctica de Antropología Aplicada*. Lima: Editorial Estudios Andinos.
*1966b "Del Paternalismo a la Democracia: El Proyecto Petú-Cornell." Vicos, Método y Práctica de Antropología Aplicada. Lima: Editorial Estudios Andinos.

Peasants, Power, and Applied Social Change

*1966c "El Procedimiento de Investigación y Desarrollo para el Cambio Cultural." Vicos, Método y Práctica de Antropología Aplicada. Lima: Editorial Estudios Andinos.

*1966d "Un Simposio de Tenencia de la Tierra y Cambio Social Planeado: Un Caso de Vicos, Peru." Vicos, Método y Práctica de Antropología Aplicada. Lima: Editorial Estudios Andinos.

1967 "Algunas relaciones entre la privación psicobiológica y el cambio cultural en los Andes." América Indígena, 27 (Enero) 3-24.

1969 "Dynamic Functionalism." in A. A. Rogow (ed.), *Politics, Personality, and Social Science in the Twentieth Century*. Chicago: University of Chicago Press.

HOLMBERG, ALLAN R. and HENRY F. DOBYNS

1962 "The Process of Accelerating Community Change." Human Organization, 21 (Summer) 107-09.

*1966 "El proceso de acelerar cambio comunal." Vicos, Método y Práctica de Antropología Aplicada. Lima: Editorial Estudios Andinos.

*1969 "The Cornell Program in Vicos, Peru," in C. R. Wharton, Jr. (ed.) *Subsistence Agriculture and Economic Development*. Chicago: Aldine Press.

HOLMBERG, ALLAN R., HENRY F. DOBYNS and MARIO C. VAZQUEZ

*1960 *Métodos para el Análisis de los Cambios Culturales*. Lima: Ministerio de Educación Pública, Dirección de Educación Fundamental y del Adulto.

1961 "Methods for the Analysis of Cultural Change." Anthropological Quarterly, 34 (April) 37-46.

HOLMBERG, ALLAN R. y CARLOS MONGE M.

1952 "Acuerdo celebrado entre la Universidad de Cornell y el Instituto Indigenista Peruano. . . ." Perú Indígena, 2 (Enero) 85-86.

*1957 "Prórroga del Acuerdo Celebrado entre la Universidad de Cornell y el Instituto Indigenista Peruano." Boletín Indigenista, 17 (Diciembre) 358-63.

HOLMBERG, ALLAN R. y MARIO C. VAZQUEZ

*1951 "Un proyecto de Antropología Aplicada en el Perú." Revista del Museo Nacional (Lima) 19 y 20.

HOLMBERG, ALLAN R. and WILLIAM F. WHYTE

1956 "From Paternalism to Democracy." Human Organization, 15 (Autumn) special issue on human problems of U.S. enterprise in Latin America.

HOMANS, GEORGE C.

1941 *English Villagers of the Thirteenth Century*. Cambridge: Harvard University Press.

HUENEMANN, RUTH L.

*1954 "Nutrition and Care of Young Children in Peru." Journal of the American Dietetic Association, 30 (June) 554-58.

HUENEMANN, RUTH L., CARLOS COLLAZOS C., D. M. HEGSTED, Y.
BRAVO DE RUEDA, A. CASTELLANOS, A. DIESELDORFF, M.
ESCOBAR, I. MOSCOSO, P. L. WHITE and H. WHITE
*1955 "Nutrition and Care of Young Children in Peru, IV: Chacan and
Vicos, Rural Communities in the Andes." Journal of the American
Dietetic Association, 31.
KAUFMAN DOIG, FEDERICO
*1956 "Las ruinas de Chopijirka (Vicos, Ancash)." Revista del Museo
Nacional (Lima) 25.
KENNEDY, JOHN L. and HAROLD D. LASSWELL
*1958 "A Cross-Cultural Test of Self-Image." Human Organization, 17
(Spring) 41-43.
KLEIN, RALPH
1963 "The Self-Image of Adult Males in an Andean Culture." New York
University Ph.D. Thesis.
KUBLER, GEORGE
1947 "The Quechua in the Colonial World." in J. H. Steward (ed.),
Handbook of South American Indians, Vol. II: The Andean
Civilizations. Washington: Bureau of American Ethnology Bulletin
143.
LASSWELL, HAROLD D.
1962 "Integrating Communities into More Inclusive Systems," Human
Organization, 21 (Summer) 116-21.
*1963 The Future of Political Science. New York: Atherton Press.
*1965 "The Emerging Policy Sciences of Development: The Vicos Case."
American Behavioral Scientist, 8 (March) 28-33.
*1966 "Integración de Comunidad en Sistemas más Inclusivos." Vicos,
Método y Práctica de Antropología Aplicada. Lima: Editorial
Estudios Andinos.
1968 "Policy Sciences." in D. L. Sills (ed.), International Encyclopedia of
the Social Sciences, Vol. 12: 181-89. New York: Macmillan and Free
Press.
1971 "The Continuing Decision Seminar as a Technique of Instruction."
Policy Sciences, 2, No. 2: 43-57.
LASSWELL, HAROLD D. and ALLEN R. HOLMBERG
1966 "Toward a General Theory of Directed Value Accumulation and
Institutional Development," in H. W. Peter (ed.), Comparative
Theories of Social Change. Ann Arbor: Foundation for Research on
Human Behavior.
1969 "Toward a General Theory of Directed Value Accumulation and
International Development." in R. Braibanti (ed.), Political and
Administrative Development. Durham: Duke University Press.

LASSWELL, HAROLD D. and A. KAPLAN
1950 *Power and Society*. New Haven: Yale University Press.
LASSWELL, HAROLD D. and DANIEL LERNER (eds.)
1965 *World Revolutionary Elites: Studies in Coercive Ideological Movements*. Cambridge: M.I.T. Press.
LOMAX, A.
1959 "Folk Song Style." American Anthropologist, 61 (December) 927-54.
LYNCH, THOMAS
*1967 "Quishqui Puncu: A Preceramic Site in Highland Peru." Science, 158 (10 November) 780-83.
McCLELLAND, D. C.
1966 "Does Education Accelerate Economic Growth? " Economic Development and Cultural Change, 14.
MACMILLAN, ALLISTER
1957 "The Health Opinion Survey. . . ." Psych. Reports, vol. 7 Monograph Supplement.
1959 "A Survey Technique for Estimating the Prevalence of Psychoneurotic and Related Types of Disorders in Communities," in B. Pasamanick (ed.), *Epidemiology of Mental Disorder.* Washington: American Association for the Advancement of Science.
MALINOWSKI, BRONISLAW
1945 *The Dynamics of Culture Change*. New Haven: Yale University Press.
MANGIN, WILLIAM P.
1954 "The Cultural Significance of the Fiesta Complex in an Indian Hacienda in Peru." New Haven: Yale University Ph.D. Thesis.
*1955 "Estratificación Social en el Callejón de Huaylas." Revista del Museo Nacional (Lima) 24.
*1957a "Hacienda, Comunidades and Strategic Acculturation in the Peruvian Sierra." Sociologus 7: 142-46.
*1957b "Drinking Among Andean Indians." Quarterly Journal of Studies on Alcohol, 18 (March) 55-66.
*1958 "La bebida entre los Indios de los Andes." Perú Indígena, 7 (Julio-Diciembre) 14-22.
*1960 "Organización Social en Vicos." Etnología y Arqueología (Lima) 24-37.
*1961 "Fiestas in an Indian Community in Peru," in symposium: Patterns of Land Utilization and Other Papers. Seattle: American Ethnological Society.
MARTINEZ A., HECTOR
1959 "Vicos, las fiestas en la integración y desintegración cultural." Revista del Museo Nacional (Lima) 28: 189-247.

1960 "Vicos, los hábitos alimenticios." Revista del Museo Nacional (Lima) 29: 129-51.
MEAD, MARGARET
1956 *New Lives for Old.* New York: William Morrow.
MOGROVIEJO, TORIBIO DE
1920 "Libro de Visitas, 1593," Revista del Archivo Nacional del Perú, Tomo 1, Entrega 1.
MONGE MEDRANO, CARLOS
*1952 "Editorial." Perú Indígena, 2 (Enero) 3.
*1957 "Discurso de Carlos Monge M." Boletín Indigenista, 17 (Marzo) 74-81.
*1966 "Introducción." *Vicos, Método y Práctica de Antropología Aplicada.* Lima: Editorial Estudios Andinos.
MONGE MEDRANO, CARLOS and MARIO C. VAZQUEZ
*1957 "Antropología y Medicina." Perú Indígena, 7 (Julio) 19-33.
*1963 "El Proceso de Aculturación de Vicos." Perú Indígena, 10: 9-15.
MONTALVO VIDAL, ABNER
*1957 "Salud Pública y una película en Vicos." Lima: Talleres Educación Sanitaria.
MONTOYA R., RODRIGO
1963 "Elección de Dirigentes: Aceptación y Resistencia." Cuadernos (Lima) 2 (Julio) 60-82.
NEWMAN, MARSHALL T.
1960 "Nutrition, Disease, and Physical Status of the Indians of the Peruvian Sierra, based largely on Data from Vicos." Washington. Ditto.
1960 "Blood Group Systems in Latin American Indians." American Journal of Physical Anthropology, 18: 334-35.
NEWMAN, MARSHALL T. and CARLOS COLLAZOS CHIRIBOGA
*1957 "Growth and Skeletal Maturation in Malnourished Indian Boys from the Peruvian Sierra." American Journal of Physical Anthropology, 15 (September) 431.
NEWMAN, MARSHALL T., CARLOS COLLAZOS CHIRIBOGA and CARMEN DE FUENTES
*1963a "Growth differences between Indians and Mestizos in the Callejón de Huaylas, Perú." American Journal of Physical Anthropology, 21: 407-08.
*1963b "Physical and Clinical Changes in Vicos Indian Boys with Improved Dietary Status." American Journal of Physical Anthropology, 21:
NOMAD, M.
1961 *Apostles of Revolution* (rev. ed.). New York: Collier Books.
ORTIZ R., ALEJANDRO
*1963 "Enfermedad y Organización Social en Vicos." Cuadernos (Lima) 2 (Julio) 39-53.

PARSONS, TALCOTT
1954 *Essays in Sociological Theory* (rev. ed.). New York: Free Press.
PATCH, RICHARD W.
*1957 "The Hacienda Becomes a Community." American Universities Field Staff Newsletter October 4.
1962 "Life in a Peruvian Indian Community." American Universities Field Staff Reports Service, West Coast South America Series IX (Peru).
1964 "Vicos and the Peace Corps." American Universities Field Staff Reports Service, West Coast South America Series, II (Peru).
PAYNE, E. H., L. GONZALES MUGABURU and E. M. SCHLEICHER
1956 "An Intestinal Parasite Survey in the High Cordilleras of Peru." American Journal of Tropical Medicine and Hygiene, 5 (July) 696-98.
PEASLEE, A. L.
1965 "Elementary Education as a Prerequisite for Economic Growth." International Development Review, 7.
PERU, MINISTERIO DE GOBIERNO
1878 *Resumen del Censo General de Habitantes del Peru Hecho en 1876.* Lima: Imprenta del Estado.
PERU, MINISTERIO DE HACIENDA Y COMERCIO
1944 *Censo Nacional de Población de 1940,* Vol. III. Lima: Imprenta Torres Aguirre.
PRICE, RICHARD
1965 "Trial Marriage in the Andes." Ethnology, 4 (July) 310-22.
RITTER, ULRICH PETER
*1965a "Vicos; ein Experiment der Landreform auf genossenschaftlicher Basis in Peru." Archiv Für Offentliche und Freigemeinmitzige Unternehmen, 7: 264-76.
*1965b *Comunidades Indígenas y Cooperativismo en el Perú.* Bilbao: Ediciones Deusto.
*1967 "De hacienda semifeudal a comunidad de aldea: Vicos." Economía y Agricultura, 3 (Lima) 56-69.
ROMAN UNZUETA, PELEGRIN
1963 "Informe de actividades del Plan Nacional de Integración de la Población Aborigen en el periodo del 1 de Enero de 1962 al 30 de Junio de 1963." Perú Indígena, 10.
1964 "Plan Nacional de Integración de la Población Aborigen: Informe Actividades Enero 1963-Junio 1964." Lima: Ministerio de Trabajo y Asuntos Indígenas.
1965 "Plan Nacional de Integración de la Publación Aborigen: Informe Actividades Julio 1964-Junio 1965." Lima: Ministerio de Trabajo y Asuntos Indígenas.

RUBENSTEIN, ROBERT and H. D. LASSWELL
1966 *The Sharing of Power in a Psychiatric Hospital.* New Haven: Yale University Press.
RUSSELL, BERTRAND
1938 *Power.* London: Allen & Unwin.
SAENZ, M.
1933 *Sobre el indio peruano y su incorporación al medio nacional.* México: Secretaria de Educación Pública.
SANDELMAN, J. C.
1955 "Agricultural Extension Work Through the *Servicio* in Peru," in H. M. Teaf and P. G. Franck (eds.), *Hands Across Frontiers.* Ithaca: Cornell University Press.
SCHRAER, HAROLD and MARSHALL T. NEWMAN
*1954 "Quantitative Roentgenography of Skeletal Mineralization in Malnourished Quechua Boys." Science, 128: 476-77.
SHARP, LAURISTON
1952 "Steel Axes for Stone Age Australians," in E. H. Spicer (ed.), *Human Problems in Technological Change.* New York: Russell Sage Foundation.
1958 "People Without Politics," in *Systems of Political Control and Bureaucracy in Human Societies.* Proceedings of the 1958 Annual Spring Meeting of the American Ethnological Society.
SNYDER, JOAN C.
1957 "The Changing Context of an Andean Community," in *Cultural Stability and Cultural Change.* Proceedings of the 1957 Annual Spring Meeting of the American Ethnological Society.
STEIN, WILLIAM W.
1961 *Hualcán.* Ithaca: Cornell University Press.
*1971 "Nuevas semillas de papa para Vicos." América Indígena, 31 (Enero) 51-84.
STEWARD, JULIAN H.
1955 *Theory of Culture Change.* Urbana: University of Illinois Press.
STRODTBECK, F. L.
1951 "Husband-Wife Interaction Over Revealed Differences." American Sociological Review, 16.
TAWNEY, R. H.
1931 *Equality.* New York: Harcourt, Brace.
TRIGOSO P., JORGE
*1963 "Instrumentos Musicales de Vicos." Cuadernos (Lima) 2 (Julio) 53-59.
VAZQUEZ VARELA, MARIO C.
1952 "La Antropología Cultural y nuestro Problema del Indio: Vicos, un caso de Antropología Aplicada." Perú Indígena, 2 (Junio) 5-157.

Peasants, Power, and Applied Social Change

1955 "Cambios en Estratificación Social en una hacienda andina del Perú." Revista del Museo Nacional, 24: 190-209.

*1957 "Sexto Informe del Proyecto Perú-Cornell." Perú Indígena, 6 (Julio) 222-25.

*1959 "Proyecto Perú-Cornell, VII Informe." Perú Indígena, 8 (Enero-Junio) 232-52.

1961a *Hacienda, Peonaje y Servidumbre en los Andes Peruanos.* Lima: Editorial Estudios Andinos.

1961b "Local Authority on a Peruvian Andean Hacienda." Paper delivered at the 1961 Annual Meeting of the American Anthropological Association, Philadelphia.

*1962 "Cambios Socio-Económicos en una Hacienda Andina del Perú." América Indígena, 22 (Octubre) 217-231.

1963a "Proceso de Migración en la Comunidad de Vicos, Ancash," in H. F. Dobyns and M. C. Vázquez (eds.), *Migración e Integración en el Perú.* Lima: Editorial Estudios Andinos.

*1963b "Autoridades de una hacienda andina peruana." Perú Indígena, 10: 24-36.

1964a "The Varayoc System in Vicos." Ithaca: Cornell University Department of Anthropology, Comparative Studies of Cultural Change. Mimeo.

1964b "The 'Castas' Unilinear Kin Groups in Vicos, Peru." Ithaca: Cornell University Department of Anthropology, Comparative Studies of Cultural Change. Mimeo.

*1965a "The Interplay between Power and Wealth." American Behavioral Scientist, 8 (March) 9-12.

1965b *Educación Rural en el Callejón de Huaylas: Vicos.* Lima: Editorial Estudios Andinos.

*1965c "Actitud y Conducta hacia una inovación tecnológica." Procesos de Integración. Primer Tomo del V Congreso Indigenista Interamericano. Quito: Talleres Gráficos Nacionales.

1967 "Un caso de discriminación en las elecciones municipales de 1966." Wamani (Ayacucho) 1: 30-44.

VAZQUEZ VARELA, MARIO C. and HENRY F. DOBYNS

*1964 "Transformación de las haciendas con peonaje y servidumbre en cooperativas de producción." Economía y Agricultura, 1 (Diciembre 1963-Febrero 1964) 89-92.

VAZQUEZ VARELA, MARIO C. and ALLAN R. HOLMBERG

1966 "The Castas: Unilineal Kin Groups in Vicos, Peru." Ethnology, 5 (July) 283-303.

WALLACE, A. F. C.

1951 "Some Psychological Determinants of Culture Change in an Iroquoian Community," in W. N. Fenton (ed.), *Symposium on Local*

Diversity in Iroquois Culture. Washington: Bureau of American Ethnology Bulletin 149.

WHYTE, WILLIAM F. and LAWRENCE K. WILLIAMS

1964 "The Use of Questionnaire Surveys for Community Studies of Culture Change and Economic Development." Paper read at 1964 Annual Meeting of the American Anthropological Association. Mimeo.

WILLIAMS, ROBIN M., Jr.

1964 *Strangers Next Door.* Englewood Cliffs: Prentice-Hall.

WILSON, GODFREY and MONICA

1945 *The Analysis of Social Change.* Cambridge: The University Press.

WOLF, ERIC R.

1955 "Types of Latin American Peasantry: A Preliminary Discussion." American Anthropologist, 57 (June) 452-71.

1966 *Peasants.* Englewood Cliffs: Prentice-Hall.

1969 *Peasant Wars of the Twentieth Century.* New York: Harper & Row.

WOLFE, D. M.

1959 "Power and Authority in the Family," in D. Cartwright (ed.), *Studies in Social Power.* Ann Arbor: University of Michigan.

INDEX

ABOUT THE AUTHORS

Dr. J. Oscar Alers is a representative of The Population Council assigned as advisor to the research and evaluation unit of the Thai national family planning program in Bangkok.

A native of New York, Alers received the Ph.D. degree from Cornell University in 1966 after studying at City College of New York, Harvard, and Michigan. He served as Lecturer in Sociology at C.C.N.Y. during the summer of 1958. He was Research Associate in the Cornell University anthropology department in 1964-65, having conducted research at Vicos in 1963-64. Dr. Alers then became Visiting Assistant Professor in the New York State School of Industrial and Labor Relations at Cornell University in 1965. He spent a year in Peru at the Institute of Peruvian Studies, where he acted as Associate Director of the Project for the Study of Change in Peruvian Communities. Dr. Alers then taught at Boston College as Associate Professor from 1968 to 1971.

Dr. Henry F. Dobyns is Professor of Anthropology at Prescott College. A native of Tucson, Arizona, he received the Ph.D. degree in cultural anthropology from Cornell University in 1960 after earlier studies at the University of Arizona. Dobyns received the Bronislaw Malinowski Award of the Society for Applied Anthropology in 1951, and shared in the Anisfield-Wolf award for writing in race relations from the Saturday Review in 1968. He served successfully as Research Associate, Senior Research Associate, and Lecturer in the Department of Anthropology at Cornell University before becoming chairman of the Department of Anthropology at the University of Kentucky from 1966 to 1970. In the Cornell Peru Project Dobyns served as Research Coordinator in Peru in 1960-62, and Assistant to the Director in Ithaca in 1962-66, where he also coordinated the Comparative Studies of Cultural Change in the anthropology department, 1963-66.

Dr. Paul L. Doughty is Chairman of the Department of Anthropology at the University of Florida. Born in Beacon, New York, Doughty studied at Ursinus College and the University of Pennsylvania before receiving a Ph.D. degree in cultural anthropology from Cornell University in 1963. Earlier, Doughty worked as a claims adjuster and served as a community development worker for the American Friends Service Committee in El Salvador and Mexico. He conducted anthropological research in Peru in 1960-61, 1962-64, and 1966-67, and represented the Peruvian Earthquake Relief Committee there during the summers of 1970 and 1971. While associated with the Cornell Peru Project, Doughty coordinated area studies for the Peace Corps Training Program (Peru III) conducted by Cornell in 1962, and from 1962 through 1964 he acted as Research Coordinator for the Project in Peru, leading an evaluation of Peace Corps volunteer achievement in the Peruvian Andes. Doughty joined the Indiana University faculty in 1964, becoming Director of the Latin American Studies Program there. He assumed leadership of the University of Florida anthropology department in 1971.

Dr. Allan R. Holmberg was Chairman of the Department of Anthropology and Scarborough Professor of Social Sciences at Cornell University at the time of his death in October, 1966. A native of Renville, Minnesota, Holmberg received the Ph.D. degree in anthropology from Yale University in 1947 after earlier study at the universities of Chicago and Minnesota. He gained wide research experience in various societies in Bolivia and Peru over a twenty-five year period. He served as a cultural anthropologist in the Institute of Social Anthropology of the Smithsonian Institution (1946-48), was Professor of Anthropology at the University of San Marcos in Lima, Peru (1947-48), and joined the Cornell University faculty in 1948. Holmberg was a fellow of the Social Science Research Council, Sterling Fellow at Yale, and fellow of the Center for Advanced Study in the Behavioral Sciences. He served as president of the American Ethnological Society and as treasurer of the Society for Applied Anthropology, and for many years was frequently consulted by U.S. government officials.

Dr. Harold D. Lasswell, Ford Foundation Professor of Law and Social Sciences at Yale, is one of the most distinguished methodologists and theorists of the social sciences. Trained as a political scientist at the University of Chicago, he made his professional mark with early studies of propaganda and political psychology. His later works have ranged far and wide into the development of content analysis and depth interviews, the application of psychological methods to the study of political behavior, and theory of a science of public policy, the international law of space, and legal sanctions. He is Ford Foundation Professor Emeritus of Law and the Social Sciences at Yale University, and Distinguished Professor of Policy Sciences at the John Jay College of Criminal Justice, City University of New York. Among his numerous offices Dr. Lasswell is President of the American Society of International Law and Chairman of Development Administration Seminars at SEADAG; he has also served as president of the American Political Science Association. His chapters in the present volume are a revision of a paper he originally gave as his vice-presidential address to the 1964 Montreal meeting of the American Association for the Advancement of Science. Lasswell's interest in the Vicos project dates from his contact with Allan R. Holmberg when both were Fellows of the Center for Advanced Study in the Behavioral Sciences in 1954-55. He later conducted research in Vicos.

Dr. Mario C. Vázquez is Director of the Bureau of Peasant Communities in the Peruvian Ministry of Agriculture, a position he assumed in August of 1969. He holds a Doctorate in Letters from the University of San Marcos in Lima in addition to an M.A. in Anthropology from Cornell University. Vázquez initiated a study of Vicos in 1949 with Allan R. Holmberg, and was associated with the Cornell Peru Project from its organization in 1951 to its termination in 1966. In 1957 he became Field Director of the Project in Vicos, and in 1964 acted as Research Coordinator in Peru. In 1966 Vázquez led the Cornell anthropology department's research-and-development team in Bolivia, personally making a study of a nationalized tin mining settlement in that country. Vázquez has taught at the National University of Mexico and served as instructor for students in the Interuniversity Summer Program in Latin American Cultures of Cornell, Columbia, Harvard, and Illinois universities. In his own country he joined the faculty of a special institute at the National Engineering University in 1966, later heading the anthropology program in the Pontifical Catholic University of Peru.